POET'S WORK, POET'S PLAY

Poet's Work, Poet's Play ·

Essays on the Practice and the Art

Edited by
Daniel Tobin and Pimone Triplett

THE UNIVERSITY OF MICHIGAN PRESS
Ann Arbor

2010   2009   2008   4   3   2   1

A CIP catalog record for this book is available from the British Library.

Library of Congress Cataloging-in-Publication Data

Poet's work, poet's play : essays on the practice and the art / edited
    by Daniel Tobin and Pimone Triplett.
        p. cm.
    Includes index.
    ISBN-13: 978-0-472-09997-9 (acid-free paper)
    ISBN-10: 0-472-09997-3 (acid-free paper)
    ISBN-13: 978-0-472-06997-2 (pbk. : acid-free paper)
    ISBN-10: 0-472-06997-7 (pbk. : acid-free paper)
    1. Poetry—History and criticism.   I. Tobin, Daniel.
    II. Triplett, Pimone.

PN1111.P66   2007
809.1—dc22   2007019157

Acknowledgments
Special thanks to Christine Walsh for her keen extra set of eyes.
The editors also gratefully acknowledge Kerry Skemp for her
invaluable work indexing *Poet's Work, Poet's Play*.

Contents

DANIEL TOBIN AND PIMONE TRIPLETT

Introduction

This collection of essays represents a selection of craft lectures given over the past decade by new and returning faculty to the Warren Wilson College Master of Fine Arts Program for Writers. Since the publication in 1996 of *Poets Teaching Poets,* edited by Gregory Orr and Ellen Bryant Voigt, that first volume of essays from faculty regularly associated with the program has made its way into the hands and classrooms of novices, practitioners, and those interested in the art of poetry. The essays collected in *Poet's Work, Poet's Play* continue the ongoing conversation that began with *Poets Teaching Poets,* a conversation that explores the contemporary poet's responsibilities, challenges, and joys in the practice of making poems. At the same time, the present volume also represents the evolution of the program itself, as well as its commitment to including new faculty who joined the ranks of those who established the program thirty years ago as the country's first low-residency MFA program. Of the seventeen essays included in this volume, fewer than half are by poets whose work appeared in the previous volume; ten are by the program's "new" faculty. *Poet's Work, Poet's Play,* therefore, should be read as a companion volume to *Poets Teaching Poets,* and not as a collection that eclipses the previous work. Serious-minded students of the art would be well served in apprenticing themselves to both collections of essays.

The essays included here have been written with a keen ear, and eye, for the way poems are orchestrated. As such, each essay has been informed by the contributing poet's daily challenge of facing the blank page with the often daunting task of poetic making, and they do so by offering a diversity of approaches and perspectives by serious and dedicated teachers. Moreover, as the Warren Wilson program does not ascribe to any particular aesthetic doctrine, this collection reflects a wide variety of poetries and interests, with contributors engaging all manner of poetic techniques, as well as writers ranging from Shakespeare to Charles Olson, Robert Frost to Harryette Mullen. Perhaps what most links these essays is a pragmatic, yet dynamic, approach to the art, where close readings of poems by practicing poets often model how the reading process informs the writing process through attention to detail, vision, and craft.

In addition to the daily challenge of making poems, in the ten years since the publication of *Poets Teaching Poets* the milieu of contemporary American poetry appears to have become even more eclectic than during the two decades preceding the new millennium. Since we have approached and passed that historical milestone, the explosion of writing programs, conferences, poetry clubs, and reading venues, as well as journals (both Web and print) and independent presses devoted to poetry bears witness to the art's vitality—apparently there is no shortage of people writing poems, despite the wider culture's relative indifference to the poet's work. At the same time, the range of distinct approaches to the art, from the New Formalism to L=A=N=G=U=A=G=E to all manner of lyric and narrative observance, suggests that American poetry has not only become multifarious but "professionalized" and entrepreneurial to an extent that even Pound—the P. T. Barnum of modern poetry—might never have imagined. While there are modes and schools that surely come to the fore in local periods and regions, and a wide array of ethnic and cultural influences, there appears to be no majority style in American poetry, nor, on the contrary, does there appear to be any kind of poem anathema to the increasingly plural nature of American poetry. There seems to be now no mainstream but multiple currents that assume degrees of prominence depending on where one stands and one's aesthetic assumptions. In short, the mainstream has become a matter of perspective as well as currency, and above all there appear to be a variety of contemporary strategies from the experimental to the traditionally formal. Over the past two decades, the self-proclaimed outsiders of postmodernist or "theory-based" poetics have been embraced by critical theorists and enshrined in positions in the American academy. Formalist presses promote their latest avatars beside those of the experimental houses in the pages of *Poets and Writers*. Rather than embracing any mainstream, conservative or avant-garde, the essays included here might best be characterized as inhabiting a vital space within American poetry, engaging both the art's rich and evolving traditions and its most stimulating prospects, and they do so dynamically with practical attention as well as theoretical seriousness. That said, for the aspiring poet devoted to learning and practicing the art there may never have been such a wealth of choice and opportunity.

Nevertheless, the perceived necessity to "brand" oneself in order to make one's way in the ramifying world of contemporary American poetry can, potentially at least, distract even the most serious practitioner with matters of less artistic significance than the work and the poet's hard-won pleasure in the work. Perhaps at least as potentially compromising to the growth of the poet's practice is the sheer plethora of voices and the concomitant haziness about quality and reputation. A recent American issue of the British journal *Agenda* summarizes one view from abroad: "Speaking generally, an accurate comprehensive overview of American poetry today is impossible. Such an overview would have been possible thirty years ago, but not now."[1] Were Tocqueville milling among the throngs of poets writing today, would he caution us to be aware of "a tyranny of no majority" in addition to "the tyranny of the majority" as a trend that could undermine what is most valuable to our collective artistic well-being? Great diversity, great opportunity, and great doubt. Perhaps the state of contemporary American poetry, simply by reflecting how and where we live, manifests what is most vital and distressing about the present state of the culture.

The present collection, *Poet's Work, Poet's Play,* intends both to speak out of this circumstance and to speak to the need for a renewed focus on the essential purpose and practice of the art of making poems, as well as on the varieties of poetic expression—an insouciant play of multiple voices speaking to one another across intentions and expectations. The title also intends to suggest the notion that the essays are the play, and the poems we write the work, sitting in tension with how it is also the other way around. Both require our hearing. As Frost said in a letter to his friend John Bartlett, "It is so and not otherwise that we get the variety that makes it fun to write and read. *The ear does it.* The ear is the only true writer and the only true reader."[2] In the same letter, Frost opines against "eye readers," those who only get the meaning of poems by glances. In a world ever more shaped by visual stimuli and new utilitarian iconographies that permit us to "surf" digital media without plumbing the deeper currents of what it means to be alive, the caution against eye readers, and, perhaps more important, "eye writers," remains at least as relevant today as we move forward into new technologies of literacy and dissemination we are only beginning to imagine. Although the Program for Writers at Warren Wilson College represents a range of orientations to the art form, different ways of working and playing, the poets teaching there remain dedicated to the deep aural resources of poetry in every sense while likewise seeking to extend the art's possibilities.

In that spirit, the essays in part one of the volume tackle first principles of poetic aspiration, technique, and effort, as well as the art's relation to the world. Eleanor Wilner's insightful distinction between aesthetic distance and analytic detachment opens a moral framework for the functions and privileges of the imagination through the poems of Robert Frost and Karl Shapiro. In turn, Marianne Boruch examines poetry's need for "heavy lifting," its burden of takeoff given the timeless burdens of love and death in the poetry of Robert Hayden, T. S. Eliot, John Berryman, and others. Laura Kasciske locates the transcendent poem in the mysteries and hard realities of being alive, the Venerable Bede, and the local barfly and the stories she finds in between. Finally, Pimone Triplett reexamines the sublime tradition, with its dual concerns of place and surpassing place, in light of those whose sense of home is multiple, fractured, and contemporary.

Part two expands and develops what William Carlos Williams called "the American Grain," considering the art in terms of the forces—historical, inspirational, even metaphysical—that have gone into the making of our nation. A. Van Jordan's essay provides and examines contexts for some of the major writers of the Harlem Renaissance and the international movement of Negritude through his astute definitions of poetic time as synchronized, chronological, psychological, or suspended in "fermata." The late Larry Levis connects the injustices of class and birth in America to those of Seamus Heaney's Ireland in his powerful meditation on the responsibilities of the act of elegy and the poet's need for passion. Alan Williamson, in turn, considers the motives, complexities, and necessities of cynicism as a tonal mode in contemporary poetry through his multifaceted readings of Mark Halliday and Jane Mead. Dean Young's essay explores the rich and complex ideas that continue to generate the surrealist tradition in poetry. The late Agha Shahid Ali follows with his provocative exploration of poetic standards and canon formation under the shadow of imperialism and history. In turn, Tony Hoagland's incisive discussion of the contemporary distrust of narrative illuminates the pleasures and dangers of the current fascination with "associational" models in American poetry. Finally, Daniel Tobin's inclusive argument moves us beyond the binaries, complicating the supposed American "two-party system" of open and closed form through his subtle readings of Yeats, Frost, Charles Olson, A. R. Ammons, and Elizabeth Bishop.

Part three gathers together essays in which elements of craft and style are made visible through each writer's inspired, meticulous approach to the art. Focusing on the syllable, Stephen Dobyns traces that unit of sound from its eleventh-century English roots all the way to the work of the twentieth-century poet Philip Larkin with stops in the stream that include Thomas Wyatt, Janet Lewis, Yeats, and Robert Lowell. Ellen Bryant Voigt roundly demonstrates the balances and gyrations of syntax in Stanley Kunitz, D. H. Lawrence, Frost, Donald Justice, and others. Next, through the work of Andrew Marvell, John Donne, Emily Dickinson, Frederick Goddard Tuckerman, and Bishop, Carl Dennis investigates the way plot informs temporal and nontemporal structures in the lyric poem. Then, in his essay on the first-person pronoun, Chris Forhan complicates the poetic construct of the speaker to embrace the bewilderments of subjective experience itself in the work of William Carlos Williams, Charles Simic, and Anne Carson. Heather McHugh teases out the oxymoronic strands between poise and suspension, exquisite feeling and passionate thought, in the works by Robert Herrick, Ezra Pound, and Louis Simpson. Last, the poet's effort to place his or her art in the shaping history of tradition comes alive through James Longenbach's treatment of purity and restraint in the metrics of Yeats, Pound, Marvell, and George Oppen. The sum of these essays is an extraordinarily multifaceted reflection on the state of the art of poetry as we head deeper into the first decade of the twenty-first century, and the program's repertoire is even more wide ranging when one considers that the editors were required to limit themselves to contributors who focused on more than one poet and whose association with the program extended beyond a single residency lecture.

In its latest, most credible model, contemporary physics tells us that the universe is in a state of accelerated expansion, that, like Frost's "West Running Brook," it "seriously, sadly runs away to fill the abyss' void with emptiness," or, in Whitman's less disquieting observation from "Song of Myself," "All goes onward and outward, nothing collapses." With its explosion of practitioners, schools, programs, professional associations, publications, colonies, and regions, each gravitating to its local center, it might appear to some that contemporary American poetry is its own "runaway universe" with the gulfs between its many artistic spheres expanding. Beyond gathering together essays on craft by some of America's most impressive established and younger poets, the present volume intends to explore the binding countermotion by which poetry at once continues to hearken back to its source in the immediacy of lived language and to reinvent itself in conversation with the world and its own plurality of voices.

NOTES

1. Greg Delanty, "Letter to Patricia McCarthy," *Agenda* 41, nos. 3–4 (autumn-winter 2005): 7.

2. *Robert Frost: Collected Poems, Prose, and Plays,* edited by Richard Poirer and Mark Richardson (New York: Library of America, 1995), 677.

Poet's Work, Poet's Play

The ear does it. The ear is the only writer
and the only reader.
                    —Robert Frost, "Letter to John Bartlett"

PART ONE *Ratios of Flight*

Delight is in the Flight
Or in the Ratio of it . . .
                    —Emily Dickinson, no. 257

ELEANOR WILNER

The Closeness of Distance, or Narcissus as
Seen by the Lake

A few years ago I attended a talk by the great alternative educator, Ivan Illich, a talk whose subject I can no more describe than I could articulate the design in a Persian carpet. Yet, out of the kaleidoscopic shifting of provocative ideas whose underlying connections were not at all self-evident, moments of clarity did now and then emerge like the hidden faces in a trick landscape painting.

One such moment revealed his deep concern with the increasing dangers attendant on detachment in a world where technology enhances the ability of corporate, commercial, and centralized power to separate language from actuality, the person from the task, the act from felt awareness of its consequences, the bomber from the target he is about to obliterate. Another and seemingly unrelated notion emerged from Illich's discussion of a medieval monastic order that he required his students to study in order to give them what he called "distance," a distance he felt was a spiritual necessity, necessary to a humane understanding of the world.

A question began to form itself in my mind. "What," I wondered, "is the difference between the detachment that allows a man to push a button and calmly destroy a city and the distance that the immersion in another time and place gives his students, a distance that makes them wiser and more humane?" As I mulled it over, the difference seemed already implicit in the question's form: for to focus on the opposite outcome of these two mental actions is to bring into sharp relief the difference hidden beneath apparent resemblance, a difference in the uses of distance that has everything to do with the exercise of imagination.

"The condition of the artist," says novelist Jeannette Winterson, "is a condition of Remove." She capitalizes the R in Remove, suggesting that this is a very special kind of Remove, and since the primary subject of Winterson's art is passion, that Remove of which she speaks is somehow necessary to its exploration and expression. What kind of Remove, then, is this, which carries such intensity? And why must we now redefine and defend the aesthetic distance that has always been a condition of art?

In our common and urgent project as late-twentieth-century poets—to write close to the bone, to celebrate our real lives in the body and in the world, to speak in the language of everyday life, to bring poetry down to earth, to relocate meaning in the dance of molecular matter of which we and the world are made, and to offer an antidote to the high-flown diction and formal decorum of the literary past, as well as to the cold and calculating detachment of unregulated corporate interests who downsize human value—for all these good and sufficient reasons, I think we may at times have forgotten that imagination, the instrument of our art, of our invention—our way out of a deadly repetition, requires—absolutely requires—distance.

What, then, distinguishes aesthetic distance from analytic detachment? With clinical detachment, distance separates and frees the person from *feeling for* what he observes. But what aesthetic distance separates us from is not the emotions but the ego. With poetic imagination, it is precisely this distance from the ego that enables the emotional connectedness we call empathy—and because it is remote from ego threat, as we enter imaginatively what is actually at a remove from us, we are given both vision and connection.

In short, there are two ways of using the mind here: detached mind and aesthetically distanced perception, which we might call, borrowing the Buddhist vocabulary, nonattached mind. I borrow their usage because it has helped me make this distinction. Nonattachment does not mean indifference; it means that the mind, in distancing itself from ego or self-concern, becomes compassionate—even to oneself—and that compassion alters and opens vision.

Everyone who has ever written a real poem knows that the surprise of its significant form seems to arise in an odd in-between state of deepened attention when the will—which is the hammer of the ego—is relinquished in favor of some other shaping faculty, a passionate mindfulness. The clinical mind, detached from its objects but not from ego, looks down on and thinks to master what it sees; oppositely, in the act of imaginative remove, the intellect serves not the ego but the life it illuminates, enlarging what we can see by providing protection to what is seen.

In his poem "Atlantis," Mark Doty writes of Wally, his beloved partner, who is dying, "All those years / I made love to a man without thinking // how little his body had to do with me; / now, diminished, he's never been so plainly / himself—remote and unguarded, / an otherness I can't know." Doty makes that connection between "remote and unguarded," between distance and feeling protected, that allows a man to be "so plainly / himself" and "in an otherness I can't know." With this respect for the unknowable mystery of another being, knowledge, as it faces its limits, shades into wisdom, a wisdom suffused with love. Doty goes on to say, "Lucky we don't have to know / what something is in order to hold it."

But it is not only the word *distance* we need to recuperate; part of the problem may be in its partner, *aesthetic*. Our definition of *aesthetic* in the West had become rarefied, our notion of the aesthetic object identified, since the philosopher Emmanuel Kant at the end of the eighteenth century codified it, as something boasting its disconnection from the real world, an object defined by its lack of utility. Thus, *aesthetic* may have come to sound withdrawn from the sweat of the world's work—privileged, artificial, precious—the word *aesthetic* consorting with *distance* to suggest a contemptuous and lofty purity, a marble museum isolationism.

We have, in this century in the West, been overhauling our notions of beauty, trying to free the living figure from the porcelain of the past (because if beauty *is* truth then beauty ain't no Grecian urn). But, in our commitment to the immediate, the personal, and the bodily, we may have overreacted and injured the very instrument we need to express them; we may have become excessive in our distrust of distance—historical, cultural, spatial, formal, and intellectual—distances so necessary to the transformations of the imagination.

It is a regular refrain of workshop lingo that "the speaker" of the poem is not the same as the writer of the poem. That this statement requires constant reiteration is itself suggestive for, although it is true that the two are never quite one and that *some* aesthetic distance is built into the act of writing itself, nevertheless the distance between the speaker on the page and the author in her skin has been shrinking until it is hard for either to move freely. For with that shrinkage of distance between creator and creature has come a reduction in the amount of creative freedom— and with it some of poetry's primary pleasure and much of its point.

Further, an assumption of exact identity between writer and speaker is one held by too many of our readers these days, who want to turn poetry into gossip or psychological symptom, who try to track our poems back to some private occasion, a project that hopes to reverse the action of imagination, as if it were a simple linear function and not what it is—a transmutation of raw materials from many sources into fresh and significant form. I think of something the philosopher Bachelard said in *The Poetics of Space* about such reductive readings: "The psychoanalyst confuses the flower with the fertilizer."

At a reading some time ago, Daisy Fried introduced a poem by telling us that people invariably would come up to her later and say, "You don't seem old enough to have a grown daughter." So now she feels compelled to explain *before* she reads the poem that of course she *isn't* old enough and that the woman in the poem who speaks in the first person is actually somebody else. Imagine that!

Which is exactly what our self-saturated culture has trained us not to do. North Americans live in a culture that attempts to make itself invisible, turning us away from corporate and collective causes of behavior, creating the illusion, which our pop psychology reinforces, that both our problems and their solutions are personal. The resulting extremity of the solipsistic self is visibly depicted in a poem by Rebecca Seiferle, "Bat in a Jar," in which a bat, trapped in a glass jar, keeps sending out its radar signals but "confined to its own mind. That which enabled / the bat to select a mosquito or nip a June beetle out of the air / now sickened it."

It seems urgent to free the power of perception from the preserving jar of the self, recover the words *aesthetic distance* from those associations that may have sullied them, and return them to poetry, which, I believe, sorely needs them just now in renewing its thinking about itself. Do not misunderstand me. I am not against writing out of one's own heart and history—on the contrary. I hope I am talking about *how to do that better.* For I think that our hearts and our histories are both more capacious and less easily accessible than we might think and that aesthetic distance gets us closer to ourselves than perhaps we can get in any other way.

I want to quote the last two lines from "Ars Poetica," a poem by Constance Merritt. She begins by giving in a mocking tone the earnest advice to apprentice writers that is one of the workshop banner heads of the day: "Write what you know!" Then she follows with her questioning stance toward that advice. Here are her lines.

> *Write what you know.* And go on knowing only what
> We know? And never know the lakeness of the lake?

This sets the problem quite squarely before us in its two main aspects: the pointlessness of using writing merely "to go on knowing only what we [already] know"; and the loss of the possibility of discovering, when fixated on one's own face, what she calls "the lakeness of the lake" or what Robert Frost, in this famous little poem, calls "something of the depths."

FOR ONCE, THEN, SOMETHING

Others taunt me with having knelt at well-curbs
Always wrong to the light, so never seeing

Deeper down in the well than where the water
Gives me back in a shining surface picture
Me myself in the summer heaven godlike
Looking out of a wreath of fern and cloud puffs.
Once, when trying with chin against a well-curb,
I discerned, as I thought, beyond the picture,
Through the picture, a something white, uncertain,
Something more of the depths—and then I lost it.
Water came to rebuke the too clear water.
One drop fell from a fern, and lo, a ripple
Shook whatever it was lay there at bottom,
Blurred it, blotted it out. What was that whiteness?
Truth? A pebble of quartz? For once, then, something.

Here is a poem about the inability to achieve the distance and
angle of vision necessary for insight, and its success as a poem depends
precisely on the subtle way it achieves the distance required to deliver
that message. First, the poem's ancient prop and container is, obviously, the Narcissus myth. The speaker of the poem is looking, after all,
not just at his reflection in water but into a well, which, as a deep shaft
sunk into the earth to tap underground springs, is conventionally associated with poetic and cultural tradition.

Frost, in order to see some truth about this situation, one particular to his speaker but also characteristic of the Romantic poet and the
generic American, looks through him to an ancient and recurring
figure of the fate of the self-absorbed even while—in a charming
irony—connecting the speaker of the poem with a long line of isolated
self-seekers. Frost's poem, through this mythic resonance, and—as we
shall see—formal virtuosity and syntactic sleight of hand, finds a distance that allows for vision, one that offers a key to its own myopia.

Myopia, or nearsightedness, is, optically described, an abnormality
in the eye whose result is that light rays that come from and allow us to
see distant objects are focused in front of the retina rather than on it,
which means those objects are not seen distinctly. Extending the biological to the metaphoric, the visionary problem in the eye of the
beholder is that the focal length of his interest intersects just in front of
him, at his own reflected image, and thus more distant objects are elusive, unreadable, obscured.

But if it is himself he is interested in, and let's not fault him for that
very primary human concern, why should Frost's speaker be dis-
satisfied and want to see into the distance? In that question lies the difference between two contrasting kinds of resemblance: mirror image
versus metaphor.

The face in the mirror is, obviously, an image of the surface whose shape has no necessary resemblance to what might be behind or beneath it—so different from a metaphor whose appearance corresponds with a hidden reality below the surface, one that requires disguises to be seen at all. The water gives the poem's speaker back only "a shining surface picture," a polished-up image laid like a veneer over what lies below, that "something more of the depths."

Nothing is more difficult than seeing the truth about what is behind what both we and the world permit us to see of ourselves. Culturally induced cognitive myopia is a malfunction whose cure requires bringing the distance into the focal range of our own eyes. And if in that distance are to be found images that correspond to something of our own depths, then we are on the brink of identifying distance and closeness. Which is precisely the brink that poetry pushes us over.

Looking back at Frost's first line, we see that he begins at once to establish his aesthetic distance by having the first-person speaker describe himself as seen not by himself but by others: "Others taunt me with having knelt." Aesthetic distance is achieved in multiple ways, but chief among them is the view through other eyes, which creates a distance from the ego (or the received view) that opens our eyes to things we could not otherwise have seen. The poem's speaker says that the "others taunt" him; it is precisely their lack of charity that offsets his partiality, creating a larger perspective.

The word *Other,* with a capital *O,* has become these days a buzz-word in academic circles, but there's a real bee in its buzz. Other is nonego; to enter an Other is to gain that aesthetic distance that helps offset the difficulty of seeing and expressing what is closest or, more elusive still, inmost.

Besides the otherness that Frost imports into the I, and its mythic extension, the poem has the aesthetic distance created by formality, an adroitly handled and expressive traditional prosody, a pentameter whose insistent trochaic beat, as in "shíning súrface pícture," creates a falling rhythm that emphasizes the disappointment of vision in the poem's climax—for the surprise in this poem is precisely that disappointment. It is a fifteen-line poem, a sonnet with one extra line, even as that extra line has an extra beat, and its final word is also a final trochee with its dying fall: *sóme/thing.* The prescribed form is another distancing device, its pacing cooling down the first-person *angst* of the voice, the natural speech tone playing against the regular metric, even as feeling is held in tension with mindfulness.

As an aside here, I should add that metrical, stanzaic form may be a contributing factor but is not sufficient by itself to produce aesthetic distance. I was once at a reading where an accomplished poet read an extremely well-made, metrically impeccable, elegantly and subtly rhymed sonnet whose subject was a graphic, move-by-move description of herself masturbating. Who could help thinking, "Honey, we *know* how it's done"? I think of a line of Louise Glück's from her essay "The Forbidden" about the ease of display demonstrated by writers these days "competing in the previously un-permitted arena of personal shame."

Distance also comes from cues that indicate habitual action, for instance, the way the past progressive of the verb *having knelt* and the plural *well-curb*s denote customary, repeated instances. This is not what happened but, as Aristotle said of tragedy, what happens.

The word *always* reinforces the sense of the habitual, as does its negative twin, *never*: "Always wrong to the light so never seeing deeper," that *always* placing us in the here *and* elsewhere of the imagination, the "always-never" place of quasi-mythic engagement, abstraction joined to real action. Equally, the word *Once,* which marks the turn after the initial sestet, introduces the unique instance; against *always* with its *never* comes the hopefully dramatic "But once," a hope that draws the reader and speaker forward until subsequent action deflates it. Throughout, then, the poem is immediate and present, but it is also "elsewhere," that distanced place where concretion carries abstraction, where the intellect can remain fully operative while the senses and feelings are also engaged.

Now there is a third actor in the poem beside the man and the others who taunt him—water, the very medium in and through which he is trying to see. This subversive power is carried in the sonic system of the poem in the almost involuntary repetition of the *-ur* sound: *curbs, never, deeper, water, surface, picture, fern, summer, curb, discerned, picture, picture, uncertain, water, water, fern, blurred. Blurred* is the finale of this soft murmur of sound—as if uncertainty itself were given voice. In this soft blur of sounds arrives another notion of truth than that for which the poem's speaker had been looking: "Water came to rebuke the too clear water."

In order to explore this tantalizing statement, let's consider what the speaker thinks he glimpses: "a something white, uncertain," "whatever it was lay there at bottom . . . whiteness." And he asks what it was: "Truth? A pebble of quartz?" Now, while the pebble seems to mock with its littleness the word *truth,* it also adds substance to his sense of what there is "at bottom." Indeed, the very notion of solving life and identity by the finding of a single "something there at bottom" is itself a particular philosophical position.

The language is unmistakable: he is an essentialist, that is, his notion of truth is of some essence not unlike that white stone—some absolute, pure, and fixed center, a chip off the old rock of ages. To this vision of truth there is added the rebuke of falling water to still water: one drop will do it—a "ripple shook" the image of what might be below—and we are left with the ripple and its "blur," the motion of water set against the notion of something unmoving and unmoved at bottom—the fluidity and interconnectedness of the mediating waves of the real, undoing the stasis and detached singularity the speaker looks for as if it were synonymous with truth.

The pebble of quartz both embodies and critiques this ultimately reductive and nonsensical notion of some pure essence of self down to which we could get. And "whiteness"—well, that has been in trouble since Moby Dick ate Ahab's leg and terror stalked the southern night in white satin sheets.

Finally, *what* he sees is not unrelated to his stance as a single self trying to see through his own image to something essential. The vision is all of a piece, really, and it is the water that tips us to another sense of truth, as "it shook whatever it was lay there at bottom." To be so shaken may be the beginning of wisdom. We are reminded that new vision comes not from the old center on which we are fixated but from the periphery—what grows beyond the curb, where we neglected or were trained not to look. Which brings us to the other Frost poem I mentioned earlier, one that takes up the same narcissistic dilemma but looks outward to the periphery of vision on the other side and enlarges the aesthetic distance—and with it the amount of vision that the poem enacts.

THE MOST OF IT

He thought he kept the universe alone;
For all the voice in answer he could wake
Was but the mocking echo of his own
From some tree-hidden cliff across the lake.
Some morning from the boulder-broken beach
He would cry out on life, that what it wants
Is not its own love back in copy speech,
But counter-love, original response.
And nothing ever came of what he cried
Unless it was the embodiment that crashed
In the cliff's talus on the other side,
And then in the far distant water splashed,
But after a time allowed for it to swim,
Instead of proving human when it neared

And someone else additional to him,
As a great buck it powerfully appeared,
Pushing the crumpled water up ahead,
And landed pouring like a waterfall,
And stumbled through the rocks with horny tread,
And forced the underbrush—and that was all.

The aesthetic distance is more overt in this poem than the last. The main actor is not a first- but a third-person speaker—a "he," a position that gives the writer more distance from his subject, even as that subject, by looking into a distance on the other side of where he stands, will see something about himself he could not have seen by looking at himself up close. It is what Barbara Tuchman called "the distant mirror" in her history by that name, a book in which she showed the twentieth century something of its own image by writing about the fourteenth. Frost places his character in the spacious landscape of the poem in such a way that his subject's posture, like the figure kneeling by the well, is a conscious attitude as well as a physical position.

He is alone, he stands at the edge of a lake across which he calls, demanding response, and, from a hidden cliff on the other side, gets back (like Narcissus in the myth) only "the mocking echo" of his own voice. The subject, we are told in the first line, "thought he kept the universe alone," a rather overweening sense of personal possession, but the line "for nothing ever came of what he cried" shifts the cause of his sense of isolation onto the universe itself, a nature that simply echoes his calls rather than responding to his demand for a genuine response. The egoistic tendency is to blame the other side, and with the truth of that tendency the poem begins.

But another truth lurks in the odd detachment of the lines "He would cry out on life, that what *it* wants / Is not *its* own love back in copy speech." Frost could have said "what he wants" but he says "what it wants." The man speaks of his own life as something alien, an "it"— neutral, impersonal, missing the very life it names. So when something takes shape out there, though fleshed out and revealing in its shape and action, it remains a nonhuman it.

As in the other poem, a unique occasion erupts in what seems to be a chronic condition as the verb shifts from the simple past tense to the conditional "he would cry out." The conditional shifts from the usual to the possible, a "might be" that opens the mind to suppose and thereby *not to remember an experience but to imagine an event*—one that happens in, and only in, the poem and offers an insight that all the recitation of actual experiences could never provide.

This freeing of the imagination by means of the conditional tense is further enhanced by the very offhandedness of the phrase "unless it was": "And nothing ever came of what he cried / Unless it was the embodiment that crashed." So something new enters the visual field from the periphery of both attention and scene—this "embodiment." I love Frost's nerve in using the word *embodiment* to remind us of the virtuality of this virtual reality, to undermine the literal minded for whom a buck is a buck is a buck (*pace* Gertrude Stein). For in metaphor, as you know, the "embodiment" is both a buck and not a buck—it can neither be simply resolved into that single animal nor solved like an equation by substituting paraphrase for presence.

I remember the textbook interpretation of this poem from years ago—something to the effect that the buck represented "Nature" in America, the untamed wilderness and its indifference to man. But, of course, the forcing of the underbrush, and the generally rude way this buck forces its way through the very nature it is supposed to represent, also tears its way through such a facile reading.

This distant mirror into which the subject looks is not a passive surface but some active disturbance on the other side of the lake. The poem is set up as a kind of long-distance reflecting device: on one side, the demanding subject, alone on "a boulder-broken beach" on the "far distant" shore its mirror image, the "cliff's talus"—broken-up rocks at the foot of a cliff—out of which comes the stony, unfeeling "embodiment," itself a kind of animate stone whose action opposes water, crumpling it in passage, then shedding it as rocks do.

We first know this *it* by its loud and discordant sound: it "crashed / in the cliff's talus," a rather violent disturbance that continues throughout its passage—it crashed and splashed, and pushed and landed and stumbled and forced. For six lines after it first emerges, neither the poet nor the reader knows what it is—and the full and significant embodiment of the apparition rests on this listening-and-watching-but-not-knowing. We sense that Frost set his created man to call out across those waters, the poem depending on the poet's not knowing what his call might elicit.

The protagonist of the poem, whose inner life demands of external life an "original response," gets exactly that, even as he also gets a kind of "copy speech"—for it is both something alien and something alienated in himself that comes back to him, he who demands but offers nothing. This is the central irony of the poem. The buck is both copy and response; the man gets yet another echo from the cliff, but this one, being embodied, is also an "original response." What Frost's character gets back is not what he wants but what he is—or what, at least, explains and maintains his isolation.

What is troubling about too much of our poetry is that, without aesthetic distance, it remains in the realm of ego, of what we think we know, or what we want or think we ought to see. Let me for a moment illustrate that point from my own experience, an incident that suggests how a self-flattering, conventional, and other-blaming poem got itself rewritten from the margins.

Sometimes when we sit down to write a poem it is to do only what we do on a regular basis: whine, show off, cast blame, blast our enemies, and congratulate ourselves. But the imagination won't have it; the poem must go otherwise if it is to be a poem, and let the chips fall where they may. I was trying, one day, to write a poem about male rage. Now, you will understand at once that I had a problem. When a woman sits down to write about male anger, I'll give you pretty high odds that she has some ego stake in the matter, which may create a serious lack of the poetic vision that depends on aesthetic distance.

So now I'll ask you to picture me at the typewriter (that anti-quated machine dates the experience back twenty years or more) writing about *his* anger without much noticing my own. You will not be surprised to learn that my imagery took a direct fall into the conventional (an almost sure sign of bad faith) and that what I was writing was, quite literally, bull. In fact, my little ersatz poem featured a large and raging bull, a mountain, a thunderstorm, and plenty of Sturm und Drang. I was using up all my powers of description on this poor bull, who was stamping and snorting and charging his way through the terrain, up the mountain and down the page, going more or less nowhere.

Now, while I was writing this, I was also doing a little something on the side. A kind of offhand thing as it were; without paying much mind to it, I had begun to write on a piece of paper that was lying on the desk to the side of the typewriter. When I finally pulled the bull from the typewriter, I turned to see what I had written on the side. I tell you truthfully that I had barely been aware of writing it, but there it was. I read it and threw the bull in the wastebasket (which I have elsewhere and frequently named as the writer's best friend). Here is the poem almost exactly as I found it. It is written in the first person; the speaker begins with her own epitaph (the form itself a warning, a fate already closed and carved in stone).

EPITAPH

Though only a girl
the first born of the Pharaoh,
I was the first to die.

Young then,
we were bored already,
rouged pink as oleanders
on the palace grounds, petted
by the eunuchs, overfed
from gem-encrusted bowls, barren
with wealth, until the hours of the afternoon
seemed to outlast even
my grandmother's mummy, a perfect
little dried apricot
in a golden skin. We would paint
to pass the time, with delicate
brushes dipped in char
on clay, or on our own blank lids.
So it was that day we found him
wailing in the reeds, he seemed
a miracle to us, plucked
from the lotus by the ibis' beak,
the squalling seed of the sacred
Nile. He was permitted
as a toy; while I pretended play
I honed him like a sword.
For him, I was as polished and as perfect
as a pebble in a stutterer's mouth.
While the slaves' fans beat
incessantly as insect wings,
I taught him how to hate
this painted Pharaoh's tomb
this palace built of brick
and dung, and gilded like a poet's
tongue; these painted eyes.

Well, here we have a poem that is more to the point—a poem about
female complicity in male rage—and, unlike the bull, this one did go
somewhere. This poem doesn't cast blame but explores motive: it does
suggest why the daughter of a king makes the perfect nurturer of the
leader of a future slave revolt for it reveals a thwarted female power,
bondage in its privileged form.

    The roots that this poem exposed were not particular to me, nor—
frankly looked at—are those of most of our dilemmas, though they

need a set of particulars to express them. When the Pharaoh's daughter speaks, it's with an intersubjective or transpersonal voice out of an ancestral story, but, freed from her own time's restraints, she speaks with the personal and confessional passion of a singular, present woman—reminding me that in focusing in the bull poem on *his* anger I had more or less forgotten my own. In his book *Poetic Diction,* Owen Barfield says that there are emotions too powerful to be only personal. So it is that we find ourselves, in expressing our own conventionally denied or hardest to touch feelings, in a transpersonal realm to which the depth of our expressive needs drew us.

When the Pharaoh's daughter spoke from her distance out of the margins of my attention, her heretofore untold story not only changed a collective memory but changed the way I looked at certain things that had baffled me before. The point of changing the cultural memory that sanctifies the past, besides the joy of freeing the spirits of our sisters from their silence in the histories of the past, is, obviously, to keep from repeating that past, to leave the future more open. Perhaps we shall never be wiser. But need we be stupid in precisely the same, murderous way?

In the poem "In the Kingdom of Pleasure," by Alan Shapiro, the same biblical figure rises to confront that question and confound the old categories.

> Unwitting accomplice in the scheme of law
> she thought to violate, man-set as it was,
> and, here, inconsequential as the sun
> at midnight, drought at flood-time—
> when she heard a baby in the tall reeds
> at the river's brink, she was nobody's
> daughter, subject of no rule
> but the one his need for her established
> as she knelt down to quell his crying
> with a little tune just seeing him there
> had taught her how to hum.
>   Now as then,
> it is the same tune, timelessly in time,
> your mother hums as she kneels down
> beside your little barge of foam,
> smiling to see you smile when she wrings
> out from the sponge a ragged string
> of water over the chest and belly,
> the dimpled loins, the bud so far
> from flowering, and the foot slick

as a fish your hand tries to hold up
till it slips back splashing
with such mild turbulence that she laughs,
and you laugh to see her laugh.

Here now, as it was then, it is still
so many years before the blood's smeared
over doorposts, before the Nile clots
with the first-born, and the women
wailing, wailing throughout the city;
here now again is the kingdom of pleasure,
where they are safe still, mother and child,
from the chartered rod of the Fathers,
and where a father can still pray, Lord,
Jealous Chooser, Devouring Law, keep
away from them, just keep away.

The poem begins in the deep, storied past with the biblical Pharaoh's daughter, the word *here* planted like a stone in time's stream for footing. As the poem unfolds, we realize that the speaker is the poet, meditating as he watches his wife bathe their new baby son. The depth of the speaker's feeling takes him to that place, supersaturated with meaning, where the personal, present configuration corresponds with and is viewed through an ancient one: Pharaoh's daughter, who takes up the baby Moses from the reeds where he was hidden to save him from the Pharaoh's edict to kill the Hebrew firstborn. When she sees the baby, his sweet helplessness frees her from all former allegiances: she becomes not Pharaoh's but "nobody's daughter," which sets up the poem's temporal merge: "Now as then," while erasing the egoistic, old, and bloody tribal demarcations of "us and them," Hebrew and Egyptian.

These distant but correspondent figures provide a form for otherwise inexpressible feelings, allowing the poet to approach his deep and intractable fear and also to reveal the historical ground that amplifies a father's natural apprehensions for his infant son, the Jewish heritage that is a factor in the depth of his paternal anxiety. Thus does historical distance naturally become intimate present, the political and the personal merging as the poem expresses and attempts to allay painful contradictions—among them, a man's ardent desire to protect those he most loves and his dreadful fear that, inevitably, he will be helpless to do so.

By invoking the old story, he invokes the fearsome pattern that the forces of history marshal, again and again, against the nurturing values the poem espouses. Yet, at the very same moment, his love for his wife and new son, his contemporary historical awareness, and his redefinition of the role of father all fuse in the crucible of his imagination, and, although the ancient story recurs as part of the figure, it is stripped of its essential chauvinism: its divine sanction of the slaughter of the innocents. For whereas the Bible celebrates the victory over the Egyptians—including the God-ordained death of the firstborn of their children—the poet, as he sees his own wife through the figure of the once-alien Egyptian daughter, makes of all women sisters in their motherhood. And when he describes, in the last stanza, how "the Nile clots / with the first-born, and the women / wailing, wailing through- out the city," he makes equivalent both sets of murdered children— Hebrew and Egyptian—and both sets of wailing, grieving mothers.

This is a vision of human equivalence that, were it to become gen- eral, might create a future different from that engendered by the old tribalism and the biblical patriarchy (what he calls "the chartered rod of the Fathers"). But, equally, the dread of what lies ahead, informed by past history, shadows the innocence of this "kingdom of pleasure" and makes it appear momentary. The poem balances exactly on this ful- crum of hope and despair. So here is that "intimate immensity" of the imagination, where distance and closeness, past and present, repetition and change, intellect and feeling, fear and pleasure, pattern and matter, paternal and maternal, abstraction and concretion, us and them, the singular "I" and the collective "we" are rejoined in a single, complex entity—its driving force the desperate need to protect that which, in the life of the poet, is most precious and most vulnerable.

Which leads me, in closing this essay, to reinforce the function and privilege of the imagination, for, though there be nothing to hide, there is something to protect. What prompts this statement is the false but fashionable assumption that shame is the only reason to protect pri- vacy, and require aesthetic distance, as if a secret were the same as a mystery. I would say that, in fact, there has been a shift in the frontiers of shame, and now the autobiographical imperative in America (in our poetry as in many areas of the culture) has reached such a pitch that writers are (ironically enough) being made to feel ashamed if they have no particular inclination to write publicly of their private lives.

If something is essential to us to see, it will get into whatever we write, and if—through the various means of language I have been dis- cussing—we find the right aesthetic distance to invite the imagination, then may deeper, inmost matters become visible. Although the present piety is that everything is a legitimate subject for poetry and is open to the gaze, a tyranny of sorts may hide under this banner of openness. When the imperative of the day, the unwritten and even unacknowl- edged but nevertheless powerful edict about what is "authentic" poetry, pushes you to write what you already know, or to violate your soul's sense of privacy, to confess rather than to create—you have every right to cherish the aesthetic distance that transmutes suffering into art, that makes it possible to outwit the tedious ego, to use water not as a mirror but as a medium, to make poetry a way of knowing. And to those (including the imperious social voice in your own head) who want you to write against your own deepest inclinations, you have every right to say, as Shapiro's speaker said to the Devouring Law, *keep away . . . just keep away.*

NOTES

First appeared in *Writer's Chronicle* 31, no. 3 (December 1998).

MARIANNE BORUCH

Heavy Lifting

"*. . . don't pick it up.* The law of gravity
is the law of art."

—Karl Shapiro

Before there's a *thing* at all—fire station, airplane, bicycle, poem—
there's probably a blueprint. Before that, a drawing in a sketchbook—
on the verge of, about to. That's a beginning, at least a way to think
toward roof or wing, a turning wheel or something as quick as
metaphor in a poem, wily wayward device for digression or *viola!* One
thing leading to another as structure makes meaning strange and immediate and possible. And dense perhaps, the hand with a pencil suddenly
filling up the page, a roof turning into a gable, a wheel linked to a chain
and then to another wheel, or metaphor forgetting a while, for how
many stanzas, it's *like* anything at all. Of course, I'm already stymied at
this X-marks-the-spot, already lifting too much. It's too heavy.
"Everything is made out of everything," Leonardo da Vinci records in
his journal in what must be half praise, half exhaustion. So say this *thing*
is a poem. I have to get smaller, down to the simplest definition. A
poem is a box, then—see it in that sketchbook? In the hovering blue
of that blueprint? A poem is a box, a *thing,* to put other things in.

For safekeeping. Okay. Or it's a time capsule, or even a catapult,
for poets with more public ambitions, overarching, or just arching
enough. (Sorry, there it goes, getting bigger . . .) So, again, just this:
as a box, the poem contains. As a box, it is carried place to place. And
closes. And has secrets. And can weigh quite a bit. You pack and
repack it languidly or with exact intention. Or with hopeful indifference (back up, see *languidly* again, and float there with a little more
gravity). You forget to include your favorite things in that poem, or
you don't forget to forget, on purpose, putting old habits of beauty
aside each time, so it's new. Maybe it has to be new and sound different. It still weighs a lot. You can hardly lift it to the table, the porch,
the car. But the truth is you can always open the box. You can always
look down into it, and take things out, and rearrange its not-at-all-

like-little-furniture in there, the whole time lifting it, about to lift. Because the poem is lighter now; it's going up. And now it *is* up and out of your hands. You can hardly make it out up there, but you know the shape of its shadow down here where we live. It darkens the ground.

I need that darkness first because that's the happy outcome and perhaps the demanding, default position, start or finish. Let's face it: a poem matters because it's about eternal things—death, love, knowledge, time—however these are disguised. The great subjects are endless, never used up. But each waits there in shade. Each weighs at least four thousand pounds. Too much. It's awful, really. How can we stand it? Such melodrama could be—is!—offstage, pacing in the wings, heavy-handed moves ready to prove a point, certain half-seconds clenching up as if underscored three times with a thick black pencil. Maybe. But at times it's so believable, up there in the air. It's impossible, isn't it? Getting such mysterious, monstrous things to lift and keep going? Question: how the hell to do that? "There is no art to flying," said Wilbur Wright, "only the *problem* of flying." So there are ways, I suppose. Or maybe, for starters, it really is a matter of birdseed, Thomas Edison as a boy convincing another boy that eating a handful or two would make him smart about it all. He'd abruptly know *how* and launch himself right out the window into perfect flight. *Come on, just a few!* I imagine Edison telling that kid, thinking like a wise guy, but scared a little, past that, almost believing himself. And is it that simple, the old certainty that poems beget poems, something I've heard and absorbed and insisted for others, for years? We read all our lives toward poems we wish to write: black oil sunflower Dickinson and Bishop, thistle seed Hopkins and Whitman, the hard suet of Jeffers or Larkin or Kees or Plath. That work humbles and empowers, two things at once. Then at the window, looking down to our own city and mountain and farmland, to personal grief, into our own wonder about anything—this hesitation, this screwing up of courage, forgetting for a moment that we've eaten at all. Because our own hunger is crucial.

But crucial to what in poems? Their dark? Their light? What presses down or lifts up? Or, in Leonardo's terms, is it related to *weight,* this thing that is "corporal" and "changes its position unwillingly," is stable and stays with us, and lasts forever? Or is our hunger something he calls *force,* which is terrible and angelic, utterly "spiritual," he writes, the "true seed in sentient bodies," its energy always a "violence," *fortuitous* and *transforming* and *fleeting?* It desires only "flight from itself." And "death," he adds. This "force" that "willingly consumes itself.

. . . From small beginnings, it slowly becomes larger, a dreadful, mar-velous power."

Open any book about flying and one reads first about *angle*. Of wing, yes, but the ascent *into* and *up*—the "angle of attack," pilots call it—and *downward* eventually, even that cautionary no-doubt-about-it *sideways,* almost idling, just living a life for most of the journey. On the instru-ment panel—that airborne dash—so many small, important-looking faces loom up, clocking altitude then "heading"—the direction you thought you were going. Then the "turn and slip" one to balance, to stay put or at least level, by the old-fashioned charm of needle and ball; certainly the straight ahead speed, the vertical speed, each has its own dial and is busy. You can get such a thing in a kit these days, for as lit-tle as ten grand to do a whole airplane in wood or metal, or *composite,* which is strictly man-made. You can't predict how long it will take, though you can make a W.A.G., a WAG—*a wild ass guess*—says the book I'm reading about such vessels called "homebuilts," all put together, it seems, right down the street in anyone's neighborhood. But how many of those planes lie half finished, for years in how many garages, this minute? I'll venture a WAG: hundreds, maybe thousands. And someone might be walking through the yard now, thinking to turn on the light in there. Someone thinking to do some sanding, some welding, a little work on it; the wing needs to be set in place, just so.

Because the angle focuses everything. The incline, the turn, the deepest human wish: to rise, to get out of bed. Then later the second great longing, to be dark and descend. We'll never get over those two brothers at Kitty Hawk, the hard sand there autumn after autumn into winter, four years of failure and half failure, those Wright boys from Dayton, so far across the country, men who never married, self-taught mechanics and bicycle makers, their hunger large and dogged as their patience. In the old photographic stills, one is running, the other so careful about balance, shifting his weight in *their* homebuilt, a glider, then a motorized glider aloft one day in 1903, four flights' worth, those 12, 13, then 15, then the famous 59 seconds, an honest-to-god off the ground moving through space, on its own. But so ingenious, that they angled the wing by way of the bird, by way of its delicate, steely wise, hollow-boned pressure.

And poetry? That remains to be seen, but angling up like that, oddly lighter than air, it alters what one sees and *is*—looking down and across now, listening for something else, which might resemble the silent, largely selfless focus right before any poem kicks in. "Something, somebody, is trying to speak through me," Adrian Stoutenberg begins her "Séance," already in a forward pitch through patient guesswork.

> Ant or ape or a great grandmother,
> perhaps a voice even older,
> perhaps the sea, perhaps a throat in the sea.
> perhaps a shape without eyes or thumbs,
> dust maybe . . .

To such an eye, by way of such distance, all can seem altered, multiple, and odd. *Everything is made of everything.* But there are rhythms and patterns, and all starts simply, with one word or two or three. But—*news flash, key point*—this "lift" engineers talk about, the way air pushed down by the wing's slant must push up and up, it's physics, it's Newton's third law of motion—"for every action, an equal and opposite reaction"—and thus the rise, this heavy thing lighter, abruptly, into air. But what force pushes down in a poem? Which, in turn, turns furious, pushing up?

"Sundays too my father got up early." So Robert Hayden begins his well-known poem, "Those Winter Sundays," with something remembered, pretty large, and already under way. *Sundays too,* he says, as if we know about the other days, the boy, this son listening from a nearby room, from half dream perhaps, to his father's daily ritual in "the blueblack cold" as he fires up the stove to heat the house. *Already under way:* you can hear that lift in the cool assertion about this supposed day of rest—"Sundays too"—no commas for the natural pauses after "Sundays" and "too," the *of course, of course* of statement pushing here, this heavy thing, habit, made lighter by its seemingly automatic again-and-again, day-after-day. We are stopped, nevertheless, by the emphatic semi-inversion, a press downward on the wing—flying directly now *into* the wind for greater lift—with that structural decision to put the day first, in that clipped, near shorthand way, a trochee here, the poem launched on that initial no-doubt-about-it heavy stress. After all, it's not "On Sundays, my father got up early," the graceful rise of a more iambic beginning, and definitely not the prosaic get-the-job-done "My father got up early on Sundays." This is fierce. There's strain in the phrasing—"Sundays too"—a resistance that releases, one line later, the lingering, triple-weighted "blueblack cold," this "blueblack" suddenly older than anything we've thought about for a while, the two words flush against each other, as a *kenning* works, right of out of *Beowulf,* its "cold" flooding father, son, the memory itself.

It's the final two lines of this poem that show its true mettle, though one can't praise enough how this steady unsonnet sonnet moves toward that closure, accounting for the father's predawn labors—his cracked and aching hands, his polishing of shoes—but never sentimentally. From the start, the harder truths—including the boy who speaks "indifferently" to this father—are not airbrushed out.

> I'd wake to hear the wild splintering, breaking.
> When the rooms were warm, he'd call
> and slowly I would rise and dress,
> fearing the chronic angers of that house . . .

And so on, to the well-known ending of this poem, which takes those hard truths and weighs them so hopelessly—"What did I know, what did I know / Of love's austere and lonely offices?"—lines often recited, committed to memory, and for good reason; they stand by themselves. And maybe it's natural that we'd cherish and roar them out loud, then and now. I'm remembering again, years ago in Indianapolis, a car making its way through snowy streets, a handful of us in there, caught up like this. Out of nowhere, those words. And again, just this summer, in a friend's kitchen two states away, those lines in the air. They keep doing that, coming back. And maybe not *why*—that's a matter for more private places—but how exactly?

The given, bony rise in any question—the open, wondering built-in aerial view offered by that particular sentence structure—immediately gives these lines their initial internal power, and the repetition too, so by its second utterance—"What did I know, *what did I know*"—all is rattled and urgent, secret really, this speaker fully unto himself now. No longer directly hearing, we are suddenly secret ourselves, just *over*hearing. And what do we catch there, past lament? He stares again into that lost flash of childhood: "what did I know / Of love's austere and lonely offices?" One word, or two. So a poem starts, and finishes. *Austere* has to have one of the most violently beautiful effects in English, distant and vulnerable at once, public and hidden, held upright by enormous pressure, inside and out. And here its sound—its iambic lift—the second syllable stressed, adds a brief and expansive counter-rhythm. We hear in that both contraction and expansion.

But it's *offices* here that compels, and is brilliant, a word going straight into ancient practice. I remember a young priest in my childhood parish at dawn, reading the matins from his Divine Office, walking the streets as he read, never looking up as we biked by to early Mass. Something vast, nearly incomprehensible looms up in that word. In

Hayden's poem, it brings humility—what's been done and done again; one merely partakes of that. But nobility's there, too—ditto, done and done, this time into tradition and so heavy we no longer even know how to weigh it. The power of a single word can be staggering. And finding it, trying to figure out why it works—really why other choices do not—can take a long time and is the writer's most essential, brain-fracturing job. After all, a poem is a box to put things in, and with that comes the task of taking things out, then it's all over again, putting the radiant things, however dark they are, back in. Which is to say, in my friend's kitchen this summer, we gratefully remembered the poem, singing out those last two lines. And *offices*—I blurted out as any Catholic would, even one as long lapsed as I am—that's great in there, isn't it? *Offices!* I mean, what if—god, here's a terrible thought—what if he had written *promises* instead? "love's austere and lonely *promises*"? And my friend, her face suddenly screwed up in that funny gag-me way, her index finger already miming that half-way-down-the-throat thing.

Because *promises is* awful for about a half-dozen reasons. Which, of course, makes at least that number of ways to prove *offices* so remarkable here. But it's not a matter of meter, really, since both words are dactyls, three syllables whose first comes down hard before moving forward unstressed, first emphatic then that suggestion of *falling,* "a descent" Paul Fussell calls it, the critic who has written with such smart crankiness about these things. This downward move is especially dramatic against the *rising* shape—and hopeful, one might read that—of the line's earlier words, *austere* itself and *"love's"*—no—*Of love's,* both iambic moves, stepping lightly *up,* into the stressed second syllable. Or, if you hear a spondee there—two equal beats, *Of love's*—it only deepens the gravity, those two beats stretching time, Fussell's claim for that particular rhythm, suggesting weariness, he says, or fullness. But the words *promises* and *offices* are metrically similar; the difference in their power must lie elsewhere, maybe in what a pilot considers, the four elements that keep any plane going: lift and weight, thrust and drag. So the airborne wish, sometimes for thousands of miles.

Mileage—and certainly altitude—in a poem is harder to gauge, though one can start any first line in Seattle and land in Chicago or Philadelphia, most likely the same day. And—considering metrics again—the downward press, that first syllable's trochaic/dactylic hit that colors the very end and beginning of this poem, lifting and darkening in near equal amounts. Drag, though, is an aerodynamic force that resists the object as it moves through a fluid, which both air and water are, and which, I'd argue for a long time, thought is, too—a fluid, a near viscous dream. To land in any of these, one needs drag, which is to say, the plane routinely drops down its lumbering wheels not only to soften the impact but simply to add a needed baseline trouble, to get heavier and bigger at closure, thus to slow this last possible moment of the journey.

Words themselves drag behind them plenty of history, numerous other identities brought to the mix. And poets worry everything from the start. So back to *promises* versus *offices*. At first glance, the former has, well, promise. Anyone might *promise* a lot or a little: to pick up ice cream and avocados at Payless, to stop the mail for a few days, to make dinner, to keep a secret, to stay married. But the word can feel coy, even precious, especially following any reference to love, as it would in Hayden's poem if we forced our bad revision. A shaky choice—*promises*—and pretty much predictable, evoking the classic June wedding froth or worse, that pink icing turning petulant à la *but you made a promise,* says Tiffany to Chad (or Ryan or Trevor), wringing her hands in *Days of Our Lives* or *Guiding Light* (my mother's favorite, now celebrating its seventieth year on the air on radio and TV—the longest-running show in history). So melodrama is more than a suggestion of danger. With certain words, such as *fraught,* it's fraught with it, too willfully weighted, too much drag, I suppose, and not enough thrust to keep going, however right and graceful it is to hesitate here, at the end of Hayden's poem, where threat is genuine. Because there's already so much *falling* buried in those key words, and—double whammy—closure itself supplies a natural big bang and weight written right into the contract of the "meter making argument" that Emerson claimed a decent poem always has to be. In short, word choice is a tricky business. Such endless shifting Orville Wright needed at first, his body this way and that, to fly that delicate vessel! One needs drag, but not too much; thrust, but of a certain kind. It must surprise, however small that messing now with the angle of the wing to bring it all down, and in. Where it continues its haunting.

Offices then—because at heart that word hasn't quite the heavy-handed personal confinement that *promises* does, ticking off and getting (*look-at-me!*) credit for its duty-bound minutes and hours. Instead, *offices* goes back and back, past counting, almost courtly in its historical reserve, and will go on without, even in spite of us, thank-you very much—though not so very much. That's the lonely part, in part (*lonely,* yet another word with a first-syllable stress in this line, its second syllables unstressed, just a shade or two going under, so Fussell might declare it all the more dark, the descent even steeper). Thus this poem, this huge shuttering machine, is tiny, intricate—only fourteen lines!—coming to a sudden, albeit still moving stop.

In Leonardo's journals, you can find many curious pages on flight. "I have divided the 'Treatise on Birds' into four books," he writes, this treatise not strictly on birds (though a great deal of it is wing work— flapping versus gliding, taking off, coming down). He eventually gets to bats and fishes, flying machines, of course, and famously (their linen and sinew and pulleys, the staring figure drawn seated in the center between sticks and rope), then into the straight mechanics of such mechanics, where many of us might blur, glaze over. Always, though, "the heaviest part will become the guide of the movement." So watch out, I suppose, where exactly you put that part.

In the litany, one of our oldest literary shapes, *where,* and even *when,* seems hardly a choice, that "heaviest part" just there at the start of each line, and after that it's like the astronauts' famous floating-through-air, their arms and legs flailing as they speed far away from gravity's pull. Thus one more of Leonardo's dictums on flight: "Those feathers . . . farthest away from their points of attachment will be the most flexible." I read *flexible* here as lighter, as more subtle, as the variation Ezra Pound claimed every form needs to escape its essential fixed point, though it's exactly that shifting, back and forth, that makes art. "Repetition makes us feel secure," Robert Hass has written, "and variation makes us feel free." And it's hard not to think first of Whitman in this context, his reverence for, and brilliance at, these two sides of litany pushing out, then back, each line a miniature of the whole trip, keeping a kind of sweet stall here, back here, as the poem pushes forward.

But I'm not considering an overall habit. I'm thinking *midpoem* really, *midflight,* where so much of the journey takes place. Which is to say for a moment I'm trading Whitman for T. S. Eliot, two you'd never find in the same bomb shelter, though both would be alert and wary enough there, counting down water jugs and cans of beans to the last thirst and hunger ahead. In Eliot's "Four Quartets," the second one, the "East Coker" section, litany comes in abruptly, a surprise, not the given instrument it is for Whitman. It's a way for Eliot, already aloft, already up there, to hover soundlessly and still make noise. And because this is Eliot we enter *big,* through pure incantation: "O dark dark dark," he writes, "they all go into the dark." And so we have our anaphor, the repeated word in any litany, the fixed point to which at least some of those flexible tip-of-the-feather moves will return.

What's surprising in this section is how flexible those feathers are. Eliot is looser in one way than Whitman. The compulsion to return to that *dark* and *dark* is not so demanding, not the default setting every time as Whitman might do it. Eliot doesn't load the line *as line* so meticulously. And what's swallowed by this dark? Everyone, all, that is.

The captains, merchant bankers, eminent men of letters,
The generous patrons of art, the statesmen and the rulers,
Distinguished civil servants, chairmen of many committees,
Industrial lords and petty contractors, all go into the dark,
And dark the Sun and Moon, and the Almanach de Gotha
And the Stock Exchange Gazette, the Directory of Directors.

The accumulation here jumps categories, large groups of people, then how vast it gets with "Sun and Moon," then back to its daily inch by inch with "the Stock Exchange Gazette." Eliot's human beings are cast by where they work, high and low, and are far more generalized than Whitman's, for whom a prostitute, say, has accessories and "draggles her shawl" as his sign painter carefully letters "in blue and gold." Still, the more specific Eliot gets the more he simply *moves*—and the less he's characteristically ponderous. We get a little air, some release and sideways flight in that rapid but squarely paced shifting, that piling up before it all goes "into the dark and dark" and finally into the "moment of darkness on darkness."

Eliot does something else to lift and hover. Suddenly *cold* takes over *dark* in that cadence—"and cold the sense," he writes. Then *lost, too*—"and lost the motive for action." Steady, steady, we even rise on that move, a change in the repeat of *dark*—now this *cold,* this *lost*—a break in the weather, a new kind of breathing, more urgent. By it, we're upright, still gliding, before Eliot drops completely out of litany and into *story,* as poets sometimes tend to it, on an extended image working sideways both to evoke a moment out of human time and to make metaphor. He evokes the theater first, whose backdrop scenes go up then vanish nightly, their "distant panorama" of "hills and trees" all "rolled away," and then his next great passage, where all disappears in the "underground train," London's subway, the tube, that fabled site of so much longing and symbol for this poet. There they sit, the city's blank, staring citizens, and "behind every face" the "growing terror of nothing to think about." Of course, we descend in the weight of that image. This is Eliot, after all, whose genius loved most the dark default of such things. In the meantime, though, we were orbiting a little, and had that vision, looking with such sweep at everyone, at ourselves, so busy and doomed down there.

In fact, more ways exist to stay aloft, another set of *creature* ways to manage that. I know Leonardo was obsessed with birds and stared them through. And the Wright brothers, too, kept watching gulls, taking notes, reportedly flapping their arms, bent at elbow and wrist—no, it was buzzards and gannets at Kitty Hawk that swooped and dove. But at Berkeley, not long ago, biologists glommed onto a less in-your-face flyer. They've made a very high-tech minirobot, a giant gnat—a fruit fly, really—calling it a "robofly"—to see how the smallest of animals do it, stay up there, minus the powerful wings of hawk or jet. Some insect strategies then, and here one of their first techniques, the so-called delayed stall, where tiny wings dash forward and up (something neither bird nor plane can do), the fiercest angle. And how fast? Very fast, but Robofly is slower and larger; the human eye can see it. And would Philip Larkin mind the thought of certain moves in his "Sad Steps" flush up against this airborne feat? This poem, which initially moves off a sixteenth-century sonnet from Sir Philip Sidney's "Astrophel and Stella" and that poet's own "sad steps," which evoke the moon, quickly become Larkin's own night-bound invention. I'm counting out his six tercets, three movements really, on one of the great subjects—time (our getting old, our looking back, our right here, right now, our way of going back and forth)—not to mention the other perennial moments here—the early-hour sky or how anyone might rise midway through sleep to pee. In this shift of high to low, sacred to profane, there's humor, its automatic buzz and rise. We know at once we're reading Larkin—not Eliot, not even Whitman. So maybe Robofly is semiproper, a way of paying homage.

Larkin first gives us time and place. "Groping back to bed after a piss," he writes,

> I part thick curtains, and am startled by
> The rapid clouds, the moon's cleanliness.
>
> Four o'clock: wedge-shadowed gardens lie
> Under a cavernous, a wind-picked sky.
> There's something laughable about this.

Is this what anyone might see? The moon's up there, and clouds like "cannon smoke," and "roofs below." And heavy, clean, this stall, that won't let that moon go, this staring, quick, that keeps it coming (wings cutting forward, a steep, then steeper angle) in Larkin's pronouncements.

> High and preposterous and separate—
> Lozenge of love! Medallion of art!
> O wolves of memory! Immensements!

That sudden angle, this "delayed stall," is mimed hard by the fragmentation here, more, by his precise jabs at definition, be they wild and tongue-in-cheek. Real or imagined, it's still triumphant. Exclamation points, count them: four! They push everything higher, lighter. And the simple repetition—"of love . . . of art . . . of memory. (Knock on wood: here's the heft of litany again, though shrunk down and in its locket.) That *of of of* cuts up at an urgent angle however playful. (Can you see that intricate, fuzzy, wired creature—moon or fruit fly or poem—hovering there? And so much bigger for it?) Such high invention to make real that moon before the *no* comes, and "one shivers slightly, looking up there," the poet now dropping abruptly to a more level tone, shifting from his mock heroics to something more felt and nagging about this moon. Which is to say, worlds sadder.

> The hardness and the brightness and the plain
> Far-reaching singleness of that wide stare
>
> Is a reminder of the strength and pain
> Of being young; that it can't come again,
> But is for others undiminished somewhere.

In writing once about Auden, Larkin linked the words *funny* and *dreadful*—*dreadful* in its first straightforward meaning, that is, full of genuine dread. "High and preposterous," Larkin reminds us in his own poem, this "lozenge of love," calling up the "wolves of memory" and so many "immensements," none of which will "come again." So humor finds its weight in such an unlikely mix, and so that darker weight finds lift, fracturing itself *endurable,* even radiant for a moment. We find ourselves looking down and up and past that moon and its usual guises now into a very different—and unsettling—expanse.

In the history of flight, there are thousands of stories, and quite a few belong to the Wright brothers, though one is legendary, coming out of their bicycle shop in Dayton, Ohio. Two elements are memorable—an empty inner-tube box and Wilbur Wright leaning in the doorway, talking idly to a customer not too long after the century turned. I see him there. He's picked up the box. He's fiddling with it; it must feel good in his hands as he keeps talking, listening, nodding his head, turning the cardboard this way and that. Then he's looking down. No, he's *more* than looking down. How this simple movement—his twisting the box—superimposed itself on the rigid wing of their not-yet-flying machine shows metaphor in its most heightened—and practical—moment. *What thing is shaped as this thing is shaped?* That's William Carlos Williams decades later, from his poem "Asphodel, That Greeny Flower," a question I've loved too much, and quoted too often, but it narrows to an absolute in poetic thinking: we learn by the leap, the comparison, the analogy; two unlikely things together make a third thing, and so we move forward. *A wing could do this,* Wilbur Wright must have thought, maybe vaguely at first, but more and more, it must have taken hold under the talk-talk about whatever, the storm last night or the new brick work going in to make east Third a wider street, this deeper kind of mulling over that runs on and on under the surface fact, almost by itself, the sort of lucky thing that *comes to us,* these *glimpses.* So poems are twisted, too, drifting there, in progress regardless, kept alive even when those who write them are distracted, not particularly honed to the task.

As for aviation, Wright's fiddling that day was the key to "wing warping," the brothers' name for this great gift and innovation, so simple really, to solve the problem of control, their craft now too heavy and past the point one of them piloting could merely shift his weight left, right, forward, backward to *will* the plane through air and so avoid disaster. The Wrights' sketch and blueprint of the design was stunning. In it, we see the beauty of pure form. And the plane itself seems almost whimsical now, the wings' edges made bendable by runs of two bicycle chains jerry-rigged to a couple of levers. But the point is this: what seemed forever rigid to everyone—the airplane wing—was not. And the larger point: was it really possible? Yes. We would fly.

To warp something then. To make flexible what all along was kept as *rule,* committed in the mind to stone: the very thought, even in theory, is a great relief, a lightening of both inside and outside pressure. Applied to poetry, sometimes it's dramatic, such warping, denoting a sea change in a poet's work, John Berryman's, say, his messy and vernacular move to *The Dream Songs* from a more formal habit in *Homage to Mistress Bradstreet* or his *Sonnets,* a twisting of that inner tube box, a serious wing warp. And the nature of that particular flight—its drag and thrust, its lift and weight? "A creepy, scorching book," Adrienne Rich wrote, reviewing it for the *Nation.* "He uses any conceivable tone of voice and manner to needle, wheedle, singe, disarm and scarify the reader." Can you see Orville Wright up there at his levers? The bicycle chain angling the wing just barely, tragedy averted by a couple of degrees. No crash this time. Not yet.

Because tragedy is all over *The Dream Songs;* its threat presses down on every line. Which is why, perhaps, we think of the deep play in these poems as a kind of resistance—Newton's countermotion coming up by way of Berryman's comic brilliance. It's Larkin again, mixing dark and light, thrust and drag—to keep aloft and believable. "Life, friends, is boring," Berryman announces straight away in Dream Song

14. "We must not say so." But some of the pieces are less stagy, just painfully wry or simply edgy, which is a balancing, too. Number 29 is an example of this, taking on one of poetry's great subjects—regret, guilt, remorse, three curses of memory that make one curse in the poem. With characteristic dark grace, line-to-line, this poet twists and warps and finally convinces. Note the music here. Note Berryman's feel for a big-voiced but tentative sound, a point-counterpoint managed by inversion, fable, surprise, omission.

> There sat down, once, a thing in Henry's heart
> so heavy, if he had a hundred years
> & more, & weeping, sleepless, in all them time
> Henry could not make good.
> Starts again always in Henry's ears
> the little cough somewhere, an odour, a chime.

How huge then small this begins—*There sat down, once*—the cadence so familiar, as if this were the oldest story we have to tell. But where? In "Henry's heart," and so this very public utterance turns personal, private, and "so heavy," this *thing*—too horrible to be named—and to prove that weight, a kind of piling up—years of this thing, "& more, & weeping, sleepless, in all them time." This could be pure melodrama so easily, but it's rushed, its shutter speed so fast, even tiny decisions— quick! screw up the grammar, go slipperier, enjamb! enjamb! or use an ampersand, not the proper "and"—to loosen, to lighten before the line break quiets everything for a second, then the fall via so many hard single stresses: "Henry could not make good." So we're down—it's Fussell's lamenting spondee again—and seriously end-stopped. Which is to say, real pause. Silence. Until "Starts again always in Henry's ears / the little cough somewhere, an odour, a chime." This is a large measure of Berryman's power, his willingness to move. His rapid juxtaposition makes weighty complexity here almost lacelike, delicate. Where to go? To the triggering agents, these bad charms—a cough, an odour, a chime—to bring this *thing* back.

His sleight of hand continues, this expert shifting—it's Berryman's famous hairpin control of tone. It's wing warp taking us through time, his flashing in reverse to Italian sculpture in the next stanza, its profile's thousand-year look of reproach unchanged. Next it's the very clipped, the fragment, "all the bells:"—a colon placed after "bells," Berryman forcing an equation: "too late," he says. Under such a load, there's only retreat. "This is not for tears; / thinking." Then "but"—that word of sweet suspension, signal for every reverse turn, rise, second thought.

But never did Henry, as he thought he did,
end anyone and hack her body up
and hide the pieces where they may be found.
He knows: he went over everyone, & nobody's missing.
Often he reckons, in the dawn, them up.
Nobody is ever missing.

Juxtaposition, the bendable wing—we're up, then down—a long sentence undercut quick by a shorter one. Or the surprise of the misplaced prepositional phrase, severing a warmer, more expected rhythm—"Often he reckons, in the dawn, them up," a kind of startle, a small, awkward leap in the line before the repeated phrase here, its automatic quieting the second time around. *Nobody is ever missing.* Violence cast into dream and bewilderment by metaphor—that third thing—in the secret half light that metaphor always is. And it's a draw now, the day just beginning, night still hanging on.

Leonardo's notion that "the heaviest part will become the guide of the movement" seems reasonable and just, but is it? Certainly we feel for that weight as we write, writing toward it, at least our side vision alert for it. After all, gravity is one of the three basic forces on earth, earth itself its center because—I quote chemist Robert Wolke here—"the more mass a body has—the more particles of matter it contains—the stronger its aggregate attractive force would be. That's why," he points out, "when you jump off a ladder, earth doesn't fall upward to meet you." This is maybe the best argument I've seen for work whose center of gravity, its focus, is the world and not the self. We know that ladder, after all. We've fallen off many a time. Because it's the mysterious huge *other* out there that pulls us to itself. But this perhaps is another matter.

Meanwhile, there's that other Leonardo thing, weight versus force, *weight* so stable and unchanging, those huge subjects of poetry, for instance—love, death, knowledge, time—and *force* working through that weight, a more wily spirit, out and about, "in flight" and "transforming," terrible and angelic both, violent. The voice in a poem seems also to transform, to do this give and take, to draw itself through the heaviest part, though often, and often effectively, it's not straight on, not an easy matter of calling up the lowest chords out of the string section to make sense of the speechless moment *after* the car crash in some overwrought made-for-TV movie. Such a force, this voice, works more powerfully much of the time by inference, a sort of ruse, where we look away for a second, pretend *this terrible thing is not the point, not really*. Though it is. And I may be half eyeing Larkin again, and perhaps Berryman, in this since irony and outright humor work this sideways way. In either case, Leonardo's *force* becomes a lifting device to get whatever overwhelming ache and baggage across, making it less, not more, so less *is* more. And then we're impossibly up there, in flight.

I don't know exactly how to approach what Emily Dickinson did with her "flood subject," one of the great ones, death, which was everywhere in 1862 when she wrote so much, the Civil War upping its bloody count daily. Leonardo's weight here is surely in that fact—the end in store for all of us, a stable, immovable element if there ever was one. But Dickinson, like Larkin and Berryman, is distracted and in her best work refuses to belabor the obvious in any ponderous, expected way. There's her famous and unbelievably odd take on the deathbed scene, Poem 465, with its fly—its *fly!*—as the key figure, its "Blue— uncertain stumbling Buzz—" that comes between the dying speaker and the light, until the windows *fail,* a run of image that would almost be whimsical if it weren't so dark.

Such oddity—if not comic, at least surreal—works because it isn't quite satire, which is to say, the speaker isn't grandstanding, isn't holding forth or looking down. That's not the *force* that makes this so chillingly accurate. When asked about his own use of humor during an interview with Robert Phillips of the *Paris Review,* Larkin was clear about the distinction: "To be satiric, you have to think you know more than anyone else. I've never done that."

Not knowing more, perhaps, but not responding to certain things in the same old, same old as everyone else: that might be the key, this force that Leonardo relished, a matter of surprise and angle. Which is to say, be just a little *off*—the bendable wing again—and so deflect. And invent something called flight. In Dickinson's poem 467, what's going on seems, at first anyway, less dramatic. "We do not play on Graves," she begins, this "we" apparently a group of children and this speaker the self-appointed leader of the group. The voice continues in that most superrational, reasonable way that such children often have.

> Because there isn't Room—
> Besides—it isn't even—it slants
> And People come—
>
> And put a Flower on it—
> And hang their faces so—
> We're fearing that their Hearts will drop—
> And crush our pretty play—

One can see instantly how this vessel stays in the air—pure pretending, ruse because surely the heaviest part of the poem cries out not so secretly: *This is a grave, damn it. Dead people live here. We'll all get this address sooner or later.* But Dickinson's pilot turns this so patiently, laying out reasons through the earnest explanation of a child impatient with the clueless adult who must stand there listening. "Besides—it isn't even—it slants" we overhear. Such grounded certainty in the language, so painfully missing the point—which is the point, of course. But it's like Dickinson to tweak the darker vein here eventually. So we land, drawn back to the most dire fact, a more adult shadow suddenly on the language. And, yes, back to Leonardo's heaviest part.

> And so we move as far
> As Enemies—away—
> Just looking round to see how far
> It is—occasionally—

It's that one last look, that "occasionally," that reweights—and lifts—every word here. As if we forgot what poetry is really about.

NOTES

First appeared in *American Poetry Review* 35, no. 5 (September-October 2006).

WORKS CONSULTED

Berryman, John. *77 Dream Songs.* New York: Farrar, Straus and Giroux, 1993.
Da Vinci, Leonardo. *The Notebooks of Leonardo da Vinci,* edited and translated by Edward MacCurdy. New York: Braziller, 1954.
Dickinson, Emily. *The Complete Poems of Emily Dickinson,* edited by Thomas H. Johnson. Boston: Little Brown, 1970.
Eberhardt, Scott, and David Anderson. "How Airplanes Work: A Physical Description of Lift." *Aviation,* February 1999.
Eliot, T. S. *The Complete Poems.* New York: Harcourt, Brace and World, 1962.
Fussell, Paul. *Poetic Meter and Poetic Form.* New York: Random House, 1965.
Hass, Robert. *Twentieth Century Pleasures: Prose on Poetry.* New York: Ecco, 1984.
Hayden, Robert. *Collected Poems.* New York: Liveright, 1985.
Jakab, Peter L. *Visions of a Flying Machine.* Washington, DC: Smithsonian Institution Press, 1990.
Larkin, Philip. *Collected Poems.* New York: Farrar, Straus and Giroux, 1993.
Larkin, Philip. *Required Writing.* Ann Arbor: University of Michigan Press, 1999.
Phillips, Robert. "The Art of Poetry, no. 30." *Paris Review* 82 (summer 1982). Interview with Philip Larkin.
Rich, Adrienne. "Mr. Bones, He Lives." *Nation,* May 25, 1964.

Sanders, Robert. "'Robofly' Solves Mystery of Insect Flight." www.berkeley.edu/news/media/releases/99legacy/6-15-1999.

Shapiro, Karl. *Collected Poems*. New York: Random House, 1978.

Stoutenberg, Adrien. *Land of Superior Mirages: New and Selected Poems*. Baltimore: Johns Hopkins University Press, 1986.

Walter, Donald H. *Building Your Own Airplane*. Ames: Iowa State University Press, 1995.

Whitman, Walt. *Leaves of Grass*. New York: Dutton, 1971.

Williams, William Carlos. *Selected Poems*. New York: New Directions, 1969.

Wolke, Robert L. *What Einstein Told His Barber*. New York: Random House, 2000.

Wright, Wilbur, and Orville Wright. *The Published Writings of Wilbur and Orville Wright*, edited by Peter Jakab and Rick Young. Washington, DC: Smithsonian Institution Press, 2000.

Many thanks to Elizabeth Adcock for introducing me to the work of Adrien Stoutenberg and to Brooks Haxton for reminding me of Sidney's "Astrophel and Stella" and its trace in Larkin's poem "Sad Steps."

LAURA KASCISKE

The Transcendent Poem

I

In a famous story in Bede's *Ecclesiastical History,* one of King Edwin's
unnamed nobles, in making a case for a national conversion to Chris-
tianity, describes the "life of men here on earth" as if

> a sparrow should come to the house and very swiftly flit through;
> which entereth at one window and straightway passeth out through
> another.[1]

It's winter and night. Outside, in the darkness, there's wind and snow.
Inside the house there's a fire kindled and people sitting at dinner. The
sparrow glimpses, experiences, this shift from darkness to light, cold to
warmth, solitude to companionship, obscurity to clarity in a flash of
intensity, flying through.

> So the life of man here appeareth for a little season, but what fol-
> loweth or what hath gone before, that surely we know not.[2]

In other words, not only is life short, but it's a brief physical interlude
between the great, dark, amorphous unknown or unremembered
experiences of prebirth and death, which stand like grim bookends on
either side of it. We fly into the middle of something that's been going
on for quite a while without us and will continue after we're gone. It's
real, but how can we grasp the whole of it with such a quick glimpse?
   We can't. Just flying through. In one window and out the other.
   Only a very small percentage of sparrows would not prefer to stay
with the company by the fire. But here we go, ready or not.
   If we agree with Aristotle that all art in its general conception is a
mode of imitation, I would propose that there is a kind of poem that is
both narrative and lyric, grounded in reality but also surreal, personal
and persona, both fully realized and merely hinting at all it might be,
that best imitates the experience of "the present life of men here on
earth," and that the writing and reading of such a poem is one of the

44

most transcendent of human activities—and that such a poem has definable qualities with which it achieves its precise effects.

II

Okay. You're the sparrow. You've just flown in from the dark.

> In Amsterdam there dwelt a maid,
> *Mark well what I do say;*
> In Amsterdam there dwelt a maid,
> And she was mistress of her trade.
> *And I'll go no more a-roving*
> *With you fair maid.*
> *Since roving's been my ruin,*
> *I'll go no more a-roving*
> *With you fair maid.*
> Her cheeks were red, her eyes were brown,
> *Mark well what I do say;*
> Her cheeks were red, her eyes were brown,
> Her hair like glow-worms hanging down,
> *And I'll go no more a-roving*
> *With you fair maid.*
> *Since roving's been my ruin,*
> *I'll go no more a-roving*
> *With you fair maid.*[3]

Now you fly back out.

A correct response, I think, to the tone and detail in this poem, is to pause and wonder. At the same time that I know nothing about what happened between the speaker and the Fair Maid of Amsterdam, I know everything that happened. I've been directly handed a slice of life, and it contains not only the experience of one but the experience of many, a single instance in a life that contains the essential essence of it. Regret. Chagrin. And yet a hint of obsessive longing, too. I'm not fully convinced that there won't be more roving, are you?

We can probably guess with some accuracy as to what the Fair Maid's trade was, but "her hair like glow-worms hanging down"? And then, of course, the big unknown: what roving, what ruin? We've come into the middle of a moment of intensity and passed through it and taken its impressions with us. The song is a moment of consciousness, of illumination and connection, in the way that a life is.

The combination of mystery and specificity, complete confession and withheld information, revelation and implication, is typical of most old English, Irish, and Scottish ballads, as well as many of the lyrics of the Middle Ages. Some of their mystery is, of course, the result of a loss of context for the people and events to which the mysteries refer. I would say that this loss of, or neglect of, *context* is one of the salient features of the transcendent poem, that it's the absence of *context* that allows for the experience of transcendence, the bird-flying-through-the-room richness and mystery of the transcendent poem.

III

Once I was in a pretty rustic bar in northern Michigan. There was a woman, probably in her late twenties, sitting at one of the high stools against the walls on the opposite side of the pool table from where I was sitting. She was smoking and drinking strawberry wine coolers. There were two or three empties lined up on her table. (At this particular bar, they cleared away your debris, apparently, only after you were out the door.)

She had long red hair and pale freckled skin and might have been a bit overweight, but she was wearing a really pretty blue spring dress, and, given the backdrop of this place, she was phenomenal to look at. Radiant, and also heartbreaking, because the man she was clearly there to see—the bartender, a scrawny mustached fellow in a white shirt with sleeves rolled up to reveal what looked like a homemade tattoo in the image of either a four-leafed clover or a turkey—the man she stared at almost without blinking as she smoked and drank in the corner by herself was devoting all of his attention to another woman, a woman who was sitting at the end of the bar, laughing at his jokes, leaning over the bar to kiss him hard and long on the lips. The favored woman was also smoking, also drinking wine coolers, and she also had long red hair and pale freckled skin. I can't remember what she was wearing, but it wasn't a beautiful blue dress.

The resemblance between the two women didn't end at hair and coloring, although that would have been strange enough. The two women had identical features in every way. Eyes, nose, eyelashes, ears, and even the gestures with which they knocked the ashes off their cigarettes and poured half inches of wine cooler into their glasses before knocking them back like whiskey rather than spiked Kool-Aid.

Clearly, these were sisters. If not actual identical twins, they were at least sisters so close in age and appearance that all their lives they would have been taken for twins.

In the half hour or so that I was at this bar, the woman in the corner never took her eyes from the handsome bartender, who never looked at her or seemed even to notice her, and the woman at the bar never looked behind her at her "sister" drinking by herself at a high stool on the other side of the pool table.

When I left the place, I knew that I knew exactly what was going on there, though I also knew absolutely nothing. Similar things had happened to me and never had. The band was dragging its equipment in as I left, and I knew what would happen next, have always known what happened in that particular bar that night, though I wasn't there and never heard a word about it and never went back. (Incongruously, it looked as though one of the band members, a man with silver hair and a goatee, was pulling an accordion out of the back of a van.) It was all there. It was all in place. I flew out of the window, back into the dark.

Of course, there were other characters in the bar that night, too. They might have had much more interesting stories than that of the redheaded woman, but I didn't have enough information about them to feel the thrilling urgency of narrative behind the details and also the tug of mystery, the possibilities present in the "loss." Those people, whom I've forgotten if I ever noticed them at all, were also like a kind of poem. An utterly personal poem, a self-contained poem, full of self-reference. A man in a suit chewing on a straw thinking his private thoughts, the significance of which I would only ever be able to guess at and come away feeling emptied, uninvolved—a kind of poem I'm less interested in.

Go in fear of abstraction, especially in bars.

But that red-haired woman. So much there in what I'd never know and, therefore, knew intuitively. I went through a million equally true meanings as I drove away from that bar, even getting so far (perhaps as I grew more tired as the road got darker and farther from any town) as wondering if, perhaps, the red-haired "twin" at the bar was not an actual woman at all but was the projection of the other, her fantasy made flesh being kissed by the bartender she loved. If you love someone who doesn't love you, love him with enough passionate intensity, could you send out, across a pool table, a kind of hologram of yourself? A projection of yourself being loved?

Well, probably not, or it would happen more often. But that was in the scene, too, that potential inserted as a "loss," not of detail (there was plenty of detail) but of *context*.

I transcended any simple meaning, any one interpretation, any literal experience of the woman I saw because I did not have, and never would have, context for it. She was not sitting there in a blue dress staring at the bartender as a reference in any way to my life. The mystery of the situation was not a poetic device. Still, there was a narrative there that resonates even now, a lyric or ballad that will probably continue to unfold for me in the same way a transcendent poem unfolds in the mind upon reading it, rereading it, and in recollection.

IV

This loss became, or always was, one of the valued qualities of the ballads. I believe that Edwin Muir is writing about this potential in those poems, in their deepest nature, in *The Estate of Poetry*.

> I am trying to describe what poetry meant all those years ago, to an uncultivated but in a real sense civilized community, a more civilized one than you will easily find now. What did we think of poetry? We did not *think* of it at all. If we had chanced to do that, probably the most we could have said would have been that it was both strange and natural, that it was different from any other kind of speech—but why not?—that the meter and rhyme resembled music, so that poetry appeared to be something halfway between music and speech. If there was any mystery about it, that was a natural mystery.[4]

Here the idea of mystery is taken down to the very words, the very *sounds,* with which a poem is written or spoken, the context of tongue and teeth. The halfway world in which a poem might function is implicit in every aspect of its nature, the place it comes out of neither speech nor music, ordinary nor alien, revelatory nor secret.

Here is a famous medieval lyric, the enigmatic character of which lends it much of its power and makes it a poem of the type I'm trying to define.

> Maiden in the moor lay—
> In the moor lay—
> Seven-night fulle,
> Seven-night fulle.
> Maiden in the moor lay—
> In the moor lay—
> Seven-nights fulle and a day.
>
> Well was here mete.
> What was her mete?
> The primerole and the—
> The primerole and the—
> Well was her mete.

What was her mete?
The primerole and the violette.

Well was her drinke.
What was her drinke?
The colde water of the—
The colde water of the—
Well was her drinke.
What was her drinke?
The colde water of the welle-spring.

Well was her bour.
What was her bour?
The rede rose and the—
The rede rose and the—
Well was her bour.
What was her bour?
The rede rose and the lily-flour.[5]

Hundreds of pages have been written in speculation as to the meaning of the poem, but really all we know of it is the strange narrative it offers: A maiden lay in a moor for seven days. Her food was primrose and violet. Her drink was cold water from the spring. A rose and a lily provided her shelter. And these were good things.

We have flown through the poem, and it's a life, full of the sensual details of a life and its psychological complexities, the ungraspable nature of its nature, the nuances that imply a richness beyond what the rational can grasp—the exact experience, imitated, of a life.

V

A few years ago, in a strange (for us) burst of home-improvement enthusiasm, my husband and I decided to get new carpet in the upstairs hallway. I say "new," but there was "no" carpet at all in the upstairs hallway, which was covered with rough pine boards with gaps between them through which you could conveniently look downstairs to see if you'd left a light on in the kitchen or living room. And there were unfinished nails sticking up here and there where, it seemed, some previous occupant of the house had decided to tear the boards up, before realizing that there would be no way to walk from one room to the other upstairs because those boards *were* the hallway, and then stopped without bothering to pound the nails back down. It hadn't bothered us. We simply wore shoes all of the time, but our toddler had learned how to walk, and making him wear hard-soled shoes at all times seemed wrong.

I went to Carpet World. I looked at some carpet and spoke to a salesman who told me he would give me a much, much better deal on the carpet than the Magic Markered ticket pinned to it claimed was the lowest price I'd ever find for such carpet again in Christendom. He'd throw in a carpet pad, too—but it wouldn't be the greatest carpet pad, and installation, naturally, would be extra on such a magnificent deal.

I felt grateful. I liked the carpet. Like the bargain, it seemed unusual. It was dark red with a complicated floral design, and I felt I'd never find anything to match it. Then my two year old started to scream so loudly that the other customers at Carpet World were actually plugging their ears with their fingers. I thanked the salesman. We exchanged phone numbers. We didn't shake hands. I swear, I was not in Carpet World for more than ten minutes. I only took about five minutes of that salesman's time. No pledges, plans, or promises were made at Carpet World that afternoon.

A few days later, I found the same carpet at Merkel's for thirty-five cents per square foot less with a higher quality carpet pad and free installation, and I signed on the dotted line.

A few more days passed before the salesman from Carpet World called. He asked what I was going to do about the carpet. I'm not sure why, but I couldn't bring myself to tell him that I'd found the same carpet for less money elsewhere. I felt, I think, that it would put the lie to his and my whole interaction, that it might embarrass him. I'm being generous here to my own motives—most likely I was just in a hurry to get off the phone and flip the burgers—but it explains why I said, "Oh, I think I've changed my mind about the carpet, but I appreciate your calling."

There was a terrible silence. In it, I could hear other conversations taking place on the wires strung darkly between us. People being polite, talking to each other in their phony telephone voices. Civilization conducting itself in a civilized manner.

Then the salesman said, with what sounded like sincere disappointment and also tremendous rock-gut bitterness, "I don't know what's not glamorous enough here for you, Laurie," and then he hung up on me.

I feel quite certain that all the therapists in the world couldn't tell me why, years later, I still think about that sentence nearly every day. People have said harsher, truer things to me in my life, believe me. And the interaction ended there. I fought the urge to call him back and explain myself, defend myself, and he never called again, and when we got carpet in the bedroom a year later I didn't go to Carpet World.

The mystery. What was said, certainly: *I don't know what's not glamorous enough here for you, Laurie.* And all that wasn't said.

I swear I didn't go in there that day in a black dress and pearls, running my French manicure along the pile. I remember vividly that I was wearing jeans with day-old ketchup on them because I wished, walking into Carpet World, that I didn't have ketchup on my jeans because I thought they'd take one look at me and think, Bad Risk, she eats at McDonald's, doesn't have a washing machine, and won't be able to pay off her carpet, and all of these things were more true than not at the time. My kid had a Kool-Aid stain on his face, which made him look as though he had a permanent red grin from ear to ear, like a ventriloquist's dummy, that I hadn't bothered to wash off before leaving the house because at that point in his life whenever I came near him with a wet washcloth he would scream and run away as if I were approaching his face with a pad soaked in chloroform.

The mystery was made more mysterious by the salesman's calling me Laurie. The only other person who ever called me Laurie was my mother and only when she was being affectionate. I must admit my mother *did* (although I hadn't thought of it much until then) comport herself around Grand Rapids in high heels much of the time, looking as if she felt the place weren't quite glamorous enough for her.

Was *I* not glamorous enough for her either? Or had I taken on some posture of hers without knowing I had, one that sent a message that was actually a strange echo of a message from another time and place?

And what of the salesman?

Without trying very hard, I can somehow imagine:

He is a child lying in a crib in the dark. His mother peers over the slatted rail. She's wearing a mink stole over her strapless jade green dress. He gurgles up at her, but she doesn't smile back.

And, all the while, traveling invisible in their ghost clothes, other voices in the air beyond us, between us. The sky through which the phone lines cut is a broken loom with something always in the process of being partially weaved or unraveled on it.

The word *context* comes from the Latin *contextus* "to join together, to weave." This story and the stories on the phone lines, the interaction between myself and the carpet salesman, will be always without context—hence, the mystery, the reverberation, my continuing interest in the meanings of the event.

Jack Kerouac said, "Things do not connect; they correspond. . . . That is how we dead men write to each other."

We die without ever seeing the whole pattern, the context, but the details and the quality of attention we give them is always determining its potential.

VI

On the movie posters for Fellini's *Satyricon,* the director is quoted as saying (in reference to his film, I assume), "There is no beginning and there is no end, only the infinite passion of life."

It's a wonderful epigraph to the *Satyricon,* which is, of course, a sort of adaptation for the screen of what's often referred to as the first novel ever written, a novel that has survived only in fragments but in its fragmentation evokes a whole world in all of its "infinite passion." There is certainly no beginning or end to the film or the fragments of the novel, but I take Fellini's quote to make reference to *life* as well as the *Satyricon.* To my mind, his statement would be the perfect epigraph to all the greatest poems of the type I am trying to define. Imagine it as the epigraph to "The Love Song of J. Alfred Prufrock," to "Disillusionment of Ten O'Clock," to "Fern Hill," to Lawrence's "Ship of Death," Duncan's "My Mother Would Be a Falconress," Plath's "Daddy," Roethke's "I Wake to Sleep," Larkin's "Aubade," O'Hara's "The Hunter," Jarrell's "Lady Bates"—poems that are, to use the words of Yeats, full of the "mystery and shadow in the accidental circumstances of life."

One of the things most of these poems have in common is a claim—either the poet's claim or the poem's claim through implication (tacit or stated)—of *persona.* This isn't a requirement, by any means, but it seems often to be an important aspect of these kinds of poems and their achievement of "infinite passion." No jury would be well convinced, of course, that Prufrock isn't Eliot, that Lady Bates is not Jarrell, that the disgruntled daughter in "Daddy" isn't Plath (with or without her famous BBC broadcast claiming that the speaker of the poem is an invented daughter of a Nazi who is . . . well . . . a little *angry*), but the effect created in the distance made (by greater or lesser degrees) in the tones and voices of these poems through the dreamy remove of the poet from the "I" is part of the poems' power, the transcendence of personal experience—a kind of out-of-the-body experience through poetry.

Who speaks? To whom? Even if we know what is being spoken *of*, without the answer to these two fundamental questions we are flying from window to window, gathering glimpses and bits to take with us, to build our nests back out in the dark.

The *Tibetan Book of the Dead*'s description of Dharma-Kaya, the state of perfect enlightenment, is, "Thine own consciousness, shining, void, and inseparable from the Great Body of Radiance, hath no birth, nor death, and is the Immutable Light."

I think this is a fine way of thinking about the effects of the transcendent poem and the use of the persona. The soul cannot support the weight of too much concentration on our selves any more than the poem or poet can support the weight. Hence, the heightened self in so many of the richest of these transcendent poems.

VII

In an essay entitled "Crossing into the Invisible," Laura Simms begins with the opening of a fairy tale to write about storytelling.

> There was an orphan boy whose job it was to watch the fresh threshed corn on the threshing floor of the barn. But he fell asleep and the hens ate the corn. His stepmother was furious. He exclaimed, "But I had a remarkable dream. I was standing with one foot in this world and one foot in the other. The sun was on my right side and the moon was on my left. I wore a crown and my body was speckled with stars."
> "Give me that dream," demanded the stepmother.[6]

In the fairy tale, the boy doesn't give the stepmother the dream, and therefore he ends up married to a princess, etc., etc. But it's the beginning of the fairy tale that's interesting as a metaphor for storytelling to the writer of the essay and for me for the kind of poem I'm writing about here. Laura Simms, writing about storytelling, explicates the boy's dream in terms of the characteristics of all fairy tales.

> As the characters in the fairy tale cross thresholds into other realms, we . . . are drawn inward past the boundaries of our logical minds into vast space and communal presence. The words beguile our minds with profuse detail as our imagination recreates the story. The habitual patterns of thinking that usually patrol the borders of this familiar world are engaged, and thus the door falls open inward—we feel the ever-present timeless space of mind that has always existed beneath the consciousness.[7]

The narrative structure hinted at by the transcendent poem, like metaphor and image, grounds us in this world so that the poetry can take us to another one.

In his book *Poetry and Mysticism,* Colin Wilson writes that

> the mystical—or poetic—experience is somehow very simple, like drawing aside a curtain, or turning on a light switch. But if you blunder into a completely dark room, you may feel the walls for hours before you find the switch. Turning on the light is simple only when you know where the switch is.
>
> Now the peculiarity of poetry—as also of great music and painting—is it has the same power as the sexual orgasm—of twitching aside the curtain, of pressing the switch.[8]

The poet has to give us the narrative structure so that we can find the light switch.

VIII

Laura (Riding) Jackson, before she renounced poetry, defined it this way.

> Poetry bears in itself the message that it is the destiny of human beings to speak the meaning of being, but it nurses it in itself as in a sacred apartness, not to be translated into the language of common meanings in its delivery.[9]

After her renunciation of poetry, she described her previous life as a poet in this way.

> I was religious in my devotion to poetry. But in saying this I am thinking of religion as it is a dedication to, a will to know and make known, the ultimate knowledge, a will to think, to be, with truth, to voice, to live articulately by, the essentialities of existence.[10]

If, as some critics and biographers seem to believe, her renunciation of poetry was a kind of lazy publicity stunt, then she is one of the most supreme of literary con artists. The poems lead me to believe otherwise.

"The Wind, the Clock, the We" shares some qualities with all the poems I've tried to use as examples of the transcendent poem. It has the qualities of story. There is narrative. One event follows another. The wind gets into the clock, the rain washes out the numbers, the ship goes down with its men. Until the poem's fifth stanza, there is no I, and suddenly there is the introduction of an even greater mystery than the mystery of how time can become a landscape, how the clock can devour itself:

> At last we can make sense, you and I,
> You lone survivors on paper,
> The wind's boldness and the clock's care
> Become a voiceless language,
> And I the story hushed in it—
> Is more to say of me?
> Do I say more than self-choked falsity
> Can repeat word for word after me,
> The script not altered by a breath
> Of perhaps meaning otherwise?[11]

There are too many possibilities in the poem to break them down. What we know of it is its strange landscape, a landscape that looks quite a bit like the page, a timeless place, like the poem and the hushed story at the center of it.

I don't think the poem is philosophical, nor do I think it is an ars poetica. The poem changes for me each time I read it, and I read it quite often because it wants to say something to me that I haven't quite been able to hear yet. I really think that. I think everybody has that poem, and they know it when they find it, and the poem transcends its time, place, landscape and poet when it finds you.

In his essay on magic, Yeats names three doctrines he believes have been handed down from early times and are the foundation of magical practices. The first seems to me to be relevant to the discussion of poetry as much as magic: "That the borders of our mind are ever shifting, and that many minds can flow into one another, as it were, and create or reveal a single mind, a single energy."

He goes on to describe an incident that I think might be very much like the experience of the kind of poem I'm trying to describe.

> I sat with my acquaintance in the middle of the room, and the evoker of spirits on the dais, and his wife between us and him. He held a wooden mace in his hand, and turning to a tablet of many-colored squares, with a number on each of the squares that stood near him on a chair, he repeated a form of words. Almost at once my imagination began to move of itself and to bring before me vivid images that, though never too vivid to be imagination, as I had always understood it, had yet a motion of their own, a life I could not change or shape.[12]

For me, reading "The Wind, the Clock, the We" is like that. The suggestions made by the evoker of spirits on the dais have taken on a life I can't change or shape, because someone else has created them, and which nevertheless move about with a life of their own.

The anonymously written fourteenth-century contemplative masterwork, *The Cloud of Unknowing,* compares the mystical experience to a spark flying upward. There's a moment like that in my mind when I read this poem.

IX

So what might all of this mean to those of us who are trying to write poetry as well as read it? Does it mean that we should intentionally be vague for the sake of vagueness . . . using the kind of logic that one sometimes finds in really young poets in workshops when obscurity is criticized: "But I *like* that everybody gets something different out of the poem. I *wanted* it to be confusing."

Indeed, that's the danger of even talking about the mysterious in the poem, that it might encourage the enemy of the mysterious: the meaningless. Where is the middle ground between the suggestive and transcendent and the Rorschach test poems, the kind of poem in which only the reader supplies any meaning?

I would say we only know the difference when we come upon it in our reading and our writing. In the Heikhalot Rabbati, the Jewish mystical text of the fifth century, the mysteries of existence, which "are hidden and concealed," can be explored through "the wonders of the path of the celestial ladder, one end of which rests on earth and the other by the right foot of the Throne of Glory."

In other words, we approach those mysteries that are "hidden and concealed" through the process of climbing the ladder between this world and the spiritual world. If you are strictly on one end or the other of this ladder, you are not on "the path." The path, to my mind, is the poem.

Laura (Riding) Jackson claimed to have renounced poetry in part because she found it to be "corrupted," that there was only one right reason for poetry, and that she had lost a sense of the reason. Her incredibly grouchy prose on the subject, written in a tone of (to quote her on the subject of other poets) "humanly impossible seriousness," nevertheless says something quite rich that, I think, speaks to the writing of the kind of poem I've been discussing. She writes that

> corruption of the reasons of poetry sets in—in both the reader and
> the poet—when too much emphasis is laid on assisting the reader:

when the reader goes to poetry with no notion whatever of the faculties required, and the poet is more concerned with stirring up the
required faculties than with presenting occasions for exercising
them.[13]

I think the outcome of the "corruption of the reasons of poetry" could
also be reversed, resulting in a poem that is a void rather than a *space*.
But I think the core of her statement is a very important one when we
consider our own poems and that it speaks to the sense I know I've had
when a poem has been too easy to write, when its "transcendence" is
really just an evasion, when the reason for poetry has been corrupted,
when the desire to be poetic (or be a poet) has been greater than the
desire to be with the poem.

X

Another way to think about what these issues might mean to us in the
writing of poetry could be by way of returning to another of the
famous stories from Bede's *Ecclesiastical History:* that of Cædmon, "to
whom the gift of poetry was divinely given." During his prepoetry life,
Cædmon routinely found himself in the beer hall, where they'd sometimes take turns singing.

> And so it was that sometimes at the table, when the company was set
> to be merry and had agreed that each man should sing in his course,
> he, when he saw the harp to be coming near him, would rise up at
> midst of supper and going out get him back to his own house.[14]

Then, one of these times, while trying to escape the harp, went out to
the stable and fell asleep, and he woke to a "certain man in a dream"
who said to him, "Cædmon, sing me something."
     Cædmon told him that he didn't know how to sing. That's why he
was in the stable.
     "But yet, thou has to sing to me."
     Cædmon asked him what he should sing.
     "Sing the beginning of the creatures!"
     So Cædmon did. He'd failed ever in his life before to be able "to
make any fond or vain poem," but there in the stable he sang the
beginning of the creatures and, according to the legend, became the
greatest of poets.
     "Sing me something, Cædmon," and he does.
     Just like that. Just, "Sing me something, Cædmon." Not THE

ALMIGHTY HATH COMMANDED ME TO BRING TO YOU
THE MESSAGE THAT YOU'D BETTER SING.

Naturally, God would reveal himself to the poet as just a "guy" and say, "Sing me something." Anyone who has ever sat down with a pen and a piece of paper at a desk and thought "Now I shall write a poem" knows why. It doesn't work that way. You have to be sleeping in the stable and some guy wakes you up and says, "Sing about the creatures, okay?"

You don't try to be poetic in a poem. You don't work to be mysterious or suggestive. Once, when I was in college, I'd gone to the arboretum to do some homework and I saw a couple there, probably in their thirties, and they'd brought a very large picnic basket and a blanket. They ate some sandwiches, and everything looked okay over there whenever I glanced up. Then they put the food away and took a Frisbee out of the picnic basket, and for a few minutes they sailed the Frisbee between them. Then they put the Frisbee in the basket, took out two badminton rackets and a birdie, and lobbed the birdie around for about five minutes maximum, then put that away and took out a softball. They tossed it, again for no more than five minutes, before putting it away. Then they lay on their backs and looked at the sky for about five minutes, and then they packed up the blanket and left.

By God, they were having a picnic. It didn't look very fun. We know that poem when we write it.

XI

In his big book *Lives of the Poets,* Michael Schmidt writes about the ultimate loss of context.

> Anon. is a poet without dates, parents or gender. Anon. appears in the fourteenth and in the twentieth centuries, in Britain and Australia and Africa, always with a song in the heart. Often the song is sad, as though something important—perhaps the author's identity—has been lost. . . . Anon. is the greatest of the neglected English poets.[15]

It's the loss of context we'll all come to sooner or later. Who we were will be a mystery. That's okay. It's good for poets, and good for poetry, to remember that in the end there's that ultimate untethering, unfettering, unmooring. When we write, it's to that we should aspire. To transcend our own lives. To become anon. To hope that the part of us that might last beyond this brief fly through—since we know that not much else, if anything, will last—might be something we managed to put in a poem, some music or detail that might last even after our very identities have become little mysteries.

NOTES

1. Bede, *The Ecclesiastical History of the English People* (New York: Oxford University Press, 2000).
2. Ibid.
3. Anon., "The Fair Maid of Amsterdam."
4. Edwin Muir, *The Estate of Poetry* (Saint Paul: Graywolf, 1993).
5. Anon., "Maid in the Moor Lay."
6. Laura Simms, "Crossing into the Invisible," *Parabola* 25, no. 1 (2000).
7. Ibid.
8. Colin Wilson, *Poetry and Mysticism* (San Francisco: City Lights, 1969).
9. Laura (Riding) Jackson, *The Poems of Laura Riding* (New York: Persea, 1980).
10. Ibid.
11. Ibid.
12. W. B. Yeats, *Autobiographies* (London: Bracken, 1995).
13. Jackson, *The Poems of Laura Riding.*
14. Bede, *The Ecclesiastical History of the English People.*
15. Michael Schmidt, *Lives of the Poets* (New York: Knopf, 1999).

PIMONE TRIPLETT

The "Multi-Homelanded" Sublime

By most accounts the Sublime is less sublime than it used to be. Popular usage of the word today is a quick lesson in our culture's priorities writ small, ranging from a million-selling punk/pop/ska band called Sublime to a porn site called the Sublime Directory, which offers complete downloadable ecstasy with "adult picture galleries." Gone from the cultural scene are the primary nineteenth-century listings for Reason and the Imagination, not to mention the formative experiences of nature or a poet's gothic scenes amid the Alps. Although there has been a resurgence of recent interest in the Sublime among poets and critics, it has also been considered at times to be reactionary. The traditional *Sublime* suggests ideals such as "transcendence," which we now know to be, if we follow the theorists of our time, a hopelessly totalizing and monolithic concept, something like a cheap, pine-scented air freshener that leaves the room smelling worse than when we began.

And yet, these qualifications aside, at the heart of the sublime was and is a concern with place and the sacred, with the powerful forces that can overwhelm and the rituals we invent to pay homage to them. Admittedly, the contemporary experience of nature can in part be reduced to cliché. The vastness of the Grand Canyon or Niagara Falls has gone the way of tourist postcards and the favorite fifties honeymoon. But nature's true terrors and vastness lie well beyond the powers of tourism and economic forces, as natural disasters like Hurricane Katrina and the Asian tsunami all too horribly prove. Furthermore, the sublime is not to be confused with the beautiful. Both Kant and Burke associate the beautiful with a confirmation of already held beliefs; where the beautiful consoles with harmony, the sublime disturbs with terror.

As an aesthetic experience, the sublime plays a dissonant chord, sliding on a scale between excess and exile. Kant writes in the "Analytic of the Sublime" that "The transcendent . . . is for the Imagination like an abyss in which [the imagination] fears to lose itself" (120). In terms of craft issues, the sublime supplies a rhetorical structure that is also psychological, and it tends toward certain defining, even ritualistic stages. First, there is a strong emotional response to some kind of power or authority. This power is associated by the romantics with nature, but it can also stem from an author figure. A feeling of the sublime might be prompted by one's being overwhelmed by great writing. In either case, the prompting power is indeterminate, vast, and unrepresentable, existing beyond the threshold of naming. Second, the sublime moment is usually preceded by a disruption from normal consciousness, a sense of profound exile from the authority in question. One's usual sense of scale and propriety is radically undermined, as if the correspondence between self and world is somehow breaking down. In the third and final stages of the sublime, equilibrium is apparently restored through an identification with that power or authority. The poet's sensibility leaps out of itself to make the sublime its own somehow, incorporating an enhanced vigor into her own creativity.

It's important for the practitioner of the art to keep in mind that this poetic process initially occurs by virtue of the act of description. One of the uses of trying to capture the unrepresentable in language is to see what happens to style even as something in the sublime resists the habitations of style itself. If the phenomenon of the sublime still relates to our contemporary burdens, the question becomes one of exactly how. And if our experience of the vast and powerful has changed to include such labyrinthine ungraspables as global capitalism, the split atom, or complex and multiple senses of place, how has the sublime been revised and inherited among contemporary writers, or is the sublime so materially altered as to no longer be deserving of the name?

To begin with the most famous example in the English tradition, Wordsworth's experience of the sublime provides us with the poetic blueprint from which future writers deviate or conform. Wordsworth defines *reason* as imagination in its highest form, the faculty that rises to the rescue of the poet self. It's the imagination that mounts to transcend the unrepresentable object confronting the viewer and paradoxically fills that which is fragmentary with a wholeness characteristic of the recuperative stage. The result of this personal peril is often an enlarged apprehension or insight into the hidden meanings of things, however dark and terrifying.

In *The Prelude,* upon the crossing of Simplon Pass in book 6, Wordsworth recounts the ritualistic stages of the sublime experience. After having lost the correct path while walking, Wordsworth's physical sight is first sacrificed to make way for insight; as he writes, there is a "usurpation, when the light of sense / Goes out" (217). In the Kantian paradigm, as the sensible imagination is checked in an experience of terror, it attempts to comprehend the relative infinity of phenomena. Wordsworth is faced with "black drizzling crags" and "torrents shooting from the . . . sky" (219) while in the gloomy straight of a narrow chasm. Presently, he has a recognition of eternity in the form of endurance within a pattern of change: "The immeasurable height / of woods decaying, never to be decayed, / The stationary blasts of water- falls" (219). For the romantic poet, this realization is characteristic of the ultimate form of the nature image, which seems to both participate in and go beyond the immediate workings of time, representing a sta- tionary state beyond mutability, intact at the core. Also characteristic of the Sublime here is the presence of simultaneous impressions of up and down occurring together, of the heights meeting the depths, along with the striking impact of light and dark, a vertiginous realm where opposites interact without sacrificing their essential energies. Wordsworth's physical description of the place cuts off with typical abruptness, here marked by the destabilizing dash followed by a Mil- tonic surmise.

> . . . the sick sight
> And giddy prospect of the raving stream,
> The unfettered clouds and region of the Heavens,
> Tumult and peace, the darkness and the light—
> Were all like workings of one mind, the features
> Of the same face, blossoms upon one tree;
> Characters of the great Apocalypse,
> The types and symbols of Eternity
> Of first, and last, and midst, and without end.

It's no accident that the poet's literal pathway leads to a spiritual one as image breaks into symbol. Wordsworth's experience of getting lost geographically affords his finding the intimations of an intense unity that is a hallmark of the sublime experience. What has been sacrificed is the everyday dimension of the mind, not only those aspects that are most self-conscious but also those that are most linguistically adept and in control, so that his lofty good guesses as to Eternity come sandwiched between that halting dash and the final loosening swell of "ands." Although Wordsworth's apocalyptic vision is less stylistically violent than some (Hopkins's "Spelt from Sybil's Leaves," for exam- ple), a form of conscious, even self-preserving, knowledge has given way to an epiphany of how "our destiny, our being's heart and home, / Is with infinitude." Another way of putting this is to speak of the poet's apprehension of collective memory rather than the merely per- sonal one we have been given thus far. Finally, with the arrival of the surmise, larger conceptions close with the biblical rhythms of the pas- sage's last line. Wordsworth here and elsewhere in *The Prelude* enacts the Kantian affirmation in the sublime experience, one in which identity is enlarged through, paradoxically, the loss of the ordinary sense of self. This is ultimately an aesthetic event that shapes identity rather than a religious or strictly moral one.

Well, it worked for Wordsworth. But what about the sublime now, when we think of ourselves as living in an age of doubt, beyond the assurances of absolutes? And how might this paradigm help shape the poetic concerns of our day or reveal one of the uses of description as it functions in the contemporary poem? Partly, I have to answer from personal experience. At a certain point, I felt the need to write in some way about my mother's native country of Thailand, of her and my own experience of a land both foreign and familiar. And, besides delving into the personal as deeply as possible, one way of avoiding the pitfall of the merely exotic—after all, a reader can access elephant antics and crystal blue beaches in any guidebook—was to connect my experience to an existing tradition. Here was a poetic genre that explicitly dealt not only with place but with the emotional resonance a place could trigger in memory and imagination. For me, not having been raised in Thailand but living with someone, my mother, whose every gesture, phrase, humor, and habit seemed to have to do with that place, the country became a kind of phantom world, always present and absent at once. It wasn't a lost Eden exactly, as I'd never lived there long enough in innocence to later fall from grace. And, although few writers have experienced firsthand the sweeping devastation that Paul Celan knew all too well, a phrase he once used to describe himself seems to apply to many. Roughly translated, he referred to himself as a "multi-homelanded—poly-patriotically entangled one" (Baer, 212). Perhaps for many Americans the experience of relocation and the complex relationship with place held by subsequent generations comes down to this sense of a mixed postorigin motion, a nostalgia for what was never there even as one hurls oneself into the next and next cultural moment. And, if we stretch the phrase a bit to help us account for our contemporary realities of place and how they can inspire poems, in a country as geographically vast yet locally distinct as America, couldn't some of the many who have voluntarily relocated be thought of as "multi-homelanded"—the southerner with roots in Tennessee who lands that job in Chicago, the woman who moves with her family from "back east" to "out west" or the other way around?

In speaking of the Indian writer living in Britain, Salman Rushdie addresses a more extreme version of this particular phenomenon is his essay "Imaginary Homelands."

It may be that writers in my position, exiles or emigrants or expatriates, are haunted by some sense of loss, some urge to reclaim, to look
back, even at the risk of being mutated into pillars of salt. But if we
do look back, we must also do so in the knowledge—which gives
rise to profound uncertainties—that our physical alienation from
India almost inevitably means that we will not be capable of reclaim-
ing precisely the thing that was lost; that we will, in short, create
fictions, not actual cities or villages, but invisible ones, imaginary
homelands, Indias of the mind. (10)

The recognition of the role of the imagination in re-creating the past
calls to mind Wordsworth's notion of the reciprocity between the
outer and inner worlds, when what is perceived is also half created. I
would not go so far as to suggest here that all literal displacement necessarily leads to a sublime experience. Nor would I argue that the
emigrant, exile, or expatriate has some special access to the sublime
that others lack; to do so would be to merely reverse a hierarchy in
which all parties are essentialized. But what lies implicit in Rushdie's
sense of the ambivalence of return for the culturally displaced writer
is the Kantian notion of the mind's participation in its own percep-
tions, the sense that reality comes to us not through essential objects
("cities," "villages") in themselves but through the way the mind
constitutes those objects and the processes by which we become conscious of those objects as objects in the first place. It may be argued
that the past is a country from which we have all emigrated, that its
loss is part of our common humanity, but I suggest that the writer
who is out-of-country and even out-of-language may experience this
loss in an intensified form. It is made more concrete for him by the
physical fact of discontinuity, of his present being in a different place
from his past, of his being "elsewhere." This may enable him to speak
properly and concretely on a subject of universal significance and
appeal (12).

There are limits and advantages to this recognition, a paradoxical
freedom that comes from an awareness of our own half knowledge.
When it comes to the past and the fragmentary workings of memory,
Rushdie finds more than mere loss, turning "profound uncertainty"
into a position of enhanced perspective. Certainly a powerful sense of
displacement, dislocation, or disequilibrium is characteristic of the paradigm of the sublime, although in the multi-homelanded case the dislocation is literal as well as psychological. As conceptualized by Burke
and Kant, the sublime is distinct for its disruptive, emotionally wrench-
ing effects. In a typical experience of the sublime, the subject is faced
with the infinite, with that which is literally unimaginable by the phys-

ical senses alone. Instead of being prompted by a scene in nature, however, in Rushdie's circumstances home itself has become that which cannot be fully grasped. India is not capable of being "reclaim[ed] precisely," having been transformed by diaspora into a kind of infinite realm never to be entirely represented or retrieved by the wanderer. Time and the sense of lost place make up the new vastness that challenges the multi-homelanded writer's imagination.

Another writer who engages the sublime under very different circumstances is Derek Walcott, who writes, of course, about his Caribbean homeland. Walcott has lived in America for long periods and traveled extensively, so perhaps he has begun to feel that he is from everywhere and nowhere at the same time. The burdens he inherits in the following poem, from the collection *The Bounty,* are at least twofold. First is the literary lateness of his arrival on the scene—or that Stevensian sense of poetry's many images already heaped up on the canonical dump heap. Second, Walcott is always stepping where the great historical weight of colonialism has already tread, operating in a landscape of layered strata in which the imposed images and false impressions of the new world brought by its colonizers still abound. The sublime always begins with the chord "And then I saw," following which apocalyptic cumuli curl and divide and the light with its silently widening voice might say:

"From that whirling rose that broadens its rings in the void here come my horsemen: Famine, Plague, Death and War." Then the clouds are an avalanche of skulls torrentially rolling over a still, leaden sea. And here beginneth the season when the storm-birds panic differently and a bell starts tolling in the mind from the rocking sea-wash (there is no such sound), but that is the sway of things, which has the necks of the coconuts bending like grazing giraffes. I stood on the dark sand and then I saw that darkness which I gradually accepted grow startling in its joy, its promised anonymity in its galloping breaker, in time and the space that kept it immortal and changing without the least thought of me, the serrated turret of a rock and the white horse that leapt it, that spumed and vaulted with the elation of its horsemen, a swallowing of a turmoil of a vertiginous chaos, the delight of a leaf in a sudden gust of force when between grey channels the islands are slowly erased and one dare not ask of the thunder what is its cause.

Let it be written: The dark days also I have praised.

The quotation marks of the first line sitting squarely around "And then I saw" generate an ironic tone that characterizes the poem's opening tact. Here the heft of literary history has to be lightened or joked up and saracasmed away in a kind of cinematic Hollywood version of the sublime. It's as if Spielberg took on the trope, used some stock footage of Christian apocalypse, and shot the scene by adding a close-up of the typically Romantic, particularized natural image ("that whirling rose"). Walcott's opening is outsized, over the top, even unto the gothic skulls of the second coming clouding up the skies. Adding to this effect is his mock comic use of heavily consonant alliteration ("apocalyptic cumuli curl"). This stance seems to be a necessary one for Walcott's opening gambit—to show his sophistication in a way by letting us in on his awareness of how overdone the sublime has been. What's more, his response is a comment on how natural scenes of the new, Caribbean world were partly valued for their primitive, if not pristine, effects, even as the new world's natural resources were to be tamed by its reasoning, reasonable colonizing newcomers.

But you can't step into the same sublime twice; every parody both undermines and reinscribes its object at the same time, and in this case the play gives way to prayer. This transition between the dismissive and the sincere occurs as a result of the act of description itself, for in the course of making fun of the thing Walcott is obliged to actually start to describe the world around him until inevitably the demands of accuracy and real thought press upon him. For poets, the effort of trying the catch the thing in language—the simple act of trying to get it right—invokes a potential ritual of transformation. What "beginneth" in Bible-ese becomes a metaphor than reminds one of John Donne's bell about whose toll we ask not—a phrase that reenters in echo at the poem's penultimate line, where "one dare not ask of the thunder what is its cause." In both instances, the poet's own mortality, his eventual submission to larger forces, becomes the real subject of the poem. Death, of course, is one of the last and not least of the great indeterminacies, a threshold beyond which nothing can be fully represented. Here its approach is marked by the touches "in the mind," and "there is no such sound," summoning up both the personal and the imagination itself, after which quickly follows the first local, Caribbean detail in the landscape, a turning from the generic to the genuine. The long, glorious sentence that comes next emulates the vastness of its subject through carefully managed, grand accumulation, as well as through the casual but elegant rhymes that have patterned the poem overall. Again the sublime earmarks appear: a simultaneous, paradoxical diminishment of self ("without the least thought of me") coupled with affirmation ("joy"), a dual sense of pleasure and pain, darkness and light, and downward motion ("swallowing") quick on the heals of "vertiginous chaos." In the process, the Christian clichés, too, are revised toward the physical and the local, toward believable metaphors by way of the sea waves as white horses. Finally, rather than the phallic sublime arche- type of the Alps we have the islands "slowly erased" in the final sighs of the poet's praise.

Similarly, both praise and lament spring from landscape and ruins in another multi-homelanded writer, Pablo Neruda. Chilean by birth, later serving as consul to Rangoon and Mexico, he traveled to the Peruvian Andes in 1943, spending time at the ancient Inca ruins there. His visit inspired *The Heights of Macchu Picchu,* one of his greatest poems, in which Neruda protests not only the living death of urban life but also the numbing human labor it takes to build a civilization. Writ- ten in twelve parts, each section is varied stylistically. The ninth part, in particular, is striking for its juxtapositions of scale, the large and the very small, the single moment in time beside the eternal, sweeping from bread in a star and back again.

Here are the opening verses of section nine, translated by Stephen Kessler.

> Eagle in the stars, vineyard in the mist.
> Vanished bastion, blinded scimitar.
> Shattered belt, solemn bread.
> Torrential scale, immense eyelid.
> Triangular tunic, pollen of stone.
> Lamp of granite, bread of stone.
> Mineral serpent, rose of stone.
> Buried ship, stream of stone.
> Horse of the moon, light of stone.
> Frame of the equinox, steam of stone.
> Final geometry, book of stone.
> Drumhead fashioned from lightning flashes.
> Coral reef of sunken time.
> Stone wall smoothed by the touch of fingers.
> Rooftops embattled by feathers of birds.

There is the ritual of naming the place, the over and over of stone said to make the thing come true, invoking presence through the hyp- notic rhythms of incantation. Each line is end-stopped in this section, inviting a greater sense of silence, even reverence, into the piece. As the names themselves accumulate, their multiplicity underscores the indeterminate realm Neruda tries to capture in language. It's as if we're at the end of mimesis here, a moment when description as representa- tion or imitation of nature will no longer do. Instead, Neruda is after an intensity of dreamlike expression through images that seem to melt from some primal glacier of ontological origin as he engages the work of trying to present the unrepresentable: time, vastness, history, space, nature, the psyche, power itself. And yet, with each totemic item named, there's the effort to get at a mythic whole by way of chipped fragments, like the ruins themselves, whose outlines reflect the accidents of time's wear. If Neruda's project is to make the infinite more intimate, he makes visible the cleavage between. That chasm is suggested here not only by the prevalence of the medial caesura astride his yoked contraries but also in the form of these short lines laden with multisyllabic words.

At the same time, this is one of Neruda's most profoundly political poems, and while this section forgoes the explicitly historical in favor of the imagistic shadings of anagogic time, he doesn't let us forget how the risen stones arrive at their mountain heights by way of human slavery, a topic that's central to several of the poem's other sections. Time generates its own justice as eventually the mighty man-made is reckoned to the naturally small and the "thrones [are] overturned by climbing vines." As for the return to an enlarged consciousness that marks the traditional close of the sublime experience, Neruda's denouement calls out to the souls of the enslaved to speak again through him. The sequence closes in invitation: "Come up, brother, and be born with me / . . . Enter my veins and my mouth. / Speak through my words and my blood" (111). Although this Whitmanian cry of comingling between souls is never entirely egoless, it constitutes a major revision of the more traditional sublime revelation whose starting point is the individual experience.

But not every song of history and sacred place is capable of sounding Neruda's note of bardic redemption. Neruda arrives at Machu Picchu before the tourist onslaughts that plague the place now; we live in a world that commodifies and commercializes the sites of ancient origin. What meaning lies in images when that packaging is less than benign? Further, what happens for the poet whose awareness is burdened by a history explicitly designed to silence her, partly by virtue of what Celan called being multi-homelanded and partly by the brutal diasporic history of slavery itself? M. Nourbese Philip is a black poet who was born in the Caribbean but was educated in Canada, where she eventually settled. She seems acutely aware of how sacred landscape by this time in history is marked by appropriation, a subject she addresses in a poem entitled "African Majesty, from Grassland and Forest," but subtitled as if the landscape is actually located in a museum: "The Barbara and Murray Frum Collection."

Hot breath
                    death-charred
winds
                    depth-charged
words:
          rainfall
          magic
          power
the adorn of word
in meaning,
the mourn of loss
safe   safety   save

mute
muse
          museums
                    of man—
Berlin, London, Paris, New York,
revenge seeks the word
in a culture mined
                    to abstraction;
corbeaux circle
                    circles of plexiglass
                              death;
circles of eyes
circles for the eyes—

    For Philip, there is no easy access to the original place—African
grassland and forest, majesty and memory—without facing its having
been muted, museum'd, collected, displayed, dissected, art'd up, and
stolen. There is also no mythic return, that modernist narrative more
available to Neruda, to a time before the advent of history. It is as if the
vastness to be approached is no mere literal natural landscape so much
as the self-engulfing, overdetermined weight of history's erasures, its
relentless undermining of self through culture, language, and slavery.
How, then, does one speak of the sublime when the sacred is also a site
of sacrilege?
    One answer lies in Philip's peculiarities of style. Her form is
informed by the breakages she's had to confront head on. The result is
that her fragmented spacings and partial utterances seem less content-
free experimentalism or postmodern affect and more of a personal,
albeit political, necessity. In the final prose section of her book, entitled
she tries her tongue, her silence softly breaks, she writes this of the African
artist's relation to the English language: "To speak another language is

to enter another consciousness. Africans in the New World were compelled to enter another consciousness, that of their master, while simultaneously being excluded from their own. . . . The paradox at the heart of the acquisition of this language is that the African learned both to speak and to be dumb at the same time, to give voice to the experience and image, yet remain silent"(81). For the African artist, the result of being forced to relinquish her native tongue in favor of the dominant language led to "the formal standard language . . . subverted, turned upside down, inside out, and even sometimes erased." Her spacings across and down the page lend a herky-jerky quality to our proceeding, a pacing that is perpetually disturbed out of any too straight going forward.

Yet another expression of subject through style is her rather relentless use of revision using a few letters, syllables, or smaller words. It's a kind of prismatic rhyming that makes us aware of the dangerous proximities between supposed opposites: "mute" is very nearly "muse" and the other way around; "death-charred" and "depth-charged," subtly suggest a questionable intent lurking behind the social structures she encounters. This particular tick has perhaps been much applied by our more theory-driven makers and stems in part from the present-day Derridean/Saussurian conception of language as a relay of differences or words as inherently relational rather than inherently meaningful—think of "peg/pen/pan" in which a one letter makes all the difference. Yet in Philip's hands the traces take on darker inflections, as she attempts to make one feel what it might be like to be reduced to a word without signification or significance, the human as commodity or slave, along with meaning as mere decoration or "adorn"ment, capable of easy manipulation. Similarly, the place itself, once invoked by potential sublime markers—"rainfall/magic/power" devolves to mere fashion within the museum setting. Transplanted from periphery to cosmopolitan center, the collective identity is lost now in a parody of what the sublime in its original place might have been, and with it goes the potential for a stable or even adequate self.

> wanderers
> in the centuries of curses
> the lost I's
> the lost equation:
> > you plus I equals we
> > I and I and I equals I
> > > minus you
> alone or I

alone circled
by the plexiglass of circles—
in a forest made-believe
                    filtered of fear
by light and the au courant of fashion
the wisdomed wood
stripped of reason
restored to 'living
proof' of primitive aesthetics:
"the African influence" on—
Braque, Picasso, Brancusi . . .
defies
        the blame in absolve
                    absolves
                In the elsewhere of time
head knees eyes drop
earthward—they would have . . .
not now
            feet pace
        the circumference
plexiglass of circle that circles
prisons and prisms the real in once-upon-a-time
there-was
            mask
                reliquary   fetish
                                memory
                                    ancestor
    to adorn the word with meaning
    to mourn the meaning in loss

    One of the achievements in the piece lies in its parodic element,
which occurs without the usual accompanying ironic tone. Instead, the
parody of meaningful ritual—the feet encircling the museum display
without recognition of meaning or function—generates a tone of
mourning. The displacement of magical into the coopted marginal is
thrown into relief, as the "I" stutters unanchored, encircled alone,
impossibly prism'd away from any ancestral figure that might situate
the self in place and time. If we think of personal identity as at least
partly the effect of a unification of the past and the future with one's
present—typically symbolized in the temporal integrity of the sentence—Philip's fragments enact a stumbling through the rubble left by
the blasts of a particularly brutal collective history. Race itself, and its
cornerstone, the "ancestor," has now become the unrepresentable
phantom that Kant once associated with the sublime, here stripped of

its ritualistic performance, though the lost meaning is mourned by the poet.

Philip's work generates a moral field that sheds light on our present fascination with one of the buzzwords of our time: globalization. In speaking of the parts that go missing in translation, she reminds us of the increasing homogenization of place as it goes the way of pure display, whether corporate or artistic. In our everyday world amid the contemporary cathedrals of cash, from Safeway to the local mall, we pass in and out of an artificial sense of place or meaning. Increasingly, too, this phenomenon is what we as Americans export as culture to the rest of the world. One effect is that the most common experience of "the vast" now includes the unidentifiable forces of capital, or the seemingly infinite multinational excesses of wealth and power, with the mysteries of economic "magic" beyond the control of any one individual.

From the commodification of the human being to the commercialization of the spiritual, the rituals of the sublime still obtain in highly suspect, parodic form. Here is a short prose poem by Harryette Mullen, a poet known for an astringent but playfully punning style in which she tries to recast our commonplace productions of "reality."

> With eternal welcome mats omniscient doors swing open offering temptation, redemption, thrilling confessions. The state of Grace is Monaco. A shrine in Memphis, colossal savings. A single serving after-work lives. In sanctuaries of the sublime subliminal mobius soundtrack backs spatial mnemonics, radiant stations of the crass. When you see it, you remember what you came for.

There is an implicit oedipal psychology of the sublime where the vastness at hand is associated with the powers of the archetypal father. This father figure can take the form of the authority of the written text, a linguistic paternal order that comes to us through Lacan's retooling of Freud. In the paradigm, the poet figure is at first overcome by the sublime power's greatness but later rises to that same level of greatness upon recovery of his equilibrium. In Mullen's work, it's as if the all-encompassing text is that of capitalism itself, a sign-glutted, unmappable, and vast terrain that indeed threatens the integrity of the self and seems never to end, swallowing up all that comes before it. Both her fragments and the use of prose mimic the tabloidese she speaks of, generating a peculiar sense of isolation as Elvis in Memphis and Grace Kelly in Monaco take on biblical attributes.

Here Mullen enacts the subsuming of self or even personal space by withholding until the close of the poem any introduction of the personal pronoun. Further, when the "you" does appear, it is already belated. It materializes out of the grocery's dizzying array of materials in order to remember "what it is you came for," something mundane, no doubt, such as milk or bread. But, while memory is the hallmark of the traditional sublime's return to consciousness, here Mullen suggests that memory itself is part of this environment of a manufactured past, both as mysteriously powerful and as lacking in agency as the "subliminal . . . soundtrack" that urges our passive, massive buying. Moreover, it's long been suggested that the romantic sublime in its apprehension of aesthetic power is a disguising or sublimating of political or social powerlessness. Mullen's parody or reinscription of a sublime that saves us in the Safeway amounts to a level of awareness that in itself can be construed as inherently political.

Of course, not all treatments of the sublime need be parodic to be contemporary. Campbell McGrath's urban sublime in a poem entitled "Fire & Ash, Times Square, New Year's Day," begins in noisy Whitmanian catalog and ends with a sincere appeal to divine forces.

Past "Prometheus in Teflon," patron saint of the Rock Center ice dryads
    waltzing their way to fortune & fame;
past NBC, down 50th, snare for a rootless gaggle of zanies whose skulls
    like floral Easter eggs
have been sucked high & dry by "The Days of Our Lives"; past chestnuts
    & knishes playing Radio City;
past the tattered, last-gasp Woolworth's thumbed with the stale print of
    dust & olid fudge,
tables of ski-caps & polyester jumpers, aisles of after-shave, "Attaboy"
    dog snacks, two-for-one mini-vacs,
demented shoppers thronging the discount racks while alone at the steam
    table a woebegone TV set shows
Utah State Police officers flushing outlaw polygamists from their log
    cabin hideout with high-frequency sound waves,
and John & Greg Rice, identical-twin midgets, pitching do-it-yourself
    millionaire real estate deals,
yes you can make it happen, yes you can, yes you can; past *Cats;* past
    rats; past Hawaii Kai;
past the guy offering free evaluations at the Scientology table, the
    benevolent specter of L. Ron Hubbard
risen like a bat-winged umbrella of faith from his humble birthplace in
    Tilden, Nebraska;
past the skewed grate dispensing wild jazz amid the roar of the metal-
    driven dream machinery,

passengers in the shadows like nutmeats in raisin toast stepping forth
  between the green I-beams
as the express train roars in and sodden flocks of waxed-paper wrappers
  take wing in its wake;
past the rank & file army of the porno arcades, omnivorous host of the
  stretch-pants parade,
nighthawks of the twenty-four-hour donut shops, the crippled & cryptic
  genies of despair,
town criers, lamplighters, flyboys, skyboys, lunatics & lonewolves & pie-
  in-the-sky pilgrims,
needle jerks & junk monkeys, toothless impersonators of Goths &
  Visigoths rampaging out into traffic;
past it all and down, at last, down the simmering avenues of lust to the
  belly of the beast,
where last night's crowd shimmied & shoved to wow & watch the hot-shot
  ball of light drop,
where sparrows parrot the gulls' echolalian idiocies and pigeons coast the
  exhausted air as dishwater snow
begins to boil over, or circle in soapy currents, or something altogether
  grittier, slick & oiled,
an airborne grime swirling faster & faster, cascading in waves across neon
  stars and failed resolutions,
settling on stalled cabs & broken trees struck dumb by grief, overarching
  the steeples & moribund statuary,
the electroplate giant huddled fearful in the lee of the sacrificial tree as
  the asymmetrical skaters pass:
ash, daughter of fire, the pith of a great conflagration, a mighty will raging
  against Prometheus;
fire, mother of ash, slouching toward Manhattan, slowly unlimbering her
  vast golden hands.

Past, indeed, the cynicism we might expect from name-brand allegiances and urban decay, McGrath turns to an apocalyptic but also
potentially redemptive imagery at his close. This Yeatsian final movement is a version of the imagination's leaping upward to identify with
the vaster forces of the sublime, although the poet finds no need for
pronouns of selfhood here. In fact, all along the piece has engaged the
biblical traditions behind the catalog poem. This listing form tends to
honor diversity rather than hierarchy, simultaneity rather than cause
and effect, with praise implicit even in the most mundane of names.
Yet buried in the manic glut of endless sales pitch is a mounting tenderness for the human condition signaled directly by such emotional
diction as "despair," "failed resolutions," and "grief." Meanwhile, too,
the usual phantom embrace of sound connections—alliterative, conso-

nant, and assonant—has grown to great bear-hug proportions, matching the rhythmic excesses of our cosmopolitan, late capitalist center.

This poet, like many of us, has lived in various places around the country, from Miami to Chicago, appointed as writing professor and graduate student; his sense of being multiply placed seems typical of many of our professional lives. In his second book, *American Noise,* the poem about Times Square is flanked by poems featuring the forests of the Pacific Northwest and the smokestacks of Chicago. McGrath draws consistently on the excesses of place in his writing, especially the relentless urge to make it new that is so uniquely American, along with our willingness to build and build again, restlessly, in surfeit, over the admittedly stolen landscape.

At the opposite end of the stylistic spectrum, Shrikanth Reddy is a young poet whose restraint seems to hark back to a South Asian tradition of the sublime. His first book is called *Facts for Visitors,* and, although he is a multi-homelanded writer who has worked in South India, he draws on an otherworldly sense of travel in which fabrication and fable knit together in strangely ritualistic scenes witnessed by an almost alien persona. Here he gives us a rigorously hushed lyric, "Waiting for the Eclipse in the Black Garden."

It takes long.

A wind comes worrying the candle-tip.

Our servant's teeth flicker.

His jawbone flickers.

Once I watched him cut open a goat.

Now no one can breathe.

The black disc locks into place.

Listen. Listen.

Under that box is a snake.

Listen while the unlit places hollow you out.

Action comes slow and deliberate in this ceremony of silence, which is further endorsed by the muted end-stopped, double-spaced lines. Reddy includes his servant, and there is a tradition of the poet's including a secondary figure, such as Wordsworth's address to his sister in "Tintern Abbey" or the peasant guide in the Simplon Pass episode of *The Prelude* already mentioned. In this poem, Reddy's servant figure seems to function as a stand-in for the poet in a kind of ritualistic substitution. The servant is farther along in an initiation into the mysteries at hand, ominously associated with the wind and the candle's fluctuations of light, having already acted out the archetypal violence of animal sacrifice. Like the goat whose throat was cut, the human beings of the scene cannot breathe. As the light is eclipsed, so seemingly is the possibility of whatever has passed for freedom in this enigmatic world, as the sun "locks" into place like a key closing a door forever.

At the final, surprising close of the poem, there is that sublime invocation of erasure, a penetrating emptying out of self that is the culmination of all that has been threatened thus far. Fear, in fact, has driven the piece forward all along. And if it is a commonplace of spiritual transformation that the self-preserving, desire-ridden mind fears its own annihilation, it is also a necessary component of an expanded freedom.

Reddy locates the poem in a mythic rather than geographic setting. Like many poets of his generation, he eschews the old labels and burdens of identity politics. Perhaps as a result, his notion of place/no place is expansive and mysterious beyond the need for explicit references to Indian or American landscapes. The emptiness, the hollowing out, he speaks of at the end has a transpersonal quality to it, even as the poem evolves, so to speak, moving from the personal pronoun "I" toward the universal one of "you." Of course, the notion of an enabling negative space in the self has both Eastern and Western roots, from Keats's conception of negative capability to the Buddhist sublime of a radical emptiness that removes the false veneer inherent to an unenlightened existence.

This unveiling of the mythical within the actual is close to where we began, with Salmon Rushdie's creation of his Indias of the mind. If there are those among us who would lose themselves, if they could, wholly in some single, most beloved place, there are many who carry a jerry-rigged sense of home from here to there. From the vastness of the American freeways laid flat across horizontal reaches of desert to the sweeping verticals, the flying buttressed buildings of New York City, the sublime tells us about place in the form of an impossible debt. Poems are efforts to pay part of the balance.

There are more sublimes than can be spoken of responsibly here— the urban sublime, the feminine sublime, the nuclear, the technological sublime, the domestic, the postmodern, and so on. Thus far, less critical attention has been paid to the tradition in terms of our mixed, contemporary, hybrid senses of place. Still, young poets such as Elizabeth Alexander, Campbell McGrath, Shrikanth Reddy, and others have begun to undertake some of the terms of the sublime, revising, inheriting, and making that tradition their own, and in this effort they join older American poets such as Charles Wright, A. R. Ammons, and Jorie Graham. The current movement seems informed by several traditions functioning simultaneously, from African American to the Sublime, from Tobago to Canada and the English sonnet. Although it remains to be seen how these literary contributions to the genre will develop, in terms of the sublime, Wordsworth's claims surely apply across multiple boundaries when he realizes in a flash of light that "our destiny, our being's heart and home, / Is with infinitude" (217).

WORKS CITED

Baer, Ulrich. *Remnants of Song: Trauma and the Experience and Modernity in Charles Baudelaire and Paul Celan.* Palo Alto: Stanford University Press, 2000.

Kant, Immanuel. *The Critique of Judgment.* Trans. J. H. Bernard. New York: Prometheus, 2000.

McGrath, Campbell. *American Noise.* New York: Ecco, 1993.

Mullen, Harryette. *S*PeRM**K*T.* San Diego: Singing Horse, 1992.

Neruda, Pablo. *Machu Picchu.* Trans. Stephen Kessler. Bulfinch Press, 2000.

Philip, M. Nourbese. *she tries her tongue, her silence softly breaks.* London: Women's Press, 1993.

Reddy, Srikanth. *Facts for Visitors.* Berkeley: University of California Press, 2004.

Rushdie, Salman. *Imaginary Homelands.* New York: Penguin, 1981.

Walcott, Derek. *The Bounty.* New York: Farrar, Straus and Giroux, 1998.

Wordsworth, William. *The Prelude.* New York: Norton, 1979.

PART TWO   *Various Ingenuities*

*america as much a problem in metaphysics as
it is a nation . . .*

*confess I am curiously drawn
        unmentionable to*

*the americans . . .
        their variousness, their ingenuity*
                —Robert Hayden, "American Journal"

A. VAN JORDAN

Synchronizing Time in the Poetics of the Harlem Renaissance and the Negritude Movement

One of the more daunting questions posed to me is, "What poems or poets have influenced you?" Not that I can't think of poets and poems, but I never know how to qualify the answer. The work of other poets influences my writing every time I face a blank page or the process of revision, directly or indirectly, yet, I never know what poet will visit me in these moments. Of course, there are poets I return to again and again but not consistently. As a result of this consideration, the answer to the question is always slow to come.

One of the qualities I look for in a poem—whether another's or mine—is how the poet navigates time and space within the poem. In my estimation, this is one of the more enduring qualities of poems from which I learn. I say that this is a quality I "look for," but this isn't always true; often this is a quality that, more accurately, surprises me in a poem, which makes the poem more attractive to me. This element of surprise should be a factor of influence for all poets. If we're not taken aback by the craft of a poem from time to time, we would grow tired of the art form. Indeed, when I think of great films, novels, operas, or paintings, they're often memorable over time as a direct result of the discovery—or surprise if you will—found in the experience of the work. We shouldn't know what would influence us because we'll soon try to determine what will influence readers, which will result in robbing them of the surprise. Once braced, it's difficult to catch someone unaware.

The poems of Langston Hughes and Waring Cuney from the Harlem Renaissance and the poems of Leopold Senghor and Aimé Césaire from the Negritude movement are emblematic of work, in many ways, targeted to a specific audience and reaching far beyond it. Let me begin by giving a contemporary anecdote to introduce these poems and my journey to this topic.

I had a reading in 2004 in Plattsburgh, New York. I was asked to read at "Black Poetry Day," a strange enough event by its label, but it became increasingly more provocative when they asked if I would mind also reading at a local prison, the Clinton/Dunnemore Correctional Facility. I'm always excited about opportunities to read outside of academic venues, so I agreed.

I didn't know it then, but this is a famous prison. Lucky Luciano was an inmate there, his family donated money to the prison, and there's a wing dedicated in his name. Tupac Shakur was incarcerated there, the Son of Sam is incarcerated there, and the hip-hop artist Shine was also an inmate at Clinton/Dunnemore. The head librarian at the prison, Mark Wolfe, told me this as he showed me around. The facility has a two-story, concrete wall surrounding it, topped with barbed wire. It has two guard towers equipped with marksmen. The correctional officers are not friendly to guests, especially if guests come from the college to speak in the prison library.

I was told I'd read for forty-five minutes or so, including questions. I finished reading in thirty minutes. No one uttered a word the whole time. No one laughed, no one sighed, no applause at the end. Just silence. Mark told me when I finished that I had another hour. I looked perplexed. He said that my ride wouldn't be back for another hour at least. So I could just keep going. All I could do was swallow and try to look cool. So I kept reading through the silence for another twenty or thirty minutes. When I asked again if I could stop, he said, "Yeah, if some of the men want to ask you questions they can."

There were no questions, formally. So, without applause or any acknowledgment of me, as if I weren't there, they dispersed. After a few numb minutes, an inmate came up to me with some poems he pulled from a pocket underneath his shirt. He asked me to look at them and to tell him what I thought. Soon two other inmates came over and did the same. And then I thought a fourth was coming for me to look at his poems, but he wasn't. He had something he wanted to say to me, something about which he and another inmate, one of the poets, were in disagreement. The man told me that he was fifty-one years old and had been incarcerated since he was twenty-three. He said he'd seen a lot of writers come through Clinton/Dunnemore to present to the prisoners. And then he asked me, "Why did they ask *you* to come here?" I told him I just happened to be in the area, reading at the college, so they asked me to come here as well. "No," he said, " you don't understand. Why *you?*" Another inmate, a younger man in his twenties, tried to interrupt him in my defense, but the fifty-one year old quieted him down with a stare. I told him I didn't really understand his question, and I asked him if he could just tell me what was on his mind. He said, "They always ask people to come here to read to us about women and drugs and shit like that that they think we want to hear. So I wondered if that's why they asked you to come here."

I told him I just brought the poems I had, the poems I wrote long before I ever heard of this prison. He said, "Well, good. I just wanted to say that I'm glad you had more time and that you read more of those poems about that little girl in the spelling bee. That's the kind of shit we need to hear in here. I never heard anything like that before."

As I stated earlier, when I'm asked about influences on my writing I never know how to answer. But that inmate taught me why I didn't know the answer. I simply—once again, thankfully—*never* know for whom I'm writing.

Certainly with the presence of the Universal Negro Improvement Association, the UNIA, and Jamaican-born Marcus Garvey and the Pan-African efforts of W. E. B. Dubois; certainly with the presence of Eric Walrond, from South America, and Claude McKay from the Caribbean; the immigration of Africans and Caribbeans to America and, specifically, to Harlem; certainly with the sometimes voyeuristic, sometimes worshipful, sometimes appropriating study of African art and American jazz and Negro literature by Apollinaire, Picasso, Breton, and Lorca; the writers of the Harlem Renaissance must have been conscious of, at least, a *possible* African and Antillean audience. But could they have predicted the words of Leopold Senghor, who went so far as to say, "Claude McKay can rightfully be considered the true inventor of Negritude. I speak not of the word, but of the values of Negritude. . . . Far from seeing one's blackness as inferiority, one accepts it, one lays claim to it with pride, one cultivates it lovingly."

Arnold Rampersad notes,

In March 1966, about a year before his death, Langston Hughes flew from his home in New York City to Africa, to the city of Dakar in Senegal, to attend the widely heralded First World Festival of Negro Arts. As a leader of the large United States delegation, but more so as an individual in his own right, Hughes stood out among the more than two thousand visitors who had come from all over the world to celebrate the international appeal and influence of black culture. . . . Senghor . . . singled him out for his historic contribution to the development of black poetry and the concept of negritude, the *New York Times* also reported of Hughes that 'young writers from all over Africa followed him about the city and haunted his hotel the way American youngsters dog favorite baseball players.

I doubt that the writers of the Harlem Renaissance expected this sort of treatment. It's hard to imagine that level of prescience or even arrogance being attributed to them, but, nonetheless, their reach was that long and sustained.

What's startling, though, is that poetry so aesthetically disparate—the Harlem Renaissance being noted for its realism and the Negritude movement being surrealistic—could inspire a new literary movement without the need to displace the previous movement but to honor it. This is very different from, say, the influence of the Harlem Renaissance on the black arts movement. There was no need to dethrone one group to empower the next. Theirs was a political mission to dethrone French colonialism and its threat to Africa and the Antilles.

Senghor was often criticized for being too meticulous as a poet and too faithful to the iconography of his country. The accusation of preciosity was answered with a glossary at the end of the 1961 English-language edition of his collection, *Nocturnes,* which was introduced with this statement.

> I write primarily for my own people. They know that a kora is not a harp, any more than a balafong is a piano. Besides, it is through reaching Africans who speak French that we have the best chance of reaching Frenchmen and, across seas and frontiers, the rest of men.

Some might respond that the onus of understanding of Senghor's cultural references might fall on the reader. I believe, however, that Senghor understands there is a universal element to the specificity of culture, the use of proper names of people and places, in a poem. Why wouldn't he? He was a student of French, Greek, Latin, and algebra; he obtained the highest degree in French education, the agrégé de l'Université. He was the first African to obtain this degree. This is simply to say he knew something about seeing the universal in the literature—in the aesthetics in general—of other cultures.

One of the more instructive traits of the poetry from these two movements is the use of time and space, how it differs and, at times, borrows from similar influences. Although there are a number of ways to approach the issue of temporal-spatial movement in poems, I'm going to focus on four: chronological time-space, sequential time-space, psychological time-space, and fermata, an unnatural elongation of time-space in the previous three categories.

    1. **Chronological time-space** is movement navigated by the clock so to speak. Whenever a poet employs a verb tense, it becomes an attempt to ground the reader in a temporal-

spatial logic. Sometimes this comes through other images, images that are indicative of the movement of objects through time: seasonal changes, changes from day to night, changes on an actual clock. This movement is closely related, but not always restricted to, a sequence of events.

2. **Sequential time-space** movement provides a logic of order by a numerical sequence; the order of directions on a map; or a change in velocity, an acceleration or deceleration in speed. One might argue that a change in seasons or time of day could also be sequential, but it is not exclusively so.

3. **Psychological time-space** movement is a bit harder to nail down. It mimics the slowness or quickness of time in our minds, which is incongruent to chronological time. Rhythm or meter can have an effect on how the mind perceives time. I'll delve into this by way of explanation a bit later. But, for now, understand that it can apply to chronological time-space and sequential time-space and, in a more pronounced way, to fermata.

4. **Fermata** time-space movement is simply unnatural shifts in time or indicators of time that elongate or blur temporal-spatial movement. The tools of fermata include language or imagery that does this: references to the movement of light, the idea of time being endless, time on a continuum, time periods mixing, and so on. This can be applied to all of the examples given earlier to achieve surreal effects; indeed, these shifts are usually considered surreal.

Chronological Time

In realism, we expect the poem to move with a patterned order in relationship to time. Another way of saying this is that we expect the actions, events, and objects in the poem to move with some relationship to time. There is usually some clear artifice used for chronological or sequential movement. This in many ways reinforces the suspension of disbelief in these poems, particularly if they are narrative. So it would be fair to say that if time moves in a poem *realistically* it moves as it *appears* to move in life. Of course, it doesn't, but we get, and we buy, the illusion of it, whether the poem is narrative or lyrical. Langston Hughes makes a strong argument for this in "The Weary Blues."

> Droning a drowsy syncopated tune,
> Rocking back and forth to a mellow croon,

I heard a Negro play.
Down on Lenox Avenue the other night
By the pale dull pallor of an old gas light
    He did a lazy sway. . . .
    He did a lazy sway. . . .
To the tune o' those Weary Blues.
With his ebony hands on each ivory key
He made that poor piano moan with melody.
O Blues!
Swaying to and fro on his rickety stool
He played that sad raggy tune like a musical fool.
    Sweet Blues!
Coming from a black man's soul.
    O Blues!
In a deep song voice with a melancholy tone
I heard that Negro sing, that old piano moan—
    "Ain't got nobody in all this world,
    Ain't got nobody but ma self,
    I's gwine to quit ma frownin'
    And put ma troubles on the shelf."
Thump, thump, thump, went his foot on the floor.
He played a few chords then he sang some more—
    "I got the Weary Blues
    And I can't be satisfied.
    Got the Weary Blues
    And can't be satisfied—
    I ain't happy no mo'
    And I wish that I had died."
And far into the night he crooned that tune.
The stars went out and so did the moon.
The singer stopped playing and went to bed
While the Weary Blues echoed through his head.
He slept like a rock or a man that's dead.

There are several ways in which we can chart the use of time in "The Weary Blues." Hughes begins the poem with two gerund verbs, *Droning* and *Rocking,* which might indicate that the action is taking place in the present tense, but then the narrator reveals that this is a first-person account of what he "heard," past tense. This changes the way we navigate the poem—that is, we expect it to sound more like a recollection as opposed to a play-by-play in the midst of progressive action—but we accept it without disorientation. It doesn't call for us to break the barriers of our known world to accept what we're hearing. Despite the heavy meter of "The Weary Blues," it feels realistically conversational in tone because Hughes has presented the events in the poem in a linear, chronological order that makes sense; this order also matches the psychological time of the poem, which I'll delve into later.

For now, keep in mind the order of the action in the poem. Hughes indicates that time has passed and it is indeed later: "And far into the night he crooned that tune. / The stars went out and so did the moon." What does this mean? The Negro played all night long until the sun came up. The narrator doesn't state this so plainly, but we understand that the stars and the moon, to the naked eye, are not visible during daylight. So we can surmise that chronological time has passed. In short, it makes sense and we are grounded in the moment and the progression of action, the sequential time: "The singer stopped playing and went to bed," tells us a bit about the lifestyle of this singer. He works all night when most people sleep, and he sleeps while most people work. Once again, the narrator doesn't say this right out, but Hughes knows the narrator doesn't have to put so fine a point on it. Logic tells us this by means of what we do know about the Negro singer in the poem that these other items are probably true. The stretch in our minds isn't to understand or believe the sequence of events; the stretch in our minds is to understand the experience, what this life must be like to live. Time works, chronologically and sequentially, like road signs leading us to experience. Or, to use film as an analogy, time works like a part of the scene's design or its props.

Another way to look at this is as Albert Einstein has taught us: space and time are a continuum. Spatial movement is simply moving from one place to another in a poem or to switch the point of view. Time is always connected with this movement, the movement of place, the movement of objects or the action by objects. We understand an edifice to exist in a given time, but if we don't ground existence in a time frame *it* is difficult to comprehend. Consider such statements as the war ended fifty years ago today; a child was born March 5, 1965; she's a Pisces; they met and fell in love twenty years ago; they got divorced last month. There's spatial-temporal movement because there's a spatial-temporal relationship. Spatial-temporal movement is the congruity or incongruity of the image in the poem with the time frame in the poem. This can and should be manipulated.

For instance, in film a character that has her hand on a doorknob, facing and opening the door, is shot (by the camera) from behind. We see her action as we would in life: from the perspective of someone watching her approach a door from a comfortable distance, not from the perspective of the doorknob. And once she's opened the door there's a cut. We now see her from the front, walking through to the other side, into a room or outside. This should take all of two to three seconds unless there's some conflict involved with walking through a doorway. This action also mimics our psychological understanding of the sequence of events needed to walk through a door. In film, this is known as *matching action*. If she is facing the wrong way, that is, if she is walking toward the direction she was walking away from in the previous frame, it will lack continuity. Her actions are not sequentially congruent. They simply don't match. But let's say she does approach the door and everything has been laid out as explained before, but now the cut frame shows another scene with different characters and a whole new scenario. Do we need to go back to that scene to know she walked through the door?

What if the question posed to her before she approached the door was whether she would spend the rest of her life with our hero, who has waited twenty years to ask her to marry him. We assume that her action is her answer. Our minds will assume that she walked through the door and went on about her business there. We take a little psychological leap with time and space. We assume this based on the *potential* of the action we just witnessed. This, then, is another way time and space moves: psychologically.

Often I find myself suggesting to poets in workshops that they ground the reader better by parsing out pronouns or ordering the time. This is simply a polite way of saying "make sense." This is not fair because even when the events don't make sense there might be a reason to accept them. This is to say that sometimes the options are not simply this or that but something altogether unexpected. The rhythm and the tone of the poem form a synchronicity of movement. Both tone and rhythm are by-products of temporal-spatial movement.

The film theorist Sergei Eisenstein, in his two-volume set *Film Form* and *Film Sense,* makes the distinction in film between rhythmic and tonal montage. Eisenstein connects tone to emotion and connects rhythm to the internal movement from image to image in a frame. Rhythmic movement is a measure of the "length," as he puts it, of images and their actions. By varying the length of imagery shot in a frame, he varied the rhythm of how it was received. The emotion in tonal montage, however, comes from "all the effects" of movement in the film, which includes rhythm. In this case, as in film, so in poetry: Hughes uses shorter and longer metric units to vary the rhythm within "The Weary Blues." The manipulation of meter through rhythm, that is, the use of associative imagery, dialogue, and chronological time, creates in poetry what Eisenstein calls in film a "synchronicity of senses." Every element within the frame—ambient sound, image, dialogue, and rhythm—works to make the scene more real. These elements are also at play in the sequential movement within "The Weary Blues," which in turn affects the psychological time within it.

Psychological Time

This is found in "The Death Bed" by Waring Cuney.

> All the time they were praying
> He watched the shadow of a tree
> Flicker on the wall.
> There is no need of prayer,
> He said,
> No need at all.
> The kin-folk thought it strange
> That he should ask them from a dying bed.
> But they left all in a row
> And it seemed to ease him
> To see them go.
> There were some who kept on praying
> In a room across the hall
> And some who listened to the breeze
> That made the shadows waver
> On the wall.
> He tried his nerve
> On a song he knew
> And made an empty note
> That might have come,
> From a bird's harsh throat.
> And all the time it worried him
> That they were in there praying
> And all the time he wondered
> What it was they could be saying.

Waring Cuney sounds like no one else from the Harlem Renaissance. Best known for his poem "No Images," which Nina Simone set to music and often performed in concert, and for the lyrics on the album *Southern Exposure,* by Josh White, which is often credited with having an influence on Bob Dylan and Pete Seeger, Cuney, like a number of the Harlem Renaissance writers, came from a solid middle-class background. "All the time" begins the poem, and "And all the time" ends the poem. In a sense, we have an elongation of time, the fermata, but we also have a sense of an *enduring* of time, which feels natural to the circumstances at hand.

What about the movement through space? Do we stay in the bedroom? "They left all in a row," indicates that people came and left. Maybe they came together and left together; maybe they came in tandem and left in tandem. Either way, people came, which took time, and people left, which took time. And there's the issue of where the narrator is—the narrator's locus and perspective—in the action of the poem. Does he speak from an afterlife or a dying life, still alive? The answers will vary depending on perspective, relative to the position of the reader.

Hughes also employs a psychological use of time in "The Weary Blues." And it's the psychological movement of time that pushes us closer to the fantastic, which I'll talk about in a minute. Like I said, time moves in "The Weary Blues" as if it were realistic time, but, of course, it doesn't and it can't. But how many times have we been at a party and realized, much to our surprise, that it was an hour or two later than we *thought*. Time often moves faster or slower in our minds than it does in real time. As a writing exercise in the Washington, DC, public schools, I used to ask students to pair up with someone and sit directly in front of the person. "Put your hands on your laps," I'd say. "Now, for the next two minutes, say nothing. Just sit with this person and stare directly into his or her eyes. Yes, you can blink, but don't talk, don't giggle, don't look away; just breathe and stare." Once they were done, they'd write about it. Often *thirty* minutes would pass while they did a free write about those *two* minutes. Two minutes is a painfully long time to sit with a person in our minds. The students attempted to imitate this experience in their writing exercise. The artistic problem is figuring out the mechanism to carry this through without showing where the strings are attached.

Albert Einstein's special theory of relativity explains this phenomenon in more detail. If a person riding a train drops a ball from the window of one of its cars, from that person's perspective, the ball drops in a straight line to the ground. Let's assume, however, that someone is standing fifty yards or so from the side of the train and sees the ball drop. From the stationary position of the person outside the train, the ball moves in an arc toward the ground and a bit behind the person in the window dropping the ball. Although both perspectives are accurate, it is determined by one's position of experience. To one, it seems like the ball fell in a straight line; to the other, it appears as if the ball arcs to the ground. There's a psychological relationship to space, but there is also a psychological relationship tied to the time of the events. To the person on the train, the ball seems to fall to the ground relatively fast and in a straight line; to the person outside the train, the ball falls a bit more slowly. Einstein, when pressed for an explanation of relativity, explained more simply that an hour sitting with a pretty girl feels like a minute, but a minute sitting on a hot plate feels like an hour. In *Letters to a Young Novelist,* Mario Vargas Llosa explains this quite aptly in literary terms.

> I assure you that it is the rule that time in the novel is based not on chronological time but on psychological time, a subjective time to which the novelist is able to give the appearance of objectivity, thereby setting the novel apart from the real world.

We can substitute *poet* for *novelist* and *poem* for *novel* to see that Hughes has replicated this phenomenon in "The Weary Blues." The poem is not based on chronological time but on psychological time. The night moves quickly because activity and play are both at hand. The synchronicity of senses is at play in the poem. But by the end we know that the Negro singer has had a long night.

In a sense, psychological time is an illusion of chronological time. If we want to prolong an experience, time moves more easily and pleasurably; if we don't, time moves more slowly and less enjoyably. But, like the speed of light, time also has a constant. There does exist a proper time, so to speak—one that isn't contorted for our benefit, that continues to move while we pretend to be younger than we are. Hughes has captured the psychology of how we experience time in "The Weary Blues" by using chronological and sequential clues to guide us. He doesn't have to say, "And we were having a good time and lost track of time," no more than we needed to see the woman in the film complete the action of walking through the door. It's understood and implied through the *congruity* of how the chronology and sequence of time matches the psychology of the situation in the poem. This forms a constellation that grounds the reader in its realism.

Examples of Fermata

There's a good deal of lyric poetry in works from the Harlem Renaissance as well as the Negritude movement. Hughes and Cuney both were masters of the lyric poem. Cuney was actually a trained musician and scholar of music theory, which he parlayed into the music of his poems. This is no small wonder; the temporal movement of lyrical poetry is imitative of temporal movement in music, but this is more pronounced in work from the Negritude movement once surrealism is infused into it. Certainly, we can talk about the "music" in "The

Weary Blues," but it doesn't fully explain the effect of time on the content of the poem; it simply is a way to put into words the sequence, meter, or rhythm of the poem. Waring Cuney places the voice navigating time in the third person. So "The Death Bed" contains two times: the time of the events as they happen; and the time of the telling of the recollection, which extends time in a natural manner, a manner we're used to experiencing. For this reason, I want to use a musical term, *fermata*, to describe this movement. This term loosely means a prolongation of time in music. Sometimes this is something that can be notated—and there is a notation for it—and sometimes, particularly in jazz, it is not. When musicians would show up for recording sessions with Charlie Mingus, they—Danny Richmond, his drummer, or Jimmy Knepper, his trombonist, in particular—would talk about how much of the *feel* of the music was never on the sheet music. Sometimes the swing or the bluing of a note won't be on the sheet music but in the musician. As a result, the music sounds unorthodox to the ear of someone wedded to the page, but the emotion of it is psychologically familiar. That is to say, we understand the emotion.

In these Negritude poems, time is distended in unorthodox or unnatural ways, not in ways imitative of real time, not in ways imitative of how we psychologically manipulate time, but in ways around which we cannot wrap our minds. Consider, for example, these lines from "Elegy of Midnight" by Leopold Senghor.

> Summer splendid Summer, feeding the Poet with
>   the milk of your light . . . (1–2)
>
> . . . In my eyes the Portuguese lighthouse turned, yes
>   twenty-four hours out of twenty-four.
> A machine precise and unrelenting until the end
>   of Time . . . (18–21)
>
> I leap out of my bed, a leopard in the snare. A
>   sudden gust of Simoon sands up my throat.
> Ah! If I could crumple into the dung and blood, into
>   the void.
> I pace among my books. They gaze at me from the
>   bottoms of their eyes
> Six thousand lamps burning twenty-four hours out of
>   twenty-four.
> I am standing up, strangely lucid
> And I am handsome as the hundred yards runner,
>   as the black Mauritanian stallion in rut.

I wash down in my blood a river of seed to make
    fertile all the Byzantine plains
And the hills, the austere hills.
I am the Lover and the locomotive with well-oiled
    piston. (22–37)

The pain of living, dying of not dying
The agony of darkness, that passion of death and
    light. (55–57)

Light moves at 186,000 miles per second, always. It's a constant. The thought of doubling it or cubing it is simply beyond our scope because we can't imagine anything in our natural world moving at that speed. The word *Light,* the phrase "twenty-four hours out of twenty-four," a time within a time, are used associatively as language to guide us—the road signs, the props in the scene—to accept the images in the poem.

In "Elegy of Midnight," time now works as more than a structural device in the poem; the movement of time is also content. And the content is quite unnatural. There are natural elements, but they're not used or combined in natural ways. Surprise is a tool of surrealism.

So how does this work in the poem? There is continuity even in the surprise. Time is distended through concrete imagery that represents incomprehensible time. It's not that "twenty-four hours out of twenty-four" doesn't make sense. We're not taken out of the poem by this because it *is* congruent with the images of the poem: the movement of light, which we cannot comprehend but witness. We're not taken out of the poem by the theme—"an elegy for midnight"—which stands in for darkness, which stands in for the unknown, or the death of midnight, that is a stand-in for the death of renewal. And we're not taken out of the poem by the language, "twenty-four hours out of twenty-four," which offers a common measure of time we accept as the course of a day, but now it offers the surprise of trying to consider a day—as we know it, that is—occurring within a day. Everything, its complete iconography, catches us off guard but consistently. Nonsense in the real world, but there is matching action in the poem. Once again we understand the emotion contained in the poem. We've put a finger on the intangible.

Senghor's contemporary and friend, Aimé Césaire, takes a similar approach toward making the intangible palpably clear in his incendiary "Word," translated by Clayton Eshleman, which delves into the emotion that's conjured from the utterance of the racial epithet *nigger.*

Within me
from myself
to myself
outside any constellation
clenched in my hands only
the rare hiccup of an ultimate raving spasm
keep vibrating word . . . (1–7)

and let me be nailed by all the arrows
and their bitterest curare
to the beautiful center stake of very cool stars

vibrate
vibrate you very essence of the dark
in a wing in a throat from so much perishing
the word nigger
emerged fully armed from the howling
of a poisonous flower
the word nigger
all filthy with parasites
the word nigger
loaded with roaming bandits. . . . (13–25)

The sequence of this temporal-spatial journey is stretched across an emotional terrain. Césaire manipulates the point of view and, consequently, directs the variance of the speaker's perspective according to relativity. That is to say, the speaker's emotions are moored to the perspective from which the speaker experiences the utterance of *nigger:* the amount of time it takes to utter two syllables. The *Oxford English Dictionary,* fifth edition, and *Merriam Webster's Collegiate Dictionary,* eleventh edition, scan *nigger* with stress on the first syllable, making it a trochee; www.dictionary.com scans the word as an iamb. Nonetheless, I doubt if any African American born before 1970 hears it as anything less than a spondee, which signifies a stress that does not let up in intensity. Here the relativity of race and age factor into the sonic qualities of how the "word," *nigger,* is received in the ear. Césaire sustains the moment of utterance over permutations of the word's locus, which consequently stretches the word over time. The elongation of time—its echo, so to speak, once received by the listener—mimics the motivation, to borrow a linguistic term from Ferdinand de Saussure, of the word in the ear of one experienced with its curare. Césaire's use of fermata takes a surrealistic tone in order to convey a realistic experiencing of the "word."

This is why poetry is like physics without the math. Instead of the language of mathematics, we use the language of words to make sense of that which we cannot see, of how matter and the immaterial work. Math is used to explain physical laws, and poetry is used similarly to unravel the physical and emotional laws of our lives. This makes poetry as universal a language as math; we should wield it as such.

I no longer believe that the aesthetics of a poem or the background of the poet or even a literary movement determine the audience for the poem. The poem speaks to those who can hear its many frequencies echoing over time. Sometimes these are predetermined, and sometimes the poem teaches us this as we go along and follow its logic. When someone tells me they see or feel or understand elements in a poem I've written—things I know nothing about, things I've not thought about—I often buy it. I can try to make sense of the movement of elements in the poem, but sometimes this is beyond my scope. I simply know when things don't *match*. This doesn't mean that I write without any idea of what the poem is about, but it does mean that I may not hold all the answers in my hand. I don't worry about the poem being timeless, only that it makes sense in its present time and contains some of that time's iconography. That a poem arrives in the future, carrying some of the meaning of its past, is enough.

WORKS CITED

Césaire, Aimé. *The Collected Poetry*. Trans. Clayton Eshleman and Annette Smith. Berkeley: University of California Press, 1983.

Eisenstein, Sergei. *Film Form*. New York: Harvest, 1969.

Eisenstein, Sergei. *Film Sense*. New York: Harvest, 1969.

Gilmore, Brian. "Waring Cuney." *Beltway: A Poetry Quarterly* 7, no. 1 (2006). http://washingtonart.com/beltway/cuney.html.

Kaku, Michio. *Einstein's Cosmos*. New York: Norton, 2004.

Lewis, David Levering. *When Harlem Was in Vogue*. New York: Penguin, 1997.

Llosa, Mario Vargas. *Letters to a Young Novelist*. New York: Picador, 2003.

Senghor, Leopold Sedar. *Nocturnes*. Trans. John Reid and Clive Wake. New York: Third Press, 1971.

LARRY LEVIS

Mock the Mockers after That

> Mock mockers after that
> That would not lift a hand maybe
> To help good, wise or great. . . .
> —"Nineteen Hundred and Nineteen"

My epigraph from Yeats has to do with elegies. But before I begin my discussion I want to suggest that this is not just a critical matter, mostly because I am not a critic; it is a personal one. I wrote an elegy once for a friend of mine, a friend from high school who died in Vietnam. When it has been praised, I have always felt that there was a curious injustice at work. My friend Eddie Zamora grew up where I did in central California and dropped out of junior college, therefore lost his deferment by dropping out, therefore was drafted, therefore died in Vietnam. He was Chicano—Mexican American—I was Anglo. Because my circumstances were more comfortable and because my parents could afford to keep me in college, I had a 2S deferment. It was that kind of privilege that allowed me to live and allowed my friend to die, but my poem is praised. What I am reminded of when that occurs is the considerable injustice in circumstances that allowed that to happen. There is also, quite simply, the guilt of surviving. So and so is dead, and you are alive.

Although they are not tricks, elegies are tricky things. In the study of the form in English, the poet and critic Peter Sacks suggests that not all poets escape from elegies they write without attendant feelings of guilt, anxiety, and the sense of some further obligation that comes upon them surprisingly, either within the wake of what they have written or within the elegy itself. For such feelings of guilt, anxiety, and obligation are what they have created as well, are the sometimes unforeseen by-products of the elegiac act, while the elegy itself becomes, of course, public, social, part of a culture that defines not only the conventions of the elegy but also what the work of mourning and consolation is. Insofar as elegies are also this work of mourning and consolation, they serve two significantly opposed, contradictory functions. For if they commemorate and remember the dead they also inter the dead, bury them, and, in closing, the poet, Sacks says, seeks a new object for his affection elsewhere, as in "fresh woods, and pastures new."

In short, the poet betrays the figure of the beloved or respected even as he memorializes it; "thus the source of love turns into the object of love," Joseph Brodsky concludes in his elegy for Auden. And what is apparent there is that the elegiac act has changed the one it was written for, has made of what had been so recently human a representation.

This problem, or predicament, this entire presumption of writing for the dead, presents some poets with an ethical unease similar to that of lyrical confessional poets who, for better or worse, seem capable of writing only of the self. But of all, betrayal is betrayal, even if it is only self-betrayal. (Or, as Adrienne Rich once phrased it, "What sort of beast would turn itself into words?") But the violation that occurs in the elegiac act is sometimes more serious. If the so-called confessional poet feels dismay, embarrassment, sometimes shame in showing off his scars in print, he at least harms no one but himself. The elegy always involves another, and the poet, working in his elegy toward what he expects to be catharsis and release, sometimes finds them only at the cost of being accused and reprimanded by the being whom he has turned into a figure, into a literary convention, which, by its own definition, has little alternative but to falsify the life and death it preys upon. Little alternative because it exists in words and because, as we are by now tired of hearing, words transform experience more than they record it.

Sacks makes a compelling argument in his study that this guilt, anxiety, and obligation are oedipal in origin and this may be so if one follows one's feelings to their source and if one is equipped with the proper road map to the symbolic order, that is, the one first provided by Freud and then updated by Lacan. But isn't the dilemma simpler? Aren't the guilt and anxiety a poet or anyone else experiences more akin to the remorse or guilt of the survivor? After all, the poet lives. The beloved other does not. As one of the dead friends who surfaces in Seamus Heaney's Dantean pilgrimage in *Station Island* puts it:

> I felt that I should have seen far more of you
> and maybe would have—but dead at thirty-two!
> Ah poet, lucky poet, tell me why
> what seemed deserved and promised passed me by?

Remorse, not *guilt,* may be the appropriate term for the regret one feels when one has done something wrong, and I wonder if it isn't the term here? For the sin of the survivor, poet or not, sometimes consists simply in still being alive at all. The poet's sin is compounded by the very act of writing an elegy. If elegies exist primarily as a way of completing the processes of grief, mourning, and consolation, they are then involved in processes all people have in common; processes that are private.

What are the larger implications of writing, then of publishing, such processes? Who are elegies really for and why? W. S. Merwin, in the following poem, aspires, on the surface at least, to a state of altruistic brevity. It simply goes like this.

> Elegy
> Who would I show it to?

But the very fact that the thing exists, that we read it, undermines the sentiment.

Carried to extremes, of course, all these ethical scruples become ridiculous. If elegies are so morally wrong in the first place, what should one do? Forget the dead? Leave no written memorial to their existence? Is ignoring them ethically better than writing about them? If so, while we are doing this, we can probably forget history in its entirety. It just isn't an either/or question. Poetry may be a bit more enlightening than theory on all this. As Jon Anderson writes at the end of his poem "Creative Writing" as a kind of farewell address to students:

> I don't want to trouble you; you are entering history.
> . . . .
> after death there are two alternatives,
> both heartless:
> memory & forgetfulness.

Memory recalls the dead without regard for the misery such reminders may cause us, and only by a deliberately heartless act may we forget them.

Finally, I would ask whether such moral scrupulousness in regard to the elegy is even possible. If elegies turn lives into representations, well, what, in reality, does our ordinary daily consciousness do? Don't others we know, even those we know intimately, conform in one way or another to that representation of them that we make daily and cannot help making, however biased or inaccurate or idealized it may be?

Why else would feminists justifiably complain and react against what they term a masculine essentializing of women? If elegies are so obviously not really, not entirely written for the dead, in what sense, then, is the work of mourning public rather than private and the experience worldly and held in common with the culture around it?

Sacks writes the following: "At the most obvious level, we recall Freud's suggestion that the superego is made up of the 'illustrious dead,' a sort of cultural reservoir, or rather cemetery, in which one may also inter one's renounced love-objects and in which the ruling monument is the internalized figure of the father." I note the shocking wording of this phrase—"inter one's renounced love-objects"—because I think it accurately describes Sacks's theory of the paradoxical intentions of the elegy itself. If the theory is persuasive, I suppose it is primarily because one recognizes the presence of what Freud called the superego through its symptoms. What are its symptoms? Guilt, anxiety, the sense of a further task or obligation—that is what the superego would be for most people. (If you were born as I was, and raised as a Catholic by an Irish mother, the situation is, of course, different because in that system to have been born at all is, to some extent, politically incorrect.)

Well, if these feelings of guilt, and so forth, remain wholly internal and private, they don't have much effect in terms of poetry, but what has an effect in life usually has an effect on art as well. The clearest, most abundant, recent example of how this guilt, anxiety, and obligation function after an elegy has been written occurs in the work of Seamus Heaney, where the existence of an earlier elegiac poem, "The Strand at Lough Beg," causes a visionary meeting between Heaney and his slain cousin, Colum McCartney, in section 8 of *Station Island*.

It is interesting that the dead, who often inhabit Heaney's elegies, are not just dead; they are more often victims like McCartney, a victim of factional political assassination, or are accidental, nonpartisan victims of political violence, like the fisherman in "Casualty." Their presence is striking in a poet who for years had been criticized for avoiding direct confrontation, in his work at least, with what have been called the "troubles" in Northern Ireland. In fact, the strongest criticism mounted against Heaney accused him not of political neutrality, a state of grace that even the poet admits would be impossible, but of an indifference akin to the aesthetic sensibility of the modernist artist, the kind of attitude relevant to this discussion that one notes in Joyce's characterization of his own book, *Dubliners*. To quote, "I wrote it in a style of scrupulous meanness." Yet Heaney's recognition of the conflict in Ulster, his inclusion of it in a poetry that chronicles the history of violence and injustice in his native land, that takes note of those young women "cauled in tar" on bridge railings as punishment for their involvement with British soldiers occupying Belfast ("Punishment"), is of crucial importance to his achievement and growth as a poet. It is a difficult thing to do because, on the one hand, the poet must engage a violent political dilemma without ignoring his own membership in it. On the other, he has to write poetry not propaganda.

But the question Heaney addressed in *Station Island* is far more troubling. What if the dead, including the already elegized dead, won't stay dead? Heaney concludes "The Strand at Lough Beg" in the following, rather elegiacally conventional manner.

> Across that strand of yours the cattle graze
> Up to their bellies in an early mist
> And now they turn their unbewildered gaze
> To where we work our way through squeaking sedge
> Drowning in dew. Like a dull blade with its edge
> Honed bright, Lough Beg half shines under the haze.
> I turn because the sweeping of your feet
> Has stopped behind me, to find you on your knees
> With blood and roadside muck in your hair and eyes,
> Then kneel in front of you in brimming grass
> And gather up cold handfuls of the dew
> To wash you, cousin. I dab you clean with moss
> Fine as the drizzle out of a low cloud.
> I lift you under the arms and lay you flat.
> With rushes that shoot green again, I plait
> Green scapulars to wear over your shroud.

The figuration that concludes this elegy, its abundant pastoral imagery, the elegiac action of cleansing the dead with vegetation of some kind, is as ancient, or as old, as the elegy itself. But the blood and roadside muck in the young cousin's hair and eyes are wiped away, I think, too easily. They are wiped away, not by any convincing human action but by the conventions of the elegy form itself.

Therefore, the dead won't stay dead. In section 8 of *Station Island,* the cousin, Colum McCartney, returns, reappears on Heaney's pilgrimage with a bitter family score to settle. Heaney has just been speaking with the shade of his "archaeologist," Tom, who has called Heaney "poet, lucky poet" in the lines quoted earlier. The section continues like this.

> I could not speak. I saw a hoard of black
> basalt axe handles, smooth as a beetle's back,

a cairn of stone force that might detonate
the eggs of danger. And then I saw a face
he had once given me, a plaster cast
of an abbess, done by the Gowran master,
mild-mouthed and cowled, a character of grace.
"Your gift will be a candle in our house."
But he had gone. . . .

And now—notice how quickly—follows a Dantean passage that gives
a sense of the kind of thing Heaney is able to do. Notice the immediacy, the kind of hallucinatory phantasmagoria that goes on in Dante
and in Heaney, too, as the cousin appears.

But he had gone, when I looked to meet his eyes
and hunkering instead there in his place
was a bleeding, pale-faced boy, plastered in mud.
"The red hot pokers blazed a lovely red
in Jerpoint the Sunday I was murdered,"
he said quietly. "Now do you remember?"

"You were there with poets when you got the word
and stayed there with them, while your own flesh and blood
was carted to Bellaghy from the Fews.
They showed more agitation at the news
than you did."

Now Heaney speaks.

                        "But they were getting crisis
first hand, Colum, they had happened in on
live sectarian assassination.
I was dumb, encountering what was destined."
And so I pleaded with my second cousin.
"I kept seeing a grey stretch of Lough Beg
and the strand empty at daybreak.
I felt like the bottom of a dried-up lake."

The cousin's response:

"You saw that, and you wrote that—not the fact.
You confused evasion and artistic tact.
The Protestant who shot me through the head
I accuse directly, but indirectly, you
who now atone perhaps upon this bed
for the way you white-washed ugliness and drew

the lovely blinds of the *Purgatorio*
and saccharined my death with morning dew."

Then I seemed to waken out of sleep
among more pilgrims whom I did not know
drifting to the hostel for the night.

In his essay "The Recantation of Beauty," Barry Goldensohn
argues, concerning the reappearance of the dead cousin, "It would be
hard to devise a more fundamental denunciation of the politics and
morality of "The Strand at Lough Beg." He continues, saying that this
episode of *Station Island* is a sort of moral center for the whole poem,
"Heaney is not fulminating, not accusing himself of lying or propagan-
dizing or comforting the enemy, nor grandly consoling himself for
being merely human" (although this last is maybe arguable). "The
move," Goldensohn tells us, "is towards locating where the real moral
danger lies: namely in that priestly posture that poets take on, dispensing grace and beauty when a colder and clearer vision is called for."
This is a sensitive assessment, but something else is happening besides a
moral lesson here. Something prior to the origins of ethics, something
ancient in the culture and ancient in the psyche. For why else would
the slain cousin admit that the poet, in the supposed dream fiction of
Station Island, atones for anything here? What happens is a mutual kind
of witnessing. The cousin, at the moment of his own death, sees
Heaney at a gathering of poets, and Heaney, at least in the cousin's
account, is able to see the cousin in the agony of his end. In this
moment, using only a few details to accompany the scene—tellingly,
"the red hot pokers blazed a lovely red"—the cousin's voice, its anger,
conveys the injustice of his death. And so, in this moment, Heaney
must undergo it in imagination with him. In doing so, he atones, or
"perhaps" atones, for atonement in the sense used here is never assured.
This is the ritual descent, larger than any moral lesson that Heaney is
required to make, and it is the penance beyond prayer that he is
required to write out in addition, scribed to the dead cousin he had
once betrayed, both in art and in life. In all, the episode is a leveling,
humbling experience revealing the exact Dantean limitation of art by
life. In a larger sense, such empathy is simply the necessary recognition
that others, alive or dead, are real. Part of a procedure of grief and
mourning, inside and outside art, by which a certain grace, atonement,
and liberation from guilt and anxiety are made possible.

The elegist, if his art is to be authentic, must also die, imaginatively
at least, with his subject. But if, after section 8 of *Station Island,* Heaney

has atoned for his earlier elegy and the entire arrogance of the artist in relation to the life around him, what are we to make of the end of this poem? For in section 12, Heaney encounters a literary father figure, James Joyce, and Joyce's appearance here, compelling as it is, is as troubling as it is liberating.

> Like a convalescent, I took the hand
> stretched down from the jetty, sensed again
> an alien comfort as I stepped on ground
>
> to find the helping hand still gripping mine,
> fish-cold and bony, but whether to guide
> or be guided I could not be certain
>
> for the tall man in step at my side
> seemed blind, though he walked straight as a rush
> upon his ash plant, his eyes fixed straight ahead.
> Then I knew him in the flesh
> out there on the tarmac among the cars,
> wintered hard and sharp as a blackthorn bush.
>
> His voice eddying with the vowels of all rivers
> came back to me, though he did not speak yet,
> a voice like a prosecutor's or a singer's,
>
> cunning, narcotic, mimic, definite
> as a steel nib's downstroke, quick and clean,
> and suddenly he hit a litter basket
>
> with his stick, saying, "Your obligation
> is not discharged by any common rite.
> What you must do must be done on your own
> so get back in harness. The main thing is to write
> for the joy of it. Cultivate a work-lust
> that imagines its haven like your hands at night
>
> dreaming the sun in the sunspot of a breast.
> You are fasted now, light-headed, dangerous.
> Take off from here. And don't be so earnest,
>
> let others wear the sackcloth and the ashes.
> Let go, let fly, forget.
> You've listened long enough. Now strike your note."
>
> It was as if I had stepped free into space
> alone with nothing I had not known
> already. Raindrops blew in my face
>
> as I came to. . . .

But the shade of Joyce continues, jeering.

> "The English language
> belongs to us. You are raking at dead fires,
> a waste of time for somebody your age.
> That subject people stuff is a cod's game,
> infantile, like your peasant pilgrimage.
>
> You lose more of yourself than you redeem
> doing the decent thing. Keep at a tangent.
> When they make the circle wide, it's time to swim
>
> out on your own and fill the element
> with signatures on your own frequency,
> echo soundings, searches, probes, allurements,
> elver-gleams in the dark of the whole sea."
> The shower broke in a cloudburst, the tarmac
> fumed and sizzled. As he moved off quickly
>
> the downpour loosed its screens round his straight walk.

The presence of James Joyce here is compelling and seductive. (It is like listening to the pleasure principle itself, if it had a voice, for poets anyway.) But the trouble is that Joyce here remains so much a literary ghost handing out writerly advice that, however subtly and splendidly contrived, this voice feels false to the dramatic structure of the whole poem. It acts merely as a way to escape the poem rather than end it. It is Joyce's appearance here that causes James Simmons, in "The Trouble With Seamus," to qualify his praise for the good poems in *Station Island* and for its ambitious conception. Simmons believes that the poet is not "wise or clever enough" to warrant "great ghosts from the past" advising him. The idea, Simmons says, is "vain and comic."

Well, I, for one, am just as glad that Heaney is not wise or clever here or elsewhere—although I think he is wise sometimes—for I think there are enough wise and clever poets around nowadays. But I would agree with Simmons's assessment that the ghostly literary figure here presented is vain and comic. Vain because the advice of Joyce lacks in its placement at the end of a serious poem enough contextualization, enough tone, to establish a kind of legibility. As readers, we don't know how to read this last section. We don't know whether we are meant to take Joyce's advice seriously. We aren't even sure that Heaney himself knows how to read that voice, knows whether to take that advice simply on the authority of the patriarchal master. If we do take it seriously, we are left only with the arrogant indifference of a modernist sensibility—one that lacks the ethical commitment that

Joyce's work, in fact, had. (That is, no matter how literary his reworking of the Ulysses myth is, what we remember about Joyce are these unforgettable characters, the abundantly present Molly Bloom and the invisible Michael Fury, upon whose passions fate depends.) But Joyce's advice at the end of *Station Island,* despite its political jab at England, is mostly literary advice. By telling Heaney to forget the troubles in Northern Ireland, aren't the reappearance of Colum McCartney, all of section 8, and certain other episodes that are extraordinarily powerful, aren't they all, to some extent mocked? Aren't they made to seem unimportant in contrast to this final theme of the artist's immortal destiny? In this way, the lives and deaths of others become merely mortal, insubstantial, forgettable. But isn't that Joyce's advice? Forget them? Only, if in some way Heaney's presentation, his representation of Joyce, were an implicit renunciation on the poet's part of the advice Joyce gives him could this concluding episode be moving and adequate to the questions the poem has already asked, in other words, if we heard Joyce and Heaney, and we then had the sense that Heaney would like to do what Joyce suggests, but Heaney's own location, in a political context, makes that impossible.

As it is, the advice given, looked at twice, seems selfish and impossible given the contemporary context of Heaney's Ulster. It is even more unfortunate that this end reminds us that the entire poem is a kind of contraption using Dante's form and acquiescing, if conclusions matter dramatically, and they do, to some Joycean aesthetic. The poem ultimately reinforces his literary influences' artistic authority, not Heaney's, and Heaney is in some measure disgraced and diminished by this as an artist. The ending here is a large structural mistake akin to the kind of belatedly written last ten chapters of *Huckleberry Finn,* when Tom Sawyer appears in the novel and mocks the serious theme Twain has established, namely, that love and freedom are incompatible. And it is no good insisting anymore in response to this that poetry has always been literary. Of course it has. Dante needs a Virgil in order to know hell at all. But, on the collective behalf of poets, it is clear that Hell is not populated entirely by poets. From Paulo and Francesca to Ciacco, to Ugolino, we are shown an extraordinary panorama of life, a variety. Nor am I criticizing the presence of the literary in poetry. When Philip Levine writes of García Lorca or Thomas Lux writes of Keats, there are crucial matters of human concern involved. The heart is at stake in such poems, and the heart is not a paper one.

Bear in mind that I am saying all of this within the context of a genuine admiration for Heaney, offering it perhaps as a warning to him and members of that generation of poets, now writing in their maturity, who seem at times to be writing under the influence of a heady literary criticism, at times to be writing almost for the literary critic. Heaney is one of the best poets I can think of writing in the language now, and to see him and others concerned—overly concerned—with their literary immortality is dismaying or, as James Joyce would have phrased it, "a cod's game."

Well, I make only this little gripe here about the end of a poem that is amazing and rather wonderful in other episodes. I think the poem ends before it ends, quite simply.

Still, the dreams that poets have of the great dead poets are powerful and sometimes unforgettable. I will just conclude with one of mine since it is something you should never do, write your own dreams into a critical lecture. No PhD-granting institution would approve of what I am about to do, and that is why I feel so delighted to do it.

Once, when I was living in a small studio apartment in Salt Lake, one with a Murphy bed and no color anywhere in it that wasn't grey or brown except for some brilliantly striped, rainbow sheets that my friend Mark Strand had insisted would be just the thing for the place (though they weren't and I had spent my last penny on them), I had a dream in which Yeats appeared. (The sheets, even with their wild colors, did not prevent me from falling asleep. It was, after all, Salt Lake City.) Anyway, I had been teaching there, a seminar on Yeats, and had the new Finneran edition of his poems with its vast acres of notes at the end of it open on the coffee table when I dozed off. When Yeats appeared, he simply walked into the place without knocking and, by way of explanation, said he didn't mean to disturb me but that he'd left some papers in my apartment. He had originally left them in his place in London, he said, but because of the phases of the moon and the shifting of the heavens—earth too, he shrugged—they were now here in a drawer in my tiny kitchen. He was dressed in that great white suit he had once worn, and he explained that he needed these papers, needed to finish what he had been working on in them, so that he could move on to the next "bardo." No kidding, that's what he called it: bardo. He went quickly into the kitchen and emerged again with the work in his hand and, passing by me, glanced at the new edition of his poems, the most complete and scholarly one available, open to a place where I had made a note in the margin, and paused slightly. Then he asked, "What are you reading that for?" And, looking straight at me, he said, "Passion is the only thing that matters in poetry. As a matter of fact, it is the only thing that matters in life."

NOTE

First appeared in *Marlboro Review* 3 (winter–spring 1997).

WORKS CITED

Goldensohn, Barry. "The Recantation of Poetry" *Salmagundi* 80 (1988): 76–82.
Sacks, Peter M. *The English Elegy: Studies in the Genre from Spenser to Yeats* (Baltimore: Johns Hopkins University Press, 1985).
Simmons, James. "The Trouble with Seamus" in *Seamus Heaney: A Collection of Critical Essays,* edited by Elmer Andrews (New York: St. Martins, 1992).

ALAN WILLIAMSON

Cynicism

Cynicism in, or about, poetry is a curious phenomenon. I sometimes feel it passes through the world of poets in periodic waves, like an epidemic. One such wave occurred about thirty years ago, in the early 1970s, in the mode Robert Pinsky described as "a kind of one-of-the-guys surrealism."[1] (The phrase remains memorable because it points up the disparity between the claim to depth that *surrealism* implied and the socially defensive humor or indifference that displayed itself on the surface.) Larry Levis, who began writing in this mode and then wrote many wonderful volumes as a poet in recovery from it, suggested in his essay "Eden and My Generation" that the poets in question began by taking the revelatory potential of surrealism very seriously indeed, as they admired it in poets such as W. S. Merwin, James Wright, and Sylvia Plath. But their "imitative gesture began to feel faint, inauthentic, often simply insincere or naive. And finally, as if in despair of recreating the reality of prior visions, this poetry often took on a sarcastic or sardonic attitude toward experience."[2]

Let me be clear that by *cynicism* I don't mean a pessimistic view of life or a low opinion of the possibilities of human nature. That has led to passionate poetry, of a very high caliber, from the time of Juvenal to that of Alan Dugan or Philip Larkin. What I mean is more a lack of passion toward experience in general, a certain blaséness, combined—and this is the crucial thing—with a basic, self-mocking distrust of the possibilities of art itself.

It seems to me that we have entered another such period, judging from what is appearing in the magazines, in which young poets are most discussed. One very serious young poet—embittered, it's true, by a fresh rejection—wrote me that "witty, fluffy poems à la Billy Collins or wannabe intellectual Graham clones . . . are all the rage. Strange during a time when popular journals and newspapers proclaim that we must turn to poetry for hope and insight." True, the contemporary style is very different from that current in the 1970s. For one thing, it is full of allusion and intellectual argument. Yet one does not have the feeling that these "wannabe intellectuals" are promoting any new philosophical assertions; rather, they are putting all such assertions inside quotation marks, figuratively and often literally, as if to demonstrate that they could never be so naive as to take any statement about the world as potentially true. Again, the contemporary mode is full of word- and soundplay, which the 1970s eschewed, so that its texture (as a couple of my friends have pointed out) can be curiously close to that of Gerard Manley Hopkins or Dylan Thomas. Yet there is never a sense, as with those poets, that intensification of language might convey some sort of transcendental revelation; the play remains solely, and explicitly, play. Another disillusioned young writer/reader, reflecting on the laborious complexity of these modes, suggests a "sadomasochistic" relation between poet and poem, "demanding [the poem] do certain things it is, under these circumstances, unable to perform."[3]

I'm not going to offer any examples of poems I hate. I don't like to trash poets considerably younger than myself. Besides, my concern here is really with the motives for cynicism, not with its epiphenomena. So I've taken two poems by somewhat older poets to consider, whose stance is more complex—if it manifests cynicism in some ways, it also begins to address cynicism as a problem. The first, Mark Halliday's "The Miles of Night," describes a family situation in which the mother, "[b]ack from the hospital again,"

                                        wants us
     to share something, so we're all gathered in the downstairs den
     for *Long Day's Journey into Night,* a TV special—
     my brother and I understand this is serious art
     and our sharing this serious art will be sharing on a high level.
     Except for the black-and-white screen, the den is dark.[4]

The two siblings—who, I believe, are grown-up, though they sometimes sound like adolescents—join together in a parody of the "serious art" they are supposed to "share": "Long Day's Booze into Snooze." And the speaker comes up with his own counterimage of what *is* genuinely felt and what, implicitly, *could* make good art.

                                   outside there's a dark highway
     and on the highway there is a truck
     and the driver of the truck for some reason
     releases two blasts of his horn

     into the miles of night. Image
     of courage or futility or both, and my mind prefers
     such a clean cold image to our complicated indoor warmth

I have to admit I disliked this poem intensely on first reading. The mocking repetition of the phrase "serious art" (as, later in the poem, of the sentence "the acting is so good") suggests that no one could make such judgments with a straight face or from any motive but snobbery. It might even suggest that no one, including the narrator's dying mother, could truly, unselfconsciously enjoy a work as canonical as *Long Day's Journey into Night*. And the choice of counterimage—proletarian, defiant, nonverbal—seems to be a classic instance of the self-hatred of American intellectuals. (I sometimes think all American writers begin as the bright kid who is left out, or picked on, in a conventional American high school. The only difference is that half of us grow up to emulate our persecutors; the other half try to annihilate them from the face of the earth.)

But, of course, Halliday knows all this or at least a good part of it. As the phrase "our complicated indoor warmth" suggests, this narrator is on to his own tricks; that is what makes "The Miles of Night," in its down in the mouth way, a satisfying poem. Rereading it, we see more and more clearly that what the narrator and his brother are fleeing from is not high culture but the fact that their mother is dying. The combination of "courage" and "futility," which the narrator would like to hear "outside" on the "dark highway," is right there in the "dark" den. But, of course, it is a little more "complicated," in the narrator's phrase, and more unsettling than that. The fact that this is a willed occasion ("my mother wants us / to share something") puts to the test not only the family members' ability to face death but the depth and unambivalence of their closeness as a family. "Sharing," and not just art, "on a high level" is called for. If the violent drama onscreen allows the family to feel that "at least we're not like that," it also raises the possibility that, with slightly less decorous manners, they could be. It is no wonder that so much psychic energy must be mustered to keep O'Neill inside the box. And the truck driver fantasy could now be read not as a literary preference but a classic neurotic symptom, at once fleeing from and expressing the narrator's underlying feelings—"miles of night." The joke, then, is at least as much on the narrator's tough-guy aesthetic as on the conventional aesthetic he is targeting. For his aesthetic moment makes him miss out on reality and the possibility of true connection, not hearing "something soft my mother says or doesn't say." One might almost say (from this poem and from Halliday's work generally) that his definition of an "aesthetic" is what makes you miss out on reality.

Halliday's poem, reconsidered, seems almost a conscious anatomy of the motives for cynicism. One of them—as I've already said—is the

American disease of anti-intellectualism often coupled with syco-
phancy toward pop culture. The roots of this, whether in Freud,
machismo, or the ethos of democracy, are far too complicated to go
into here. But it does provide a strong connecting link between the
"one-of-the-guys" quality of 1970s "surrealism" and a similar tone in
some current work.

On a deeper level, Halliday shows us how we use cynicism to distance ourselves from emotions we are not capable of confronting or
experiencing directly. The stakes are high in "The Miles of Night."
How will the family acknowledge, and respond to, the mother's
approaching death? What will it reveal about the strength or weakness
of their love for each other? Hard even to think about these things—
much easier to reject the "serious art" that is their outward token, as it
is easier to fantasize being a truck driver, with no family, driving away
from the scene as fast as his wheels will carry him.

But I sometimes think cynicism toward art has a deeper root than
either democratic embarrassment or defense against any particular set of
emotions. Put simply, we both like and do not like to be moved. Like
any strong disruptive force from outside the self, a powerful work of art
destabilizes our inner economy. The ego feels threatened, and it falls back
on one of its oldest, almost instinctual, strategies for mastery. It makes the
threatening force into an object, that is to say, something smaller than,
and containable by, the self. The Austrian writer Thomas Bernhard, a
master student of cynicism, puts it this way in his novel *Old Masters.*

> We only control what we ultimately find ridiculous, only if we find
> the world and life upon it ridiculous can we get any further, there is
> no other, no better, method. . . . We cannot endure a state of admi-
> ration for long, and we perish if we do not break it off in time.

Bernhard's antihero, a critic who spends years sitting in front of one
Tintoretto portrait simply to convince himself that there *is* something
wrong with it, as with all works of art, goes on to say:

> We can only stand a great, important picture if we have turned it into
> a caricature, or a great man, a so-called important personality. . . . Of
> course there are phenomena in the world, in nature, if you like,
> which we *cannot* make look ridiculous, but in art *anything* can be
> made to look *ridiculous,* . . . can be made into a caricature whenever
> we like, whenever we feel the need, he said. Provided we are in a
> position to make something look ridiculous. We are not always in
> that position, and then we are seized by despair and next by the devil,
> he said.[5]

Bernhard's insight explains for me the niggling reservation I still have about Mark Halliday's poem for all its skill and depth. The only actual detail he records about the TV performance is how "an actress apparently admired by my parents in the past"

> holds up her hands like lobster claws
> to indicate severe disability
> and I'm embarrassed by the obvious metaphor

I can't help feeling that Halliday, like Bernhard's character, would rather remember this moment of feeling superior than one in which the performer's technique succeeded, felt real: "We only control what we ultimately find ridiculous"; "in art *anything* can be made to look ridiculous."

But our cynicism belongs to our time, not to Bernhard's time in Austria or to the 1970s. So the causes for a wave of cynicism must also be specific to our own time, and they are not, it seems to me, far to seek. One, as for so much else in our culture, is the sense of media saturation. With the media everywhere in our lives, we are keenly aware of how they stage and manipulate our reactions to the things they present. The arts do the same, and our consciences are hard put to define, or indeed believe in, the difference. (As some of my friends have pointed out, it may be the fact that "Long Day's Journey into Night" appears on PBS, and not the play itself, that raises Halliday's speaker's hackles.)

Moreover, the media encourage and even force us to be spectatorial about massive human suffering—wars, murders, natural disasters. "Technology has miniaturized the world," former defense secretary William Cohen said during the buildup to the Iraq War. He meant that it had brought the world closer together, but the other meaning—diminished, made toylike—is equally relevant. If a jaded adolescent, staring at a monitor, can say "good visuals," only to be told, "That's the war, dude"—as was reported in the *San Francisco Chronicle*—clearly nothing convinces us that it is truly our size. And even if we do somehow bring home to ourselves that it *is* our size, and then conclude that we should *do* something about it, we are immediately thrown into despair because we could not possibly do something about all the suffering we are informed of. There is simply too much of it. And so we begin to doubt our, or anyone's, capacity for empathic feeling.

A second factor, I think, is the diffusion into the general culture of academic poststructuralism. In this ideology, part Lacanian, part neo-Marxist, there are no selves, or "authentic" feelings; there are only "subject-positions," and these are largely determined by language and the historical assumptions about race, class, and gender hierarchies built into language. The "author" is famously "dead," creative agency having been replaced by the unconscious, mechanical operation of these built-in, socially constructed assumptions. I am not, here, denying the poststructuralist position its virtues. It has made us aware of self-contradiction, as well as assurance, as a component of the creative process; it has made us listen to the less articulate constituencies old-style "affirmation" tends to exclude, the body in the inner economy, the uneducated and marginalized in the outer. But it must lead any writer who takes it seriously to a paralyzing feeling of impotence, of being the tool of unconscious but all too unspiritual forces rather than having anything to say about a real world. (Gary Snyder once called this view of life "solipsistic materialism.")

A decade or so ago, most poets dismissed this philosophy if they knew about it at all. They suspected, with some justice, an oedipal struggle in which critics were trying to claim the creative primacy that seemed, self-evidently, to belong to writers. Decades earlier, Randall Jarrell, already lamenting an "Age of Criticism," had recounted:

> Once, talking to a young critic, I said as a self-evident thing, "Of course, criticism's necessarily secondary to the works of art it's about." He looked at me as if I had kicked him, and said, "Oh, that's not *so!*" (I had kicked him, I realized.)[6]

But this happy obliviousness on the part of poets is gone for good, for reasons that are appropriately partly materialist, matters of economic survival. Along came the L=A=N=G=U=A=G=E poets, and the poststructuralist academics crowed with delight. Here were poets who believed what they believed and punctured all the other poets' pretensions about subjectivity, reducing them to (as the presumably self-authored copy on Mark Halliday's book jacket puts it) "an infinitesimal blip of male bourgeois anxiety." Suddenly there were panels at the Modern Language Association on L=A=N=G=U=A=G=E poetry far more than on any other (contemporary) mode; suddenly, as poststructuralists began to outnumber old-fashioned humanists in English departments, L=A=N=G=U=A=G=E poets were hired to very prominent creative writing positions. Other poets had to pay attention, and they did.

(Parenthetically, one might note that media saturation and postmodernist teaching sometimes work hand in glove. The teacher who assigns sitcoms rather than Shakespeare may have the best intentions, hoping to help the student decode ideological messages he or she encounters in daily life. But the lesson the student takes home is that sitcoms are more *important* than Shakespeare, even at school.)

I don't know whether young poets beginning to write now face the daunting sense of earlier accomplishments that Larry Levis described for his generation. But they do start with a great many reasons for believing that poetry is either a marginal or a suspect art. They are encouraged to have a bad conscience both about the motives for writing and about the value, or the effects, of the product. They feel they must at least show they are aware of these considerations, if not answer them, before they declare their own voice. That, I think, is part of what my young friend meant by a "sadomasochism" demanding that poetry "do certain things it is, under these circumstances, unable to perform."

The other poem I wish to consider, the long title poem of Jane Mead's *House of Poured-Out Waters,* interests me because it does take on all the postmodern difficulties I have discussed then bends them in an almost transcendental direction. It begins with our spectatorial involvement in scenes of horror and what it means when we tell, retell, or even think about such stories.

> First there's the
> one about the baby
> in Boston whose mother
> thought to fry him. You
>
> may have read about it
> in the papers, circa 1968—[7]

Does the speaker share, or mock, callousness when she says "the / one about," as if stories of sadism have become a category equivalent to jokes? Is "thought to fry him" a further piece of gallows humor or does it pose the essential problem—*this,* too, first entered someone's mind as a "thought," and part of the horror of existence is that the human mind can think such things? If this is so, can "the rest of us . . . relax" because the media are good at such glibly consoling phrases as "a walking, talking / miracle" or because the—in fact uncured—sufferer has "been reported" to one of the myriad agencies that are supposed to take care of such things, of which "*Hurricane Center*" is only the extreme, not the beginning, of irrelevance? The more brittle the humor in this section becomes, the more it drives home the complicity, the helplessness, and the unavoidable survival skill of indifference that are part of our condition. This is, as the poem later says, the "wedge of sarcasm / keeping you sane," which can also be called the "wedge / of cruelty keeping me / human." When the first section ends,

> Relax. This is not his story.
> I just wanted you to know

are we hearing the voice of a teasing sadist? Or the voice of conscience, insisting that we "know" all such stories even if we can do nothing about them? Or just the all too available voice of our media-trained neutrality, which needs no motive for repeating such things? And how, indeed, would we tell these three voices apart? If the first section of Mead's poem takes on the weight of media saturation, the second section could be said to take on the weight of the postmodernist critique of sensibility. It presents exactly the kind of scene L=A=N=G=U=A=G=E poets love to mock as "bourgeois nostalgia": "after my hot bath," "Mozart / on the tape machine," the speaker begins to write about

> the beach as it was this morning,
> dawn-fog, sun seeping through
> from the unavailable background
> a world all shades of gold
>
> and gray, their mixing
> and their churning

But surrounding this description is no simple aura of satisfaction but an unending anxiety about what description can provide for the writer or the reader. This act of writing is

> another
> chapter in the story of
>
> me and you—how what I want
> is to give you something—

Later she will ask the reader, "Do you believe . . . only in that . . . world as a / clutter of clichés"? And the final question, even in this section, even as the speaker becomes almost ecstatically absorbed in what she is describing, is not only "Can you hear it?" but "Do you want it?"

Perhaps the most fundamental difference between Mead's poem and a truly postmodern one is that for the latter these impasses would be ultimate. For Mead, they have contexts that can enlarge and even perhaps change them. One of these contexts is personal, even "confessional." The later sections of the poem, and indeed the entire book, repeatedly allude to a scene in which the speaker stands between an enraged father or stepfather and younger children, gets punched in the mouth for her pains, and says "*none of you will ever / own me, ever.*" This scene sheds considerable light not only on the preoccupation with bad things happening to children but on the need for "sarcasm"—"Distance how you / stay alive here"—and the countervailing need to leap beyond it, to "give something" to a "you." But it also sheds light on the speaker's distrust of her own mind and motives, a distrust that long precedes postmodern or philosophical considerations. Mead's speaker has "some knowledge of the / basic theories of the psyche" and realizes that if "Everywhere I go there is blood" there is "no way to tell the darkness outside / from the darkness within." She knows that, as Louise Glück stated in her famous essay "The Forbidden," "truth of this kind will not permit itself simply to be looked back on; it makes, when it is summoned, a kind of erosion, undermining the present with the past." Or, as Glück put it more succinctly in a poem, "a wound to the heart / is also a wound to the mind."[8] Mead's speaker knows that part of her is forever back there, standing between the father and the children: "I look down and"

> see her. I look down
> and see how the rest
> of her life is the rest
>
> of my life.

She knows that some kind of split occurred then, "undermining the present with the past," that if her sense of having a "body" is to "reappear" it must be in the bodily memory of that moment.

And yet—and this, for the poem, is the important thing—in reliving that moment

> I ask her
> to raise her eyes then, don't I.

This act of defiance is in one sense the "final betrayal," the judgment that the man's act of violence can never undo, and therefore perhaps, in Glück's words again, "the collusive, initiating desire which must have been present for punishment to occur." Yet it is also the type of the artistic act the speaker tries, for the rest of her life, to perform, the attempt to make an inhabitable "space / between" the world's terrible conditions in which she cannot be "own[ed]." Another context, surprisingly perhaps, is religious. It is first adumbrated with the introduction of a statue of an "angel in Central Park" in the seventh and eighth sections. Religion and the aesthetic—or the possibility of believing in the aesthetic—are deeply intertwined here. It is "the note . . . that / almost breaks me before / it fades" ("note" referring to the "Mozart on the / tape machine") that brings the speaker to ask "kindly what I would / have asked in anger," whether the "you" believes that "*this* is the moment / of" the angel's "final landing" in this world. (I don't think it's an accident, here, that we can't quite tell whether the "you" the speaker would have addressed "in anger" is the violent father, the unbelieving reader, or an aspect of the self; all are profoundly meshed.)

The reference is both to the Central Park statue and to John 5:2–9, the biblical passage that lies behind the title of the book.

> 4 For an angel went down at a certain season into the pool, and troubled the water; whosoever then first after the troubling of the water stepped in was made whole of whatsoever disease he had.
>
> 5 And a certain man was there, which had an infirmity thirty and eight years.
>
> 6 When Jesus saw him lie, and knew that he had been now a long time in that case, he saith unto him, Wilt thou be made whole?[9]

There are many reflexes of reference here. I suspect it isn't an accident that the man has "had an infirmity thirty and eight years," since another poem in Mead's book is called "The Seventh Revelation of My Thirty-Seventh Year." I suspect the angel's posture recalls the speaker's position in the moment of trauma, so that the question of whether the angel is "landing" takes some of its urgency from the speaker's uncertainty about reentering the world: "I may be landing, / I may be taking off." Still, the religious impulse has its full traditional force; it poses the question of whether one can be "made whole," whether a force from outside the apparent inevitabilities can work transformation. The poem seems to reach its apex of conviction near the end of the eighth section, when the speaker is able to hear music as transcendence, "notes rising up toward / elsewhere, outer hemispheres / sucking the sound in." At that moment, there comes "from somewhere the coo / of pigeons," and the speaker asks, "*How* elsewhere is it?"

I take this question to mean what Buddhists mean when they say "right here is nirvana." The pigeons' cooing, at just that moment, in this world *is* the angel arriving from the other world. Such synchronicities carry instant conviction for one kind of mind, the religious; for another, the secular, they have no more possibility of validation than the idea that "poured-out waters" could be a "house." Mead's tragedy, in this poem, is that she has both kinds of mind.

For the last section is again scathing about the escapist possibilities of a belief in transcendence. The phrase "GOD'S ANGEL," on the tomb of yet another victimized child,

> wants to mean
> there was no such child
> as Lisa Steinberg, means—
>
> without wanting to—the
> truth: there was only
> Lisa, and she belonged
> to us.

Yet I hear an immense positive, as well as negative, resolution in that "she belonged / to us." It takes back both the first section's feigned distance ("I just wanted you to know") and, more painfully, the speaker's own "None of you will ever own me." We all own, and are owned by, whatever is human. The speaker's final triumph, it seems to me, lies in owning (in yet another sense) that the boy in Boston was no random choice—"I just wanted you to know"—but a long-standing obsessive preoccupation in which she has relived the unspeakable moment when his "back curled over where he / hit the griddle." This, it seems to me, is precisely the full inhabitation of the moment, and of one's own unique conditions, that postmodern philosophy would make impossible. It is both a small and a very large act of resistance to the pressures, both personal and cultural, that insist on "distance."

Forest fires, we are now told, are good for forests. They clear away underbrush that would only burn worse later. They give the stronger trees room to grow. They may even, for certain species, release seeds whose pods or cones can only open under conditions of extreme heat. I suppose a sufficiently hardhearted Darwinian might say the same of epidemics. Dare we say it for the metaphorical epidemics of the poetry world? Group styles do tend to sweep a lot of mediocre talent into oblivion with them when they go. Most of the worst examples of "one-of-the-guys surrealism" in Robert Pinsky's *The Situation of Poetry* are forgotten names only twenty-five years later. And those whose reputations survived—Charles Wright, to take one of Pinsky's examples, or Larry Levis, to go back to mine—often changed almost beyond recognition in their later work.

The argument becomes less hardhearted when we allow that challenges to the validity of art, such as periods of cynicism represent, can also be strengthening, if unwelcome, for those who oppose them. They do not allow anyone, ultimately, to rest in overfamiliar modes. A lot of second-rate imitation Lowell also perished in the "surrealism wars" of the 1970s, and the strong realist work of the 1980s did not merely take up where it had left off. Realism had gone through its own mutations, released, if you like, its own unknown, heat-resistant seeds. It asked different questions about the relation of narrative to discourse and philosophy in the work of Robert Pinsky, C. K. Williams, and Frank Bidart; it took on its own surreal aura of myth and archetype in that of Louise Gluck and Allen Grossman.

The currently fashionable mode has many virtues the poetry of the 1970s did not. It is more intelligent, it is curious about a wider variety of topics, and it has a livelier and more interesting vocabulary. If these virtues can be joined with a willingness to be alive in the existential present, to resist both the culture's and the academy's invitations to blaséness and self-cancellation, extraordinary things can happen. I hope Jane Mead's work is a straw in the wind.

NOTES

1. Robert Pinsky, *The Situation of Poetry* (Princeton: Princeton University Press, 1976), 163.

2. Larry Levis, "Eden and My Generation," in *The Gazer Within* (Ann Arbor: University of Michigan Press, 2001), 48.

3. Thank you to Wensday Carlton and Alejandro Escude, respectively.

4. Mark Halliday, "The Miles of Night," in *Selfwolf* (Chicago: University of Chicago Press, 1999), 3–4.

5. Thomas Bernhard, *Old Masters,* translated by Ewald Osers (London: Quartet, 1989), 59, 57. Another masterly study of the destructive impulse, Yukio Mishima's *The Temple of the Golden Pavilion,* puts the essential issue still more trenchantly: "If beauty really did exist there, it meant my own existence was a thing estranged from beauty" (translated by Ivan Morris [New York: Vintage, 2001], 20).

6. Randall Jarrell, "The Age of Criticism," in *Poetry and the Age* (New York: Vintage, 1955), 84.

7. Jane Mead, *House of Poured-Out Waters* (Urbana and Chicago: University of Illinois Press, 2001), 67.

8. Louise Glück, "The Forbidden," in *Proofs and Theories* (New York: Ecco, 1994), 54; "The Untrustworthy Speaker," in *Ararat* (New York: Ecco, 1990), 35.

9. *Holy Bible, King James Version* (Cambridge: Cambridge University Press), 1053.

DEAN YOUNG

Surrealism 101

When Salvador Dalí came to the United States in the 1930s and biz-
zarely decorated a Bonwit Teller department store window, earning
himself the anagramatic name from André Breton of Avida Dollars,
what was thought of as surreal became debased to a capitalist trifle.
Fashion models wore lobsters on their heads; the rich gave dinner parties with pianos in trees. A few years ago, when one pop idol tore away
another's faux gladiatorial chest plate, exposing a breast during a Super
Bowl halftime show, the media proclaimed the event surreal. Even
given the absurd replays on ESPN the next day, in slow motion and
reverse, the avowed wardrobe malfunction between two talentless
vapidities cooked up to jolt a beer-bloated populace was about as erotic
as a potato chip bag being ripped open. Its shock was hardly fuel for the
imagination and excited only a few censors, book burners, and tele-
vangelists. On the other hand, an earlier event referred to again and
again as surreal truly was: 9/11 and not only for the strangeness of the
visions it provided. One image, of people fleeing the scene, all members of a single, united, ashen-colored race, is emblematic of the actual
aims of Surrealism. For weeks afterward, it seemed that this hideous
trauma had so destabilized our habitual assumptions that we as a people
were presented with the raw materials to bring about profound change
in consciousness and deed. Perhaps this shock, its attendant pain and
emotive flood, grief, outrage, worry, pride, nightmare, and dream,
could be the starting point for political and social revolution, for a creative examination of our foreign and domestic policies and a reaffirma-
tion of a humane attitude toward and in the world. Soon enough,
however, the guerrillas would take over, and our complicity is our failure. More people in prisons. More lies and invasions. But the surreal
has always been and always will be with us, proposing the site for
change. The movement that called itself Surrealism articulated and
demonstrated the promise that through trauma, confrontation, and
destabilization we may be set free, that life isn't tawdry and the imagination is limitless in its power. Our peril is our possibility, the surreal
insists, and its optimism is our right to hope that out of obscene nega-
tions something positive may come forth.

The tantrum of Surrealism posited a radical dismantlement of social, political, and artistic pieties through a destructive impulse given gale force. Primitive and infantile, as well as intellectually perverse, Surrealism asserted erotic value based on the efficacy of chance and the dreamed capacities of the eruptive truth of whim, of artistic expression and random happenstance that take on the radiance of ritual. For Surrealism, the path toward a state of perpetual revolution is paradisal; its negative impulses intend to wipe the slate clean so that we may enter a tabula rasa of imaginative possibility. But the essential question in this path toward the marvelous remains troublesome: what next? How can the ongoing revolution of mind, of the liberty of the imagination, be sustained and guaranteed when the means of that liberty eventually lend themselves to orthodoxy? How can recklessness be preserved?

But before we address the ends of Surrealism, its possible exhaustion and/or necessity for reformation, let's look back toward its origins.

POEM TO SHOUT IN THE RUINS

Let's spit the two of us let's spit
On what we loved
On what we loved the two of us
Yes because this poem the two of us
Is a waltz tune and I imagine
What is dark and incomparable passing between us
Like a dialogue of mirrors abandoned
In a baggage-claim somewhere say Foligno
Or Bourboule in Auvergne
Certain names are charred with a distant thunder
Yes let's spit the two of us on these immense landscapes
Where little rented cars cruise by
Yes because something must still
Some thing
Reconcile us yes let's spit
The two of us it's a waltz
A kind of convenient sob
Let's spit let's spit tiny automobiles
Let's spit that's an order
A waltz of mirrors
A dialogue in a void
Listen to these immense landscapes where the wind
Cries over what we loved
One of them is a horse leaning its elbow on the earth
The other a deadman shaking out linen the other
The trail of your footprints I remember a deserted village

On the shoulder of a scorched mountain
I remember your shoulder
I remember your elbow your linen your footprints
I remember a town where there was no horse
I remember your look which scorched
My deserted heart a dead Mazeppa whom a horse
Carries away like that day on the mountain
Drunkenness sped my run through the martyred oaks
Which bled prophetically while day
Light fell mute over the blue trucks
I remember so many things
So many evenings rooms walks rages
So many stops in worthless places
Where in spite of everything the spirit of mystery rose up
Like the cry of a blind child in a remote train depot
So I am speaking to the past Go ahead and laugh
At the sound of my words if you feel that way
He loved and Was and Came and Caressed
And Waited and Kept watch on the stairs which creaked
Oh violence violence I am a haunted man
And waited and waited bottomless wells
I thought I would die waiting
Silence sharpened pencils in the street
A coughing taxi drove off to die in the dark
And waited and waited smothered voices
In front of the door the language of doors
Hiccup of houses and waited
One after another familiar objects took on
And waited the ghostlike look And waited
Of convicts And waited
And waited God Damn
Escaped from a prison of half-light and suddenly
No Stupid No
Idiot
The shoe crushed the nap of the rug
I barely return
And loved loved loved but you cannot know how much
And loved it's in the past
Loved loved loved loved loved
Oh violence
It's nothing but a joke to those
Who talk as if love were the story of a fling
Shit on all that pretence
Do you know when it truly becomes a story
Love

You know
When every breath turns into a tragedy
When even the day's colors are laughable
Air a shadow in shade a name thrown out
That everything burns
And you say Let everything burn
And the sky is the taste of scattered sand
Love you bastards love for you
Is when you manage to sleep together
Manage to
And afterwards Ha ha all of love is that
And afterwards
We manage to speak of what it is
To sleep together for years
Do you understand
For years
Just like a boat's sails toppling
Onto the deck of a ship loaded with lepers
In a film I saw recently
One by one
The white rose dies like the red rose
What is it then that stirs me up to such a pitch
In these last words
The word last perhaps a word in which
Everything is cruel cruelly irreparable
And torn to shreds Word panther Word electric
Chair
The last word of love imagine that
And the last kiss and the last
Nonchalance
And the last sleep No kidding it's comic
Thinking simply of the last night
Ah everything takes on this abominable meaning
I meant the last moment
The last goodbye the last gasp
Last look
Horror horror horror
For years now horror
Yes let's spit
On what we loved together
Let's spit on love
On our unmade beds
On our silence and on our mumbled words
On the stars even if they are
Your eyes

On the sun even if it is
Your teeth
On eternity even if it is
Your mouth
And on love
Even if it is
Your love
Yes let's spit.

"Poem To Shout In The Ruins" was written by Louis Aragon, one of a circle of young Frenchmen gathered around André Breton, who adopted Apollinaire's neologism, "surrealism," for their explorations of poetic procedures as life lived and lived life as poetic procedure. Like many surrealist poems, this one lists in both senses of the world, it itemizes as well as lurches, its coherence is not a matter of linear development or consistency but rather one furious momentum moving by gushes and spinning in obsessive eddies. Its frenzy is both personal and political—a love affair gone sour with a you that is a particular person and a you that is the world, that souring even spreading to the very mechanisms of its own statement. Written after one pointless war and feeling the magnetism of another approaching, the poet's disgusts and self-consuming revulsions of course have nothing to say to us now, to we who have resolved our own carnal stupidities and political obscenities. Aesthetically the poem is a powerful avoidance of Eliotian anomie; even in its negative restoration of conventional associational tropes at the end, the speaker refuses of give up, to give in to exhaustion; if it approaches an elegiac timbre, it spits on that too.

In Breton's rather unclassifiable prose account of a short affair with an indigent, mysterious woman, the eponymous Nadja, he writes of the modus operandi that he wishes to guide both his life and his art. "I hope, in any case, that the presentation of some dozen observations of this order (chance encounters and events) as well as what follows will be of a nature to send men rushing into the street, making them aware, if not of the nonexistence, at least the crucial inadequacy of any so-called categorical self-evaluation." With his insistence on aleatory efficacy, Breton demonstrates a nonrational, antilogical way of reading the world and proceeding within it, a commitment and attention to an irregular system of signals that undermines conventional coherence ("all perfumes are connected by underground passageways," he writes) and replaces it with a personal, mythic consequence. It is in chance encounters that Breton finds and forecasts "the event from which each of us is entitled to expect the revelation of his life's meaning."

The job is twofold: dismantling the habituated modes of enlightenment while creating and asserting a reactivity of imagination, a volatility of awareness and receptivity, a union of interpretive and active principles that are heretical, chance derived, sexual, primitive, and profoundly artistic. Yet it is important to keep in mind that in its fundamental objectives Surrealism was not a mode of artistic production. Breton again and again throughout his writing expresses disdain for "the taint of literature" even as he labors over his prose and poetry. Art, both literary and visual, is instead a means of achieving surrealist goals that are, bluntly, complete social, political, economic, and psychological revolution. But it is art, the materials of art, that offers the best medium of provocation, havoc, and experimentation. Art is the laboratory results of surrealist activity, an activity that refuses to confine itself to the production of art. While the aims of Surrealism were political, its involvement with the conventions of political action were conflicted and often absurd. Upon offering his services to the French Communist Party, Breton was assigned to write a report on Czechoslovakian milk production.

Approximately three-quarters of a century earlier, William Wordsworth described a rather anticlimactic mountain climb in book VI of *The Prelude.* After getting lost, he and his companion ask a passerby for directions.

> Hard of belief, we question'd him again,
> And all the answers which the Man return'd
> To our inquiries, in their sense and substance,
> translated by the feelings which we had
> Ended in this; that we had cross'd the Alps.

Wordsworth has missed entirely the peak experience. Depending on a rationally expected outcome: you climb the mountain, you have the expected experience of climbing the mountain, that commodification. Instead, what in *The Prelude* is a characteristic formal device to get Wordsworth out of all sorts of philosophical and narrative corners, we get a stanza break then an ejaculation: "Imagination!" One way of reading this passage in a long poem subtitled *Growth of a Poet's Mind,* is to see it as a critique of "real world" experience, of too much dependence on experiential data in relation to logical outcome, suggesting that the real source of insight is in the energy of the imagination. "Life is elsewhere," Rimbaud will write in fifty years. Throughout, Romanticism's hunt for "the light of sense [that] / Goes out in flashes that have shewn to us / The invisible world" is in encounters with the irrational, be it Coleridge's famous narrator as voyager who has dropped off the map in *The Rime of the Ancient Mariner* or Keats bringing us to the liminal state of consciousness where dreaming and waking cannot be differentiated. In the "Preface to Lyrical Ballads," Wordsworth writes of the double task he and Coleridge shared—to make the usual unusual and the unusual usual, thereby opening the locks between the ordinary and the extraordinary and illustrating ways of knowing and experiencing outside rational systems. Romanticism begins an investigation of the imagination that will reach full, monstrous flower with Surrealism. Central to Romanticism is the power of the imagination, and many poems trace the process by which it is imperiled, found, and unleashed. As such, like much surrealist work, these poems function both as results of investigative methods and instruction manuals to those methods, very much a learn-by-doing system, the record of what happens serving as the means of achieving imaginative liberation and wholeness of being, "a sense sublime / Of something far more deeply interfused" where "We see into the life of things" as Wordsworth puts it in his great course outline *Tintern Abbey*. You can, in fact, do it on your own at home, perhaps one of the reasons why Breton referred to romanticism as "the prehensile tail of Surrealism."

Cut to a precocious sixteen-year-old French schoolboy writing on August 15, 1871, what would become known as the "Letter of the Seer." It begins with a scathing indictment of past literature: "Man was not working on himself, was not yet being awake, or not yet in the fullness of the great dream. Civil servants, writers: but author, creator, poet, this man never existed!" Now, of course, things are going to be different and "Poetry will no longer give rhythm to action: it will be in the front." Here is where the literal meaning of the avant-garde begins to take shape; borrowing terms from the military, artists will be theorized again and again in the early twentieth century as shock troops, and the casualties will be high. In fact, the high number of casualties will in itself become a model of avant-gardist authenticity. Failure is a necessity to the heroic terms the artist is conceived in. In this letter, written to his schoolteacher, Rimbaud clearly sketched out the principles of artistic activity and theory that will so dramatically mark the next century. Identity will become plastic even as the art is enacted on the self: "For I is someone else. If brass wakes up a trumpet, it is not its fault." The freeing of the self toward larger visions requires violent disentanglement, negation of self, and moral indebtedness: "If the old fools had not discovered only the wrong meaning of the I, we would not have to sweep away those millions of skeletons who, for an infinite length of time, have accumulated the products of a one-eyed intelligence, shouting they were the authors!" Instead, the new artist must be forward seeing so "The poet would define the amount of unknown awakening in his time"; he is dedicated to the new, willingly deformed: "The poet becomes a seer through a long, immense, and reasoned derangement of all the senses." The poet turns himself into a laboratory for and of the irrational in order to cultivate the unknown. The time of monsters has come.

Flash forward to July 28, 1914. A Serbian national shoots the Austrian archduke Francis Ferdinand, who bleeds to death in part because he is so trussed up in his tight-fitting regalia that the blood is squeezed from his body. One month later, having declared war on Serbia, Austria-Hungry appeals to its ally, Russia, which progresses to a general mobilization by July 31, and, through a system of alliances and reactions rivaling the absurd intricacies of the Rube Goldberg machine, Europe heaves itself into war. "The plunge of civilization into the abyss of blood and darkness is a thing that gives away the whole long age during which we have supposed the world to be, with whatever abatement, generally bettering," wrote Henry James.

At the beginning of World War I, Rupert Brooke could write of the blood of young soldiers as "The red/sweet wine of youth." Lord Northcliff remarked of "young individuals [who] enter upon their task in a sporting spirit with the same cheery enthusiasm as they would show for football." In fact, a few early charges were begun by the English by kicking a football toward the enemy, but by 1916 the stench of corpses was reaching London and Paris and Zurich and Berlin, the progress of the conflict unclear, its objectives muddled. "Bent double, like old beggars under sacks, / Knock-kneed, coughing like hags, we cursed through sludge," begins Wilfred Owen's "Dulce Et Decorum Est," presenting a much grimmer, more realistic picture of the war in which the soldiers are impoverished, sick, emasculated, and confused. Owen himself would be among the last casualties of that war, dying in a trench the day before the armistice began. In the Battle of the Somme, which would become known as the Great Fuck-up, through military incompetence, 60,000 of 110,000 allied troops were mowed down by machine guns during a single day. In the meantime, the English government issued a flyer called "What can I do? How the civilian can help the crisis. Be cheerful. Write encouraging letters to friends at the front. Don't spread foolish gossip. Don't think you know better than Haig, the British field marshal." In other words, pretend, be patriotic, shut up, and trust us. Which is precisely what Dada refused to do.

"The devising and raising of public hell was an essential function of any Dada movement, whether its goal was pro-art, non-art or anti-art. And when the public, like insects or bacteria, developed immunity to one kind of poison, we had to think of another," wrote Hans Richter of the movement. Bracketed between the suicide of Jacques Vache in 1919 and that of James Rigaut in 1929, both expressing through their self-inflicted deaths the ultimate nihilist statement of the pointlessness of life, Dada was a multinational, variously located fit brought on by the murderous hypocrisy of the status quo. *Dada,* the word, is typical of the movement in that the naming is given various accounts but all are united in the sense "that it means nothing, aims to mean nothing, and was adapted precisely because of its absence of meaning." "Dada sweeps through the world not in spite of but because of its meaning-lessness," wrote Richard Huelsenbeck. All Dada's proponents shared a profound disgust with society, politics, and culture and chose to make a celebration and debacle of that disgust. Primarily concerned with staging events, what we would now call performance art, the Dadaist choose to promote outrage by exposing through mockery (which is always primarily imitation) the bankruptcy of received opinions and accepted pieties. Out of outrage came an art that defined itself as being in permanent revolt, collapsing destructive and creative values, refusing finally to even allow for its own legitimacy. "To be dada is to be against dada," concluded Tristan Tzara. Dada's fundamental expressive mode was sabotage. Here's a description of a typical Dada soiree as recorded by Tzara.

> In the presence of a compact crowd Tzara demonstrates, we demand the right to piss in different colors, Huelsenbeck demonstrates, Ball demonstrates, . . . Janco, the dogs bay and the dissection of panama on piano and doll-shouted poem—shouting and fighting in the hall, first row approves second declares itself incompetent to judge the rest shout Who is the strongest, the big drum is brought in, Huelsenbeck against 200 . . . people protest shout smash window panes here come the police cubist dance, costumes.

Sounds like the usual military operation to me.

Explosion, hoax, confrontation, and the incorporation of accident over considered decision making; the violation of the barrier between performer and audience, between art and life; the accentuation of humor and shock; and championing the primitive and infantile and faith in the spontaneous over the reflective all point toward an antinat-uralism, an antirealism. But, if we consider realism as being that which is contrary to illusion, Dada is the century's first realism. Not only does it leave a clear trace of human presence in its rashness and harangue, but its inevitable depictions are true to the world as it is, torn open, celebrating lies over fact in the name of empty abstraction, making a dumb show of its own claims to humanity through constant carnage, concussive and profoundly confused, torn apart.

TO MAKE A DADAIST POEM

Take a newspaper.
Take some scissors.
Choose from this paper an article of the length you want to make
    your poem.
Cut out the article.
Next carefully cut out each of the words that makes up this article
and put them in a bag.
Shake gently.
Next take out each cutting one after the other.
Copy conscientiously in the order in which they left the bag.
The poem will resemble you.
And there you are—an infinitely original author of charming
    sensibility,
even though unappreciated by the vulgar herd.

Now this is the craft of poetry: explicit directions for the use of specific materials for a specific outcome. But of course it's absurd, simultaneously ascribing to how-to platitudes while pointing toward the outrageous eventuality of such an activity, an activity that sounds an awful lot like the typical creative writing exercise. Dada always has it both ways and sneers at both. Here is an aesthetic assertion of uselessness; language is torn from its most stable position as supposedly unbiased reportage, disrupted from the production of information and restored (violated) to poetry through willful derangement and chance. As with Marcel Duchamp's "Trap," a coat rack that he hammered to the floor to encourage people to trip over it, and Meret Oppenheim's mink cup and saucer, the suggestion is that art is at odds with utility; it is meant to trip us up through the disruption of the habituations of use. Also at work in Tzara's directive is a fundamental assault on the notion of the coherent self at the center of a work of art and the assumptions that that self precedes expression. The self na na na na is an accidental construction from debased materials like everything else, collaged from the wreckage of context, available to us only through sabotage and hoax. The fetishized individuality of the great work of art and the master artist is reduced to schoolboy cutting, aleatory whim, and perhaps most deliciously copying conscientiously. The self is plagiarized.

"Everything happens in a completely idiotic way," explains Tzara. A true realism would depict that "Murder and madness were rampant," as Hans Arp declared. The monstrosities of Hanna Hoch's collages and Georg Grosz's caricatures mirrored the reconstructed faces and experimental prostheses clattering through the streets and propped in cafés like the poisoned flotsam of a botched mass suicide. The cacophonous performances of simultaneously declaimed nonsense poems and piano pummelings and pictures drawn and immediately erased from blackboards only differed from the snarl of political posturings, tactical idiocies, and social lies in that in Dada no one got killed except by himself. Everyone was already limping anyway. "Revolted by the butchery of the 1914 World War, we devoted ourselves to the arts. . . . We were seeking art based on fundamentals, to cure the madness of the age," stated Arp. Or at least to trepan it.

Exhibit B: Man Ray's poem endures with a frontal assault that makes the avant-garde pretensions of today seem like wormy appeals for tenure. Has he succeeded in writing a poem that reaches the most unlikely of goals: to be understood be all? Certainly the poem is written in a universal language. You don't even have to know how to read to read it! Even the translations I have seen, from French into Italian, German, and English, preserve all its effects; nothing is lost. Its measure and musicality remain unalterable. The poem reaches a level of originality that defeats ownership and individuality. Like the ready-mades of Man Ray's henchman Duchamp, the poem slips all our forms of authentification, confounding us in self-consuming confabulations of aesthetic judgment. All poetry depends on an interchange between opacity and translucence. To some degree, all poetry must create some degree of impenetrability; otherwise the words are only indicators of things beyond them and, therefore, of diminished importance. Some poets create opacity through excess luminosity, like Gerard Manley Hopkins, whose stylistic wattage sets up impediments to getting at the poem's content. Man Ray's poem achieves opacity purely through an extremity of blackness, of ink that irrationally becomes utterly lucid. All poetry is a form of encryption, and the reading of poetry is much like breaking a code. Here the code has achieved some sort of purity; it cannot be broken, yet the severity of its encryption, its hiddenness, leads to lucidity. The poem is blunt in presenting a series of signs that stand for everything that is deleted, defeated, and cannot be divulged. Maybe there is nothing left in the graves of civilization worth exhuming. The message has already been cut from the doughboy's letter

home because finally all information is too sensitive, subject to the censor, or there is no message to send. This is the poem at the end of all poetry, when everything is crossed out, the ultimate revision, the perfected imperfection, the antipode to Mallarmé's perfect blank. Yet could it also be not the interpolated outcome of revisionist zeal, a disowning of the past, but rather a recapitulation, an utter welcoming, the culmination of a culture can that build on itself, the last density that allows nothing to escape? Shakespeare under Donne under Johnson under Herrick under Milton under Swift under Blake under Keats under Tennyson under Browning under under under. Or maybe it is just a dark joke.

Perhaps unsurprisingly, Dada exhausted itself and its own poisons and ironies. A practice that insists on the meaninglessness of itself, the fraud of art, and the pointlessness of life either becomes redundant or requires suicide as the ultimate theater. Versions of Dada will continue to appear whenever new pieties become fixed, but after a while even train wrecks become tedious, even punk rock becomes corporate. Springing from the Paris Dada group, the surrealists harnessed Dada's vigorous rupturing iconoclasm, preserving its unconditional outrage and love of scandal, to a rapture that is redemptive of the human condition primarily by accentuating and redefining the powers of the imagination.

In 1915, because of his meager medical training, André Breton was sent to the Saint-Dizier psychiatric center, whose mission was to aid "men who had been evacuated from the front for reasons of mental distress," he records in his journal. There he encountered, in the fabrications of the mad, "astonishing images on a higher plane than those which would occur to us," images that created an energy that seemed radiantly poetic. Breton leaves a rather lengthy account of one patient.

> He was a young, well-educated man who, in the front lines, had aroused the concern of his superior officers by a recklessness carried to extremes: standing on the parapet in the midst of bombardments, he conducted the grenades flying by. . . . He supposed war was only a simulacrum, the make-believe shells could do no harm, the apparent injuries were only makeup! "True," the subject calmly states, "I have stepped over corpses. They stock the dissection rooms with them. A good number more might have been made of wax."

What Breton admires here is the clarity of the imagination, its finesse in creating a convincing world, not its delusion. Breton knows as well as anyone that the war was an appalling fact, all the corpses were real, but the appalling nature of this fact was accentuated by the mad vividness of the patient's imaginative production. Here was an extreme imaginative creation that withstood the war, seemed nearly impervious to it, a recklessness that gave access to liberty. It proposed an alternative, an extreme measure to recover optimism.

"I could spend my whole life prying loose the secret of the insane," Breton will write in the "First Manifesto of Surrealism" nine years later, the single most important aesthetic statement of the twentieth century. I do not mean to suggest that Breton was alone in forming, fomenting, and developing the principles and procedures of surrealism. In fact, most of the early, pivotal work was collaborative, and the importance of collectivity was a lynchpin in the surrealist revolt. "Prisoners of raindrops, we are everlasting creatures," begins the first surrealist text, "The Magnetic Fields," jointly written by Breton and Philippe Soupault. But it is Breton alone who will so forcefully, through three manifestos, state Surrealism's aims.

The argument in the first manifesto goes like this. Imagination is in "a state of slavery" because "Our brains are dulled by the incurable mania of wanting to make the unknown known." Logic is at the center of the problem: "Experience itself has found itself increasingly circumscribed" through dependence on memory and logic, which conspire to limit possibility through a habituated sense of limited consequence. Experience of the new is impossible; every grape eaten is merely a sensation filtered through the past, a figment of some previous grape. Much of surrealism seeks to put us in a state that Breton calls in a love poem "always for the first time." The debasement of the imagination results in increasing alienation, the sense that one is befuddled and constantly wrong in one's own life, a sense of impending doom, the impossibility of not making further mistakes, and finally the inability to love. The imagination restores us to faith in rashness, the conviction of the immediacy of our own possibility, the magical reactants that every moment and encounter present us. The imagination in this formulation is fundamentally erotic as it finds itself in perpetual and ongoing mythos. Leaves sprout from our lips, our eyes fill with fire, we "put out trust in the inexhaustible nature of the murmur." The inventions of the mad and the unruly capacities of children all speak of the wellsprings of surrealism, as does, most importantly, what is still alive in us, our capacity to dream. "The waking state," he declares, "I have no choice but to consider it a phenomenon of interference." Breton isn't suggesting that we should all close our eyes and walk into walls; that's a Dada idea because it's what we're already doing anyway. For Surrealism, the dream state is a way to facilitate waking to imaginative actions that can influence reality, but it's important to keep in mind that this is a manifesto, and, like all manifestos, it is a provocation, extreme in its polarities, intending to be immoderate. "Dreaming," he continues, "is not inferior to the sum moments of reality. . . . The mind of man who dreams is fully satisfied by what happens to him. The agonizing question of possibility is no longer pertinent." Dreaming is the enactment of the fantastical, perpetually in liberation of the powers of the imagination; its concerns are primary concerns, life, terror, Eros and death. The dreamer is set free.

It is through surrealist procedures that this state of freedom and doubtlessness is uncovered. "Surrealism is based on the belief in the superior reality of certain forms of previously neglected associations, in the omnipotence of dream, in the disinterested play of thought. . . . Everything is valid when it comes to obtaining the desired suddenness of certain associations. . . . Surrealism [is] the actual functioning of thought . . . in the absence of any control exercised by reason, exempt from any aesthetic or moral concern." What this meant in practice was a lot of automatic writing, dream dictation, speaking in trances, collaborations, exquisite corpses, and "blacking paper with a praiseworthy disdain for what might result from a literary point of view." The goal isn't art production, something to market like sleeping pills for the masses; it is a change in consciousness. Much surrealist activity and the visual and written art that were generated attempts to create a breach in reality through trauma, imperiling our expectations of how art represents and responds to reality and what that reality is. It is in that split, that wound, that Surrealism sets its marvelous greenhouse: "The mind becomes aware of the limitless expanses wherein its desires are made manifest, where pros and cons are constantly consumed, where its obscurity does not betray it. It goes forward, borne by the images that enrapture it, which scarcely leave it time to blow upon the fire in its fingers. This is the most beautiful night of all, the lightning-filled night: day, compared to it, is night."

Salvador Dalí and Luis Buñuel's film Un Chien Andalou infamously begins with quick cuts between a cirrus cloud crossing a full moon and a razor passing through an eye. Aside from the shocking violence of an eye being sliced in heretical parallel with a cliché of the atmospheric poetic cliché of the cloud-crossed moon, which is brutal and crude, the movie begins with vision itself being destroyed. What occurs afterward is what is seen beyond the conventions of seeing. The blinding is therapeutic; the new eyes that the vision of the film presupposes can only be encouraged to grow by radical means. Dada ends with the jellies of the severed eye, but surrealism looks forward into a previously unseeable future.

Perhaps the most familiar vehicle of Breton's lightning-filled night is the surrealist image. Reaching back to a phrase from Lautréamont, "as beautiful as the chance meeting of an umbrella and a sewing machine on an operating table," the surrealist image seeks to create and transmit the marvelous by simultaneously hazarding disconnection and asserting reconnection, disconnecting a thing from its stagnated context, then providing another thing equally disenfranchised from the ordinary so that a spark can occur between them, creating a new, eroticized context. "Wine is flowing with the sound of thunder," writes Robert Desnos. "I describe objects and the material relationship of objects in such a way that none of our habituated concepts or feelings are necessarily linked to them," stated the Belgian painter René Magritte. While the imagery of surrealism, two objects brought incongruously together or one object given irrational characteristics (such as Dalí's infamous soft watches in *The Persistence of Memory*), is what surrealism has most commonly been associated with, I want to stress that surrealism is as much the field in which these surprising conjugations and illicit couplings occur. Surrealism is the operating table. When asked what that umbrella and sewing machine could possibly be doing, Max Ernst replied, making love, obviously. The synaptic connection is a sexual connection.

Reciprocal love, the only kind that should concern us here, is what creates between unfamiliarity and habit, imagination and the conventional, faith and doubt, perception of the internal and external object.

It includes the kiss, the embrace, the problem, and an infinitely problematic outcome of the problem. . . .

1. When the woman is on her back and the man lies on top of her it is the cedilla. . . .

10. When the woman sits, with her knees bent, on top of the man lying down, facing him with her bust either turned away or not, it is the faun.

11. When the woman sits back to front with her knees bent, on top of the man lying down, it is the springboard.

12. When the woman lies on her back and raises her thighs vertically, it is the lyre-bird.

13. When the woman faces the man and places her legs on his shoulders, it is the lynx.

14. When the woman's legs are drawn up and held there by the man against his chest, it is the shield.

This jointly written, surrealist *Kama Sutra* by Breton and Paul Eluard from "The Immaculate Conception," suggests that all namable things correspond to the arrangement of bodies in sexual relation, all things participate in an orgiastic potentiality that is collaborative and transformational. The writing of sex, about sex, is always a perversion, a turning away from silence and decorum, order and community standards (often in the revolution of the creation of new communities). Its effect is dependent on both recognition and shock, even revulsion at the sense of violation, of secrets revealed, of stripping away. It's a sad commentary that the argument supporting the sexually explicit photos by Robert Mapplethorpe in the big National Endowment for the Arts brouhaha a few years ago was based on art and titillation being incommensurate so that critical sophistication satirized itself in concentrating on hues and contours at the expense of being affected by a picture of one man putting his fist up another's ass. The primary aesthetic position in support of the NEA and Mapplethorpe was one of detachment, of disconnection, of numbness. But the life-affirming vulgarity (to use Frank O'Hara's phrase) of art is not that it promotes detachment but that it is proof of a pulse in the flooding of detail, an ability of word and image to flush the nerves to the point of lubricity, producing physiological charge by way of transubstantiation of sign, word into flesh. And it is beside the point to note any representation's inability to convey the whole of sexual desire and experience. If anything, want-more may be an indication of glut. Language isn't inadequate to the task of referring; rather, an overabundance of referential suggestion makes for the productive breakdown of any single referential stability or at least conscribes it. As proof, we have countless terms for sexual acts and organs. Witness how any phrase can become transformed by sexual energy to mean something beyond itself. Buff one's helmet, baby in a boat, groove, grotto, pearl dive, dazzle.

FREE UNION

My wife whose hair is a brush fire
Whose thoughts are summer lightning
Whose waist is an hourglass
Whose waist is the waist of an otter caught in the teeth of a tiger
Whose mouth is a bright cockade with the fragrance of a star of the
    first magnitude
Whose teeth leave prints like the tracks of white mice over snow
Whose tongue is made out of amber and polished stone
Whose tongue is a stabbed wafer
The tongue of a doll with eyes that open and shut

Whose tongue is incredible stone
My wife whose eyelashes are strokes in the handwriting of a child
Whose eyebrows are nests of swallows
My wife whose temples are the slate of greenhouse roofs
With steam on the windows
My wife whose shoulders are champagne
Are fountains that curl from the heads of dolphins under the ice
My wife whose wrists are matches
Whose fingers are raffles holding the ace of hearts
Whose fingers are fresh cut hay
My wife with the armpits of martens and beech fruit
And Midsummer Night
That are hedges of privet and nesting places for sea snails
Whose arms are of sea foam and a landlocked sea
And a fusion of wheat and a mill
Whose legs are spindles
In the delicate movement of watches and despair
My wife whose calves are sweet with the sap of elders
Whose feet are carved initials
Keyrings and the feet of steeplejacks who drink
My wife whose neck is fine milled barley
Whose throat contains the Valley of Gold
And encounters in the bed of the maelstrom
My wife whose breasts are of the night
And are undersea molehills
And crucibles of rubies
My wife whose breasts are haunted by the ghosts of dew-moistened roses
Whose belly is a fan unfolded in sunlight
Is a giant talon
My wife with the back of a bird in vertical flight
With a back of quicksilver
And bright lights
My wife whose nape is of smooth worn stone and wet chalk
And a glass slipped through the fingers of someone who has just drunk
My wife with the thighs of a skiff
That are lustrous and feathered like arrows
Stemmed with light tailbones of white peacock
And imperceptible balance
My wife whose rump is sandstone and the spring
My wife with the sex of an iris
A mime and a platypus
With the sex of an algae and old-fashioned candies
My wife with the sex of a mirror
My wife with eyes full of tears
With eyes that are purple armor and a magnetized needle

With eyes of savannahs
With eyes full of water to drink in prisons
My wife with eyes that are forests forever under the ax
My wife with eyes that are the equal of water and air and earth and fire

Breton's "Free Union" marks both a high point for surrealist imagery and its formulaic decline. On one hand, this is a dynamic tribute to the beauty of a woman, celebrating a physical instability and connection to the natural world. It seeks to achieve the rashness of sudden nudity, the explicitness of sexual tension through variety of associations, suggesting an excited faceting of subjectivity. Compare it to the more conventional evocations of beauty and you can see how exceptional and new it is.

But even before the poem ends a modern reader, rather familiar with eyebrows that are nests of sparrows, grows a bit bored, a bit too clued into the system, and the imagery itself becomes threadbare. I do not think this is a failure of the poem so much as an indication of the power and success of its method; it seems clichéd to us because as an artistic approach its successes have been reiterated and broadcast. So now this raunchy, racy poem seems a bit quaint to us. But I want to insist on its underlying commitment to disjunction, to misfit, to the inappropriate and incorrect as lasting and rich. The ongoing accumulation of analogies does not depend on aptness, on the similarity of the comparisons, so much as on a charged environment of transformational possibility so that the misfits are as communicative as the more obvious fits. Disjunction may be the most important characteristic of twentieth-century art, explored and emphasized in every art form. From the early Cubist collages to the independence of dance from music, disjunction is central to the major poetic works of high Modernism, be it the collage techniques of "The Wasteland" and *The Cantos* or the more severe semantic disjunctions of *Tender Buttons*.

The fractured self, its representation, and the notion that that fracturing is the source of art in general was an overarching preoccupation of the twentieth century. One particular form of disjunction explored by surrealism occurs in, is situated on subjectivity. I want to make a distinction between ecstatic subjectivity and pathological subjectivity. Ecstatic subjectivity, as it is articulated and extended from Surrealism (though not exclusive to it), takes the fragmentation of self as an opportunity for energetic release as well as a vehicle for new, usually temporary reformation. For the surrealists, a change in consciousness is not a static thing, not achieved so much as ongoing, an increased volatility and receptivity, the making of instability into a positive trait, a ready resource. Disjunction signals psychic tectonics in which the destructive is inseparable from the generative.

This notion of subjectivity has been rather eclipsed by the tragic disposition of modernism, be it Eliot's demonstration in "The Wasteland" of fragments shored against ruin, a sense of cultural and personal sterility in the face of overwhelming trauma (no wonder he resorted to writing doggerel about cats), or Pound's heartrending admission of failure at the end of *The Cantos,* "That I lost my center / fighting the world" (CXX) and "I cannot make it cohere" (CXVI). The futility of existence is related to the inability of identity, of subject, to take on the stability of authority and knowledge, of insight, to not be a victim of itself. That victimization receives even fuller articulation in later generations, particularly in the formidable poetry of Robert Lowell, John Berryman, and Sylvia Plath. The situation is far more complex than I'm rendering here, and Plath in particular uses the fault lines in identity to explosive, reincarnating effects, but I don't think it's far from the truth to say of these poets that the instabilities of identity their work explores are seen as pathological. "My mind's not right," writes Lowell, stating as plainly as possible one of his major themes. Literary theory, again to wildly generalize, is part in a vigorous response to a fetishization and commodification of the psychologically imperiled self, a tonic for debunking the notion of subject entirely. The self, exposed as a construct, is demoted to decentered mush; there is no subject, the word I is counterrevolutionary, and poems that pretend to relate an individual's experience are the patriarchal flimflam of capitalistic lackeys. There are only texts. And the MLA convention.

But to convince me that the self is decentered is far from convincing me that the self does not exist. Decentered it may be, and needs be, but so, too, is it constantly recentering. The self may, in fact, have too many centers, and that is the source of our psychological stress but also of our great capacity for change, creativity, empathy, love, and joy. When I cut my face shaving, it isn't a construct that bleeds. My self is constantly disrupted, constantly recentering, regrouping with each experience; when I meet one person's eyes, when I meet another's, how else to account for that voltage in those eyes meeting? Rather than seeing that process as brittle, as cause for crack-up, it may be conducted as music if we are limber and cultivate a nimble awareness that welcomes and exploits such occasions. The self is always under construction; it, too, is an aesthetic creation, and the world is always offering up its materials for garden and blast site. If there is divinity in us, it is in the process of allowing ourselves to unmake and remake ourselves. "So that understanding can begin and in doing so be undone," as John Ashbery writes in "And Ut Pictura Poesis Is Her Name."

THE VOICE OF ROBERT DESNOS

So like a flower and a current of air
the flow of water fleeting shadows
the smile glimpsed at midnight this excellent evening
so like every joy and every sadness
it's midnight past lifting its naked body
above belfries and poplars
I call to me those lost in the fields
old skeletons young oaks cut down
scraps of cloth rotting on the ground and linen
drying in farm country
I call tornadoes and hurricanes
storms typhoons cyclones
tidal waves
earthquakes
I call the smoke of volcanoes and the smoke of cigarettes
the rings of smoke from expensive cigars
I call lovers and loved ones
I call the living and the dead
I call gravediggers I call assassins
I call hangmen pilots bricklayers architects
assassins
I call the flesh
I call the one I love
I call the one I love
I call the one I love
the jubilant midnight unfolds its satin wings
and perches on my bed
the belfries and the poplars bend to my wish
the former collapse that latter bow down
those lost in the fields are found in finding me
the old skeletons are revived by my voice
the young oaks cut down are covered with foliage
the scraps of cloth rotting in the ground and in the earth
snap to at the sound of my voice like a flag of rebellion
the linen drying in farm country clothes adorable women
whom I do not adore
who come to me
obeying my voice, adoring
tornadoes resolve in my mouth

hurricanes if it is possible redden my lips
storms roar at my feet
typhoons if it is possible ruffle me
I get drunken kisses from the cyclones
the tidal waves come to die at my feet
the earthquakes do not shake me but fade completely
at my command
the smoke of volcanoes clothes me with its vapors
and the smoke of cigarettes perfumes me
and the rings of cigar smoke crown me
loves and love so long hunted find refuge in me
lovers listen to my voice
the living and the dead yield to me and salute me
the former coldly the latter warmly
the gravediggers abandon the hardly-dug graves
and declare that I alone may command their nightly work
the assassins greet me
the hangman invokes the revolution
invoke my voice
invoke my name
the pilots are guided by my eyes
the bricklayers are dizzied listening to me
the architects leave for the desert
the assassins bless me
flesh trembles when I call
the one I love is not listening
the one I love does not hear
the one I love does not answer.

The voice in "The Voice of Robert Desnos," the poet's identity, is composed by and of his capacity for calling, a performance of evoking. Supposedly taken down in dictation from Desnos while he was in a self-imposed trance, the poem's Whitmania insists on the ongoingness of self-making even as it ends in a sense of futility, unrequited. Its tragedy is nonetheless buoyant, and there is no sense of self-negating guilt or extermination; if there is any note of pointlessness, it is one of the celebration of freedom from logical constraints, an encyclopedic romp that rolls in the world of its own making. If we must end up unheard, there is still the frolic of the voice and getting drunken kisses from cyclones.

Desnos's voice, like the voice in many surrealist poems, verges on self-eradication. There is not much in writing that rivals the power of the suicide note. Its final punctuation is of such insistent finality as to assert a formal identity as irrefutable as a sonnet. Its language straddles the utterly personal and the intimate with the hermetic, a language that converses with what is beyond itself. It refers both back, from a greater and greater distance to those left behind of matters left behind, and forward with a conjectural implication that is by uncertain degrees dark and if not joyous at least released. There is nothing left out or incomplete about a suicide note; the notion is absurd. A suicide note of one word, that single word existing in radiant last form, in advance of its own definition, is always sufficient. The message is always delivered, full, indeed overfull, so that in the purest of authorial absencing that is the defining characteristic of the form there is a backwash of significance; it points back to babble. What is a poem but the management of silence and babble? The suicide note, as a form authenticated by the ultimate sincerity (no suicide note is ironic), resides in the blessed state of perfect balance between silence and babble. All that arises from the chaos of plenitude is brought into the radiant, harsh, final clarity of silence so that words lose their profane profligacy and duplicity and their inadequacy.

But is it not possible that the birth announcement, too, is a powerful form, that the urge of greeting can be as powerfully articulated as the elegiac and self-extinguishing that makes us want, in some real way, every poem to be the last poem? Why not kill yourself? Surrealism attempted to answer that question ongoingly, through whatever measures necessary, to announce the marvelous into life, to incarnate capacities dreamed of, to discover through the fecund imagination the erotics of every day. "Choose life instead of those prisms with no depth even if their colors are purer / Instead of this hour always hidden instead of these terrible vehicles of cold flame" (Breton, "Choose Life"). Perhaps the purpose of writing poetry is to maintain the spirit; be it through empathy and the amazement of finding ourselves knowable or finding ourselves so strange, it is a brilliance and glory. There are times when poetry's greatest task is to restore us to unassumed things, but there is also its primary obligation to liberty, to the invention fantastical, to a series of wildly unsupportable assertions that make life worth living at its most reckless.

The impossible is the first necessary condition of any faith. It is impossible to write poetry; therefore we do it. Without discipline. Discipline is good only for dispensing punishment. Sometimes the more impossible it is the greater the debacle, the greater the poem. Just because a thing can't be done doesn't mean it can't be did. We all look into mirrors and see phantoms. Our error is our Eros. Why is there something instead of nothing? The answer is surreal. The paramount necessary questions can only be talked back to by the surreal. Who am I? Why am I here? What is that voice inside me that is not me? What will be my conception? Why do I love? What will be my death? "Are you going to spend your entire life in this world / Half dead / Half asleep / Haven't you had enough of commonplaces yet" (Aragon, "Pop Tune"). Only dreams can wake us. Each morning we wake with the obligatory liberty to conceptually re-create the world. We fail. We despair. We try again. We try to refuse a destiny of advertising and pennies and murder. "When the traveler loses his way in the will-o-wisps / More broken than the lines in old people's foreheads /And lies down on the moving earth / The wandering horses appear / When a young girl lies at the foot of a birch and waits / The wandering horses appear" (Desnos, "Of the Flower of Love and the Wandering Horses"). The signal fades in and out, it is only always intermittent, but our art may mark it, not as a tomb but as a guidepost, a monument to toppling, a moment of doubtlessness that is impossible, of being touched that is impossible, genius that is impossible, being alive that is impossible.

SOURCES

Auster, Paul, ed. *The Random House Book of Twentieth Century French Poetry*. New York: Vintage, 1984.

Benedikt, Michael. *The Poetry of Surrealism*. New York: Little, Brown, 1974.

Bohn, Willard, *The Dada Market*. Carbondale: Southern Illinois University Press, 1993.

Breton, André, *Manifestos of Surrealism*. Ann Arbor: University of Michigan Press, 1969.

Breton, André. *Nadja*. New York: Grove, 1960.

Breton, André. *Selections*. Berkeley: University of California Press, 2003.

Breton, André, Paul Eluard, and Philippe Soupault. *The Automatic Message*. London: Atlas, 2001.

Desnos, Robert. *The Voice of Robert Desnos*. New York: Sheep Meadow, 2005.

Fussell, Paul. *The Great War in Modern Memory*. Oxford: Oxford University Press, [1975] 2000.

Jean, Marcel, ed. *The Autobiography of Surrealism*. Viking Press, 1980.

Motherwell, Robert, ed. *The Dada Painters and Poets*. Cambridge: Harvard University Press, 1989.

Nedeau, Maurice. *The History of Surrealism*. Cambridge: Belknap, 1989.

Polizzotti, Mark. *Revolution of Mind: The Life of André Breton*. Da Capo, 1997.

Tzara, Tristan. *Approximate Man and Other Writings*. New York: Black Widow Press, 2005.

AGHA SHAHID ALI

A Darkly Defense of Dead White Males

Subject matter is artistically interesting only when through form it has become content. The more rigorous the form, realized formally, openly, or brokenly, the greater the chance for content. I am not endorsing any mechanical fidelity to inherited rules. I emphasize this distinction between subject matter and content, as elsewhere one must between the political and the programmatic and, yet elsewhere, between tastes and standards, because the two are so often used synonymously. Confusion results. Often a work of little or even no depth is hailed because it asserts importance. It is certainly human and humane to feel sympathy for certain emotions as with, let's say, those of certain "surrealists who joined the Resistance in France." But, to quote Yves Bonnefoy, their poems were "insufficiently adventurous in poetry."[1] Art is indeed art; what it demands of us is a dog's life.

So what is subject matter? Certainly, those eternals: birth, sex, death, life, loss, grief. Well, even patriotism, that rather adolescent emotion, which, with Shakespeare, finds this utterance in John of Gaunt's speech in *Richard II* (2.1.40–68).

> This royal throne of kings, this scept'red isle,
> This earth of majesty, this seat of Mars,
> This other Eden, demi-paradise,
> This fortress built by Nature for herself
> Against infection and the hand of war,
> This happy breed of men, this little world,
> This precious stone set in the silver sea,
> Which serves it in the office of a wall,
> Or as a moat defensive to a house,
> Against the envy of less happier lands;
> This blessed plot, this earth, this realm, this England,
> This nurse, this teeming womb of royal kings,
> Fear'd by their breed, and famous by their birth,
> Renowned for their deeds as far from home,
> For Christian service and true chivalry,
> As is the sepulchre in stubborn Jewry
> Of the world's ransom, blessed Mary's son;

This land of such dear souls, this dear dear land,
Dear for her reputation through the world,
Is now leas'd out—I die pronouncing it—
Like to a tenement or pelting farm.
England, bound in with the triumphant sea,
Whose rocky shore beats back the envious siege
Of wat'ry Neptune, is now bound in with shame,
With inky blots and rotten parchment bonds;
That England, that was wont to conquer others,
Hath made a shameful conquest of itself.
Ah, would the scandal vanish with my life,
How happy then were my ensuing death!

Patriotism finds exciting expression in the work of Fernando Pessoa, who knew his Shakespeare according to Jonathan Griffin, and who had seen from John of Gaunt's speech that "patriotic verse can be poetry of a high order." Here is "Portugese Ocean," one of the forty-four patriotic poems in *Mensagem* (*Message*).

Salt-laden sea, how much of all your salt
Is tears of Portugal!
For us to cross you, how many sons have kept
Vigil in vain, and mothers wept!
Lived as old maids how many brides-to-be
Till death, that you might be ours, sea!

Was it worthwhile? It is worth while, all,
If the soul is not small.
Whoever means to sail beyond the Cape
Must double sorrow—no escape.
Peril and abyss has God to the sea given
And yet made it the mirror of heaven.

However, most of the poems in *Mensagem* "also go beyond patriotism: those in which King Sebastian figures are metaphors for the religious quest, and those about the ordeals of the seafarers dramatize the poet's inner perseverance."[2] For, as Salman Rushdie insists, in "the best writing . . . a map of a nation will also turn out to be a map of the world." Please do note that to establish how above subject matter one has to be, I have celebrated with you patriotic poems about two countries that colonized South Asia, one of which, through Vasco da Gama, is supposed to have "discovered" India.

Let me name some subject matters that have immediately recognizable historical stature in this century: the Armenian genocide, the

Jallianwala Bagh massacre, the rape of Abyssinia, the Holocaust. And, to come to the ebbing of this century: the American napalming of Vietnam, the Killing Fields of Cambodia, Afghanistan, Kurdistan, Bosnia, Rwanda, Kashmir, Palestine, East Timor. And then: AIDS, abortion, human rights, civil rights, gay rights, the environment. And O, NATURE!

But are all poems about the Holocaust equal? Or about Vietnam? And, even if they are of equal effort, are they of equal accomplishment? And, even more tantalizingly, is a great poem about a massacre superior to a great poem about that one art—I mean the art of losing? That brings me to content. What is content? Negative capability helps, as does the suspension of disbelief. And sometimes even an unwilling one of belief. And the objective correlative. And the recollection in tranquility. And Arnold's touchstones, which certainly should be expanded to allow for other tastes as long as they reveal the highest standards, for standards may not shift. Successful free verse is full of artifice, and weak sonnets and sestinas are not.

Content is the poet's formal investment in the subject. It is the poet's musical investment in his or her subject whereby the subject is formally implicated. Poems that rely on the stature of their subject often provide us with little more than a gloss on the poet's feelings, in aid of which the declarative sentence can often be nothing more than a crutch. Poets who rely on their subject often mistake their anxieties for principles. In many cases, we find a writer distracted from his real work into a facilely executed sense of social justice. Rather than letting his passion for justice emerge organically from the courage to implicate the writer formally and thus truly take a stand. Content is achieved sincerity. Sincerity achieved through artifice. Emotion tested by artifice.

I realize I am sounding conservative, but in matters of art I tend to be conservative. But so were Faiz Ahmed Faiz and Nazim Hikmet, two of the greatest Marxist poets of this century. Since one should not forgo the whole level of entertainment in art, let me depart now for a moment affectedly. Why do I say "darkly" in my title? Well, this adverb has an adjectival shrug. It has an attitude (like Anne Baxter's "warmly" in *All About Eve*). A crippling insistence on part-whole relationships, which makes us see poems simply as machines, does not allow for the well-realized and necessary digressions that can be built into art. Is it true, to quote *The Age of Innocence,* that it was "one of the great livery-stableman's most masterly intuitions to have discovered that Americans want to get away from amusement even more quickly than they want to get to it" (2)? Thus, the deep puritanical suspicion of wit! Notice how one is always asking for a pun to be excused.

Let me complicate the issue with a digression on South Asian writers in England given the immense attention they have been receiving since Salman Rushdie's *Midnight's Children* and the stunning success of Arundhati Roy's *The God of Small Things*. To be in a diaspora, writing the exile's or the expatriate's poetry, is a privileged historical site, sometimes indecently so today, and with that caveat let me embark on this digression.

Let me clarify that the "I" of this digression is often a composite figure beside/besides me. With modest claims to scholarship, I am shamelessly subjective, though an exile must cultivate a scrupulous subjectivity. A multiple exile, I celebrate myself. *Émigré* and *expatriate* describe me better for, as Edward Said says in "A Mind of Winter," *exile* and *refugee* imply a state into which one has been forced. Expatriates, however, "voluntarily live in an alien country, usually for personal or social reasons. [They] may share in the solitude and estrangement of exile, but they do not suffer under its rigid proscriptions." I, however, call myself an exile for its resonance, for contrast to the near clinical *expatriate* and *émigré*. And, as proof of my mind of winter, I offer my ancestor, a trader, a man of Himalayan snow, who came to Kashmir from Central Asia, his skeleton carved from glaciers, his breath arctic.

When I left Kashmir for Delhi—my first exile—I discovered what the Indian monsoons had meant to my mother. Kashmir, unlike most of the Indian subcontinent, has four clear seasons. Kashmiris respond viscerally to Shelley's "If Winter comes, can Spring be far behind?" In recounting her childhood, my mother spoke of that season in itself, the monsoons, when Krishna's flute is heard on the shores of the Jamuna and when lovers cannot bear separation. She, a Muslim from Lucknow, that cradle of the Urdu language, had Hindu folk traditions in her bones.

When I left Delhi for Pennsylvania—a more inescapable exile, the distance terrible—how was I to know that eventually I would be in the perhaps enviable position of contributing simultaneously to the new anglophone literatures of the world, the new subcontinental literatures in English, and the new multiethnic literatures of the United States? I was talking about the distance: the moon would shine into my dorm room, and I remember one night closing my eyes and feeling I was in my room in Kashmir: "It doesn't leave me, / the cold moon of Kashmir which breaks / into my house / and steals my parents' love." So I wrote. I continued, "I open my hands: / empty, empty. This cry is foreign. / 'When will you come home?' / Father asks, then asks again. / The ocean moves into the wires. / I shout, 'Are you all happy?' / The line goes dead. / The waters leave the wires. / The sea is quiet, and over it / the cold, full moon of Kashmir." However, Pennsylvania became, if not home, certainly a home, and sometimes in a bar at 2:00 a.m., like so many Americans, I felt alone, almost an exile (except when I got lucky!). Night after night, all routes to death opened up, again and again, as the bars closed all over Pennsylvania—the taxi hour of loss. Then, some years later, I left for Arizona, where it always is yesterday, no daylight savings time there, and the Sonora Desert seems strangely out of time. From Arizona to upstate New York and now Massachusetts—all this accompanied by summers in Kashmir.

These relocations meant loss. Each of them also meant creating a rhetoric of loss and, through loss, the illusion of belonging—to something, to anything. That dismal word: *roots.* As Edward Said, a Christian Palestinian from Jerusalem by way of Cairo, a U.S. citizen, asserts, "At bottom exile is a jealous state. With very little to possess, you hold on to what you have with aggressive defensiveness." I have clung to my loss, to my losses, even to my loss of losses. But wasn't I an exile of sorts even before leaving Kashmir and then Delhi? Said speaks of exile "not as a privileged site for individual self-reflection but as an *alternative* to the mass institutions looming over much of modern life." He is, of course, thinking of those on whom loss has been imposed, particularly of the great tragedy of the Palestinian nation. But as an exile in my own country—again, I use the word for its poetic resonance, for its metaphoric power—I must use the site for the privilege of self-reflection.

Formally educated subcontinentals in some ways are exiles in their own country. At the most ridiculous level, they have a pathetic "craze for foreign"—a phrase brought maliciously to light in *An Area of Darkness,* that deeply empty work by that deeply empty V. S. Naipaul. More sublimely: educated subcontinentals generally speak three languages, write in two, dream in one—English. I do not mean the dreams of one's sleep, which can occur in any of the languages they speak, but their dreams of almost anything *material.* As a privileged minority, they have maintained what the British established: English as one basic criterion for "success." (I will later show that the British created the English "canon" in India.) If an Indian wants to join the government civil service or a business firm, he or she must have an accent that approximates the Queen's "propah" English. The queen, till very lately, was Victoria.

This situation, however, is being turned around by poets and, visibly, novelists. The colonizers left fifty years ago, and subcontinental writers, particularly poets, can breathe greater confidence into Indian English (as Walt Whitman did into American English) not only because they belong to what, with qualifications, is the international-ism of the English language (in this context, note the awarding of the Nobel Prize to Patrick White, Wole Soyinka, Nadine Gordimer, and Derek Walcott) but because, by re-creating the language, by infusing into it all the traditions and forms at their command, they can make subcontinentals feel that they do not have to seek approval for any idiosyncrasy in syntax and grammar from the queens, Victoria or Eliz-abeth (the second, of course). As a matter of fact, for all kinds of rea-sons, it is gratifying to give an insult to the English language.

At the same time, I argue that history has assured me a privileged position. As a Kashmiri Muslim (an all-American Shiite, if you will) writing poetry in English, I "own" three major world cultures (Hindu, Muslim, and Western) without effort. I have a natural and profound inwardness with them; my use of them is not exotic. I feel them in three languages. I don't hunt for subjects. My position, perhaps, is not unlike Satyajit Ray's at the beginning of his career. As Pauline Kael said sometime in the early 1960s:

> Consider the Americans, looking under stones for some tiny piece of subject matter they can call their own, and then judge the wealth, the prodigious, fabulous heritage that an imaginative Indian can draw upon. Just because there has been almost nothing of value done in films in India, the whole country and its culture is [Satyajit Ray's] to explore and express to the limits of his ability; he is the first major artist to draw upon these vast and ancient reserves. The Hollywood director who re-makes biblical spectacles or Fannie Hurst stories for the third or sixth or ninth time is a poor man—no matter how big his budget—compared to the first film artist of India.

I can use the Indian landscape, and the subcontinent's myths and leg-ends and history, from within, and I can do so for the first time in what might seem like a new idiom, a new language—subcontinental English. There are no ready-made responses, as in the case of writers on old homes, to quote Charlie Baxter. Such resources as were avail-able to Ray back then are available to the subcontinental poet writing in English. Proof? Witness what Salman Rushdie has done with them in *Midnight's Children* and *Shame* and *The Satanic Verses*. If the novel has done it, poetry cannot be far behind. The Indo-English scene for some decades was so thoroughly empty and corrupt, and in some quarters continues to be (one can't forget the dreadful publications of Calcutta's Writers Workshop, which, for some time now, has been functioning as a near vanity press and which, I must embarrass myself by saying, pub-lished two of my chapbooks), that a truly gifted poet can begin anew.

The way Ray handled celluloid, so the poet can handle English and free it from its imposed and self-imposed status in India.

Often the upper classes of India adopt an unquestioning stance toward Western representations of the subcontinent, which they have internalized and unselfconsciously recycled. A passage to India? That is why Salman Rushdie is such fresh air. The upper classes of India, whose English is often more British than that of the British, have not allowed English to come into any "real" contact with Indianisms; they have, thus, not let even a pidgin English develop in India. But this is a fertile situation, almost Renaissance-like, for the truly gifted users of English. Linguists could draw comparisons between English in India and French in Chaucer's England, that is, Indian English has to liberate itself from British English just as Chaucer had to liberate English from the dominance of French and Latin. In that context, besides others, Chaucer is easily heroic, as is Rushdie. It is always good to give an insult to the English language, so Rushdie says somewhere. To quote Rustom Barucha, "Rushdie has demonstrated convincingly that a colonized language can be freed from its own tyrannies. English can be more flexible, more mischievous, ultimately more human than the colonizers who institutionalized it."

As a Muslim from the Indian subcontinent writing in English, I have three major world cultures available to me without effort, cultures that I can appropriate, mix, and exploit. I can deal with them from within. My writing in English results from my background: I spoke English at home. I attended English-medium schools. My teachers were Irish and Dutch fathers and sisters. English functions as a first language for around 40 million people in India, and, after the United States and Britain, India has the third-largest English-speaking population in the world—more than the entire population of Canada or Australia. India is also the third-largest publisher of works in English.

Because of my background, the culture of the West was and is automatically available to me. I listened to Grieg and Chopin, to Elvis Presley, the Beatles—ever since I can remember. Yes, I have sighed orgasmically to Donna Summer's "Love to Love You, Baby." But, then, who can't? I read British and European history. My grandmother read Keats, Shakespeare, and Hardy, quoting them often by heart in English. I read English/American/European literatures. My mother read Greek myths to me. I saw Hollywood films (English-language films are never dubbed in India) as well as European films subtitled in English. I read *Time* and *Life,* though I should have read less of both. The Hepburns, both Katharine and Audrey, were a part of my imaginative life, as were Madhubala, Meena Kumari, and Suchitra Sen. At the same time, my Muslim background assures me a familiarity with the cultural sensibilities, through permutations of course, of what is called the Middle East, particularly of classical Persian culture. The determining influence of Farsi, the language of the Mughal kings, on Urdu need not even be stated. Recall Rushdie's *Shame:* Old Shakil loathed both worlds, the old town and the Cantt area, a very clever use of the phrase "donon jahan" in Persian and Urdu poetry. Urdu is a language of North India much more than it is of Pakistan, where it is the official language. Ghalib, Mir, Faiz: these poets were quoted by rote in our house and in the homes of our friends and acquaintances. So were the classical Persian poets, in Farsi: Hafiz, Sadi, Rumi, Firdausi.

Finally, by virtue of being in India, I have its Hindu traditions: its music, folk culture, festivals, religion, and metaphors. I can use reincarnation as a metaphor in my poetry and be believed it is culturally innate to me even though I don't "believe" in it. Reincarnation is mine—to exploit as "realistically" as I will. (The belief in reincarnation, it has been argued, is one reason why the Indian tradition has not produced tragedy in the Hellenic sense.) So Western, Muslim, and Hindu cultures are all part of my emotional baggage. A similar sort of situation—and I have already referred to the internationalism of English—might exist for an African poet writing in his version of that language. Note the title of Ali A. Mazrui's *The Africans: A Triple Heritage.* Mazrui finds hope for Africa, despite all its faults, in a new synthesis of its indigenous traditions, Islamic culture, and Western influence. I may perhaps not allow myself hope for the Indian subcontinent in its triple (rather, multiple) heritage, but I do find a challenge, and thus hope, for its literary endeavors in English. Given this multiple heritage, why shouldn't I be envied? After all, I can use *shantih* without being exotic, as Eliot clearly was in *The Waste Land,* a use that strikes one as full of irony when one remembers his customary fuss over the mind of Europe. Wasn't *The Waste Land* supposed to serve an exclusively European tradition?

The sum or tangle of the three traditions for a subcontinental who has not lived abroad is compelling enough. But now combine them with my status as an exile in America and you have a tantalizing poetic situation. I don't have to hunt for "major" subjects: there is so much to bring to life in the increasingly fertile landscape of subcontinental English. No wonder I have no vested interest in the free verse versus formalism debate that often goes on in the United States—among, let me add, largely White poets—a debate that seems particularly petty when one knows the world is going to pieces. My situation is available to any Bangladeshi, Indian, Pakistani, Sri Lankan, or Kashmiri poet writing in English today. Many of us are now laying the groundwork for a truly major literature to emerge—maybe from writers now in their twenties. Rushdie has already pointed out a consummate way for the novelists. Notice the three sisters in his *Shame:* they recall a distinctly Western tradition—the Gorgons, the Graeae, the Fates, the Norns (there's a reference to Odin in *Shame*), Shakespeare's and Chekhov's weird sisters. The three sisters give birth to Omar Khayyam Shakil (the Persian influence), who even has a telescope, but, unlike the poet-astronomer, is uncircumcised (Hindu subversion?). The three sisters also have the Hindu element in them: at one point, they go into the pose of the three monkeys: *See no evil, hear no evil, speak no evil.* Although Rushdie says that prose writers must go to the poets for wisdom, in this case he has pointed out a way and a way out for the poets. He has "chutnified" English. The poets have an opportunity, one that results from a unique vantage point of history. Like him, they can be translated people, men and women who have been "borne across."

So it is obvious that I have a subject. Now the issue is: where and when does art begin? Many of us, hyphenated beings in particular, may think that, given the celebration, genuine or superficial, of difference these days and because historically/sociologically our stories may be seen as more interesting, we may seduce ourselves into thinking that we are automatically writing good fiction or poetry. This is indeed a danger for writers, who should always cultivate conscious strategies to formalize their dispositions and histories, and if they stumble on some unconscious ones they must locate the source of their energy and pursue them further. Rhetorical gestures are not enough, nor is simple talk, talk, talk.

To quote John Ashbery in an essay on Fairfield Porter's paintings, "politically 'concerned' artists continue to make pictures that illustrate the horrors of war, of man's inhumanity to man; feminist artists produce art in which woman is exalted and imagine that they have accomplished a useful act; and no doubt there are a number of spectators who find it helpful to be reminded that there is room for improvement in the existing order of things. Yet, beyond the narrow confines of the "subject" (only one of a number of equally important elements in the work of art, as Porter points out), the secret business of art gets done according to mysterious rules of its own. In this larger context, ideology simply doesn't function as it is supposed to when, indeed, it isn't directly threatening the work of art by trivializing it and trivializing as well as the importance of the ideas it seeks to dramatize. That is—now I quote Louis Finkelstein on Porter—"Subject-matter must be normal in the sense that it does not appear sought after so much as simply happening to one." The way it happens to Paul Celan in "Death-Fugue" or to Dan Pagis in "Written in Pencil in the Sealed Railway Car" or to Faiz in his elegy for the Rosenbergs or to James Merrill in his elegies for David Kalstone. Otherwise, what we have are various versions of exclusivisms—a gay nationalism, a feminist nationalism, a South Asian nationalism, and, O NATURE! Rushdie, whom no one can accuse of being a- or nonpolitical, warns us that these nationalisms always become debilitating where art is concerned. "Beware the writer," he writes, "who sets himself or herself up as the voice of a nation. This includes nations of race, gender, sexual orientation, elective affinity. This is the New Behalfism. Beware behalfies! The New Behalfism demands uplift, accentuates the positive, offers stirring moral instruction. It abhors the tragic sense of life. Seeing literature as inescapably political, it replaces literary values by political ones."

In this context, I was quite intrigued to read a piece by Edmund White in the *Nation* in which he defends plenty of AIDS literature and thinks it is indecent to ask whether he would be willing to vouch for it as art. The question makes him "uncomfortable whenever it's raised," and it is exacerbated "when the subject matter is AIDS and even more so when the writer has AIDS or has died from AIDS complications." I am glad that in passing White reveals the importance of art when he says that AIDS poetry "at its best benefits from almost imperceptible formal constraints and pushes right on to through to the most rigorous sincerity." He cites Thom Gunn's "Lament" at great length (he could also have cited Merrill's elegies for David Kalstone). That is, whatever the merits of his argument, and on human grounds I buy them, he chooses to cite the work of a genuine artist, a poem in which artifice is everywhere. I realize that White, whom I greatly admire, is HIV-positive, also that AIDS is war and that, to quote Wallace Stevens, in a time of war consciousness might replace the imagination in a work of art, and so on, but all these statements reveal an underlying notion of art. White may not wish to attack AIDS literature, but he knows which poems falling under the shadow of that literature constitute art and which ones don't. Yes, the cause of humanity must be served, and many stories dealing with AIDS are heartbreaking. These stories may be serving purposes greater than those of art. But they are not serving the purposes of art and the imagination.[3]

I suppose you realize that I am on my way to a defense of the canon, which to me represents artistic standards (well, I am against the ideology of standards but not against standards—that is, in levels of artistic accomplishment, achievement. I do continue to be against the imposition of tastes, however, for taste, as Picasso said, is the enemy of creativity. Something genuinely new often has to fight with everything it's got against taste. The canon—Chaucer, Shakespeare, Marlowe, Webster, Milton, and so on—represents artistic achievement at its highest. And let's not forget that every literary culture has a canon. One can't even begin to speak of Urdu without acknowledging sooner or later, usually sooner if not immediately, the all-pervasive presence of Ghalib. And Ghalib is a dead brown male. And one cannot speak of Persian literature without bringing in Hafiz and Rumi or of Russian literature without Pushkin (who was actually black I was delighted to discover). All literary cultures claim some figures as their greats.

When many of my fellow writers of a piercing brownness—ravishing shades of brown—here in the United States (the ones in India really don't say this) say that these so-called standards have been IMPOSED on us, I ask them to distinguish between tastes and standards. Further, I ask: tell me what are the criteria, if not standards, according to which you consider a work worthwhile as literature? What are your literary criteria? And how have these criteria evolved and been maintained over centuries? After all, there were many dead white males, writers, many of them courtiers, so truly privileged, whose work is not celebrated, who wrote sonnets all the time. Even if there was a homogeneous, monolithic conspiracy among the whites— the English, I mean—against us, why did they CHOOSE those white writers and not others? And, even among the individual writers, why do we call one work of theirs superior to another one? After all, Queen Elizabeth I wrote poems: do we discuss those? She was certainly a privileged white MALE, if I may! Why have Shakespeare and Milton survived, though Milton at times has suffered because of changing tastes. Whatever their shifting presence or absence in the academy, why did the writers of future generations constantly go back to them? I realize the nation, to quote Rushdie again, "either co-opts its greatest writers (Shakespeare, Goethe, Camoens, Tagore) or else seeks to destroy them (Ovid's exile, Soyinka's exile). Both fates are problematic. The hush of reverence is inappropriate for literature; great writing makes a great noise in the mind, the heart. There are those who believe that persecution is good for writers. This is false." Of course, writers "are UNABLE to deny the lure of the nation, its tides in our blood. Writing as mapping: the cartography of the imagination. (Or, as modern critical theory might spell it, Imagi/Nation.) In the best writing, however, a map of a nation will also turn out to be a map of the world." Note: whatever the argument, sooner or later a writer will talk about the best, the great, and so on. I am interested in their criteria, which they often don't spell out when they are caught in frontiers: "Good writing assumes a frontier-less nation. Writers who serve frontiers have become border guards."

If Matthew Arnold's touchstones exclude wonderful women writers, let's include them by all means. But let's not throw out the best in the service of a program to correct past wrongs. We must enlarge our sympathies, historicize simplicities and complexities, and learn even from—dare I say it?—fascists such as Pound, Wyndham Lewis, and Eliot. When I discovered Eliot's anti-Semitism, I started saying that Eliot was a horrible poet till someone asked me: "Then how come you quote him all the time?" And I had to start separating my politics—which tends to be very left wing—from my aesthetics in order to avoid confusion. Then why is it that the English canon—rather than any other canon to my knowledge—draws such heavy artillery? Well, for one thing, those who defend it did once upon a time aim pistols at our hearts. Let me refer you to the famous minute of Lord Macaulay (1835) in which he claimed that one shelf of European literature is superior to all the combined literatures ever written in the Orient and that "our native subjects" have more to learn from us than we do from them.[4] This was the arrogance of colonialism, and if the defenders of the canon are on the defensive they have their ancestors to blame. Please do remember that resistance to the canon has a very solid historical justification, a context you need to sympathize with, and easy sort of jokes against political correctness often reveal a facile and shoddy intellectual background. Just as—if I may make a contemporary departure—and I'm grateful to Robert Boswell for this insight—the nonguilty verdict against O. J. Simpson must be seen in the context of Rodney King and other cases of extremely vile racism in the Los Angeles Police Department and the California justice system. Although O. J. Simpson did not deserve their generosity, I am in sympathy with the black jurors who somewhere deep down simply wanted to fuck the system that had been fucking them.

Let me refer you now to some incredible information I have gathered from recent archival work. Gauri Viswanathan has stripped for us some masks of conquest, masks in which literature was rather heavily implicated. Noam Chomsky, one of the very few intellectual figures of our time with a genuine moral grandeur, has shown us how, while the Indians were considered morally inadequate, they were being robbed blind by the British, who had destroyed the textiles of India till the bones of Bengal's cotton weavers were bleaching the plains of India. Bengal was, in effect, ruralized by the British.

Did you know that English literature was taught in India around fifty years before it became part of the curriculum in England? Such facts should help us dispel the hush of reverence we have in our tones when we discuss the study of literature. Before that, in Oxford and Cambridge and everywhere else, really, only the Greek and Latin texts were taught. Shakespeare was not in the picture. That should certainly teach us four or five things and certainly make us strip ourselves of that easy sort of hallow that overcomes us when we talk of literature and feel it saves mankind and thus should be taught. I will be quoting Gauri Viswanathan quite a bit in the next few pages: "English literature made its appearance in India, albeit indirectly, with a crucial act in Indian educational history: the passing of the Charter Act in 1813." Whereby a new responsibility was assumed toward native education and controls over Christian missionary activity in India were relaxed. The Charter Act stated that measures ought to be adopted "as may tend to the intro- duction among" the natives "of useful knowledge, and of religious and moral improvement." In what Viswanathan calls a chilling minute issued in the Bombay Presidency, J. Farish said, "The Natives must either be kept down by a sense of our power, or they must willingly submit from a conviction that we are more wise, more just, more humane and more anxious to improve their condition than any other rulers they could possibly have." This particular policy was quite responsible for a communal writing of Indian history and for a very deliberate attempt to portray Muslim rule of any period as vicious. One way to do this was English literature—and the *discipline* of English came into its own in the age of colonialism. The Marxist critic Terry Eagle- ton has described this transformation of literature into an instrument of ideology as "a vital instrument for the insertion of individuals into the perceptual and symbolic forms of the dominant ideological formation. . . . What is finally at stake is not literary texts but Literature [with a capital *L*]—the ideological significance of the process whereby certain historical texts are severed from their social formations, defined as 'lit- erature,' and bound and ranked together to constitute a series of 'liter- ary traditions' and interrogated to yield a set of ideologically presup- posed responses." That is, once you concede such importance to the functions of education, it is easier to see that values assigned to litera- ture—such as the proper development of character and so on—serve the dynamic of power relations between those who are to be educated and those who educate. If you see a contradiction between my earlier position and this one, there is none. I am addressing the writers' need for artifice and their need to learn their art from the best in the lan- guages in which they are writing. But I have no desire to defend the ways in which the canon has been imposed on and in the academy.

Sakuntala, Kalidas's Sanskrit play, for example, was used to belittle

Indians. When the British first came to India, they hailed Indian literature as so vital, so vibrant, so new, and so on. But once they established their domination they came up with arguments to the effect that Indians lacked the prior mental and moral cultivation required for literature—especially their own—to have any instructive value for them. Oriental literature was marked with "the greatest immorality and impurity," and the native could not distinguish between decency and indecency. Nevertheless, although the native had no training, here is a paradox: they, to be brought up to the necessary level, were to be instructed in that same literature for which preparation was first necessary. The surrogate functions English literature acquired in India offer a compelling explanation for a more rapid institutionalization of the discipline in India than in the country of its origin.

The English Education Act of 1835 interpreted the Charter Act of 1813 in such a way that English was made the medium of instruction in Indian education. Of course, English had already been taught in India for two decades, but what this act did was endorse a new function for English: the dissemination of moral and religious values. Thus was pressed into existence a new discipline—English literature (note: not English language but English literature). This act officially required the natives of India to submit to the study of English literature. In 1844, Lord Hardinge, the governor-general 1844–48, passed a resolution assuring preference in the selection for public office to Indians who had distinguished themselves in European literature.

Roughly around this time, the growth of a mass British reading public had created what many alarmed critics saw as distaste for fine reading. The revolution in literary production, in both the number and nature of its publications, was brought about by the increased wealth of the higher classes and the increased literacy of the lower. There was also a fear among the "refined" of the *useful* and *ennobling* productions in France and Germany. By 1852, the historical study of English literature was firmly established in University College, London. In 1875, the alliance between literature and history was given institutional expression with the merging of the chair of English literature with that of history. You can see why the whole notion of objectivity is such a farce and the role of the novel and the omniscient narrator has its own ideological underpinnings in these formulations. The discipline of English literature was formally instituted in British *schools* only as late as 1871—and the moral motive for doing so was gaining ground in England. There were class elements also in all of this. While what I have given is a quick overview, the details are even more fascinating and often quite chilling.

This historical overview may help us see why the resistance to the European canon, particularly the English, is so politically charged. What I, as an artist in English, wish to assert is that whether English literature was taught or not in England and how it was institutionalized in India and the academy have nothing to do with the canon's position as art, as works in which artifice is charged to its utmost. For writers in England, like writers all over today, were reading one another, and they were also, unlike many writers today, reading the greats of their past and learning their ART from them. If we wish to quarrel with the notion of standards, let us find another term. To me, the artistic accomplishments of Chaucer, Shakespeare, Milton, and so on are heroic. After all, Keats, etc., were reading these very writers before the institutionalization of English literature. When some people say, of various nationalisms, that these standards have been imposed on us, I say: okay, tell me what your standards are. What are your criteria for establishing the artistic value of a piece of writing, to distinguish one level of accomplishment from another? How do standards get set in any literary culture? Note the ghazal, sonnet, and tankha, for example.

When the romantics saw Milton's Satan as a tragic figure, and they did so for extraliterary reasons—let's call them political reasons—they were choosing a text that was rich, full of surprises, constantly yielding meaning through its formal tensions. Edward Said has shown again and again that we can read texts politically while showing how a formal engagement with those texts is precisely what helps to reveal the power of their political stances and manipulations. To show the complexities of colonialism, it is certainly worthwhile to discuss Conrad's *Heart of Darkness* and show how the novel is implicated in the colonial enterprise even while at one level exposing its horrors. It is an endlessly fascinating text because of its formal tensions, its formal choices. The past is certainly not homogeneous, and the writers of the past were not in league with monolithically imposed artistic values. They were constantly examining these values, experimenting, but always returning to the greats to learn their art. Furthermore, let's assume for a minute that there was a highly conscious ruling-class male conspiracy going on regarding the privileging of dead white males. Well, there are many dead white males. The question to be asked: why these and not others?

Some sanity can be returned to this entire debate by examining literary canons of other cultures. Why is Mirza Ghalib, for example, THE *girue* of Urdu poetry? Writers, lower class, communist, upper class, women, gay, no one can ignore him or chooses to. In some ways, standards in Urdu are even more explicit, particularly in the *ghazal,* in which immediately one can detect the shoddy or the facile, as one can,

I think, with the sonnet. Trotsky asserted that first we must use aesthetic criteria to establish artistic value, though we must not stop there. And most sensible critics do precisely that, though they may talk ad nauseam about all kinds of codes and encodings. Oh! What is the power of Shakespeare that a Kurosawa makes *Throne of Blood* and *Ran?* Japan was never under the British. Why does Kozintsev film *King Lear* and *Hamlet,* certainly two of the most powerful versions on film of those plays? I hate Eliot's politics, but I would not like to be caught dead with the poems of various poets whose politics I agree with. Of course, it is a pleasure when I am able to agree with their politics, as in the case of Faiz and Hikmet and Neruda and Vallejo and García Lorca. The question, my darlings, is ART.

Art: every poem about the Holocaust is not compelling. We who are historically interesting have an ever greater responsibility to distinguish subject and content, especially when the subject has an innately powerful stature. In this context, only form should be emphasized as content. We cannot fall into the traps of nationalisms, and if we do let us still not forget artistic concerns, which may even force us by their tensions to lend complexity to the thriving simplicities of nationalisms, their need for perfect enemies. Note we often say about poems dealing with Vietnam that their content is flimsy. We don't say the subject is. Isn't what I am saying quite basic? Because of the histories of British colonialism and American imperialism, we who write in English are often in a bind of anger that we take out on Shakespeare and others. Shakespeare didn't know what terrible uses he would be put to after his death! But we must historicize and not see the past as a monolithic arrangement. And as writers we must be on guard in particular against some brands of white liberalism that will, out of condescension, encourage elements of artistic carelessness in us. I mean some critics compared Alice Walker to Faulkner. Now, really!

From the beginning, English literature was introduced—not just in India but later in Britain—for reasons other than aesthetics. It was put to politic uses in service of class and empire. That is, it was programmatically introduced. We can respond by throwing it all out, to our aesthetic peril as writers in English. Or we can see it all historically, see how texts are or are not implicated, but continue to learn our art. Of course, there is a further debate, but I don't want to go into it and wish someone would take it up. Do ponder: once we establish artistic value, let's say regarding a great poem about the Holocaust, is that poem superior to Stevens's "The Snow Man"? Are Faiz's elegies for Bangladesh or the Rosenbergs greater than Bishop's "One Art"? In that sort of debate, various passions will be unleashed, certainly, but at

least we'll be discussing poems worth talking about and making dis-
tinctions among various levels of achievement. I don't say we must not
write politically; I simply don't want us to write programmatically. I
don't say we must conform to tastes; I simply say that we must conform
to the highest standards. I don't say we must not engage ourselves with
great subjects; I say let's deepen them into content through form, language charged to its utmost. I don't want politics to be a mere conve-
nience. If we are politically engaged, as I always am, let's make sure we
deepen those concerns with content. Otherwise, with an ideology
stripped of true artistic commitment, we might find we have the air of
poetry and none or almost none of its weight.

NOTES

1. *Paris Review,* summer 1994, 117.
2. Fernando Pessoa, *Selected Poems,* translated by Jonathan Griffin (New York:
Penguin, 1974), 11.
3. *Nation,* May 12, 1997, 13–18.
4. The complete text of Macaulay's minute is found in Philip D. Curtin, ed., *Imperialism: The Documentary History of Western Civilization* (New York: Walker, 1971),
178–91.

TONY HOAGLAND

Fear of Narrative and the Skittery Poem of Our Moment

Aesthetic shifts over time can be seen as a kind of crop rotation; the topsoil of one field is allowed to rest while another field is plowed and cultivated. In the 1970s, the American poetry of image covered the midwestern plains like wheat; in the 1980s, perhaps, it was the narrative-discursive sentence that blossomed and bore anthological fruit. This shifting of the ground of convention is one aspect of cultural self-renewal. But the fruitful style and idiom become conventional and then conventionally tired.

Since the 1990s, American poetry has seen a surge in associative and "experimental" poetries, in a wild variety of forms and orientations. Some of this work has been influenced by theories of literary criticism and epistemology, some by the old Dionysian imperative to jazz things up. The energetic cadres of master of fine arts graduates have certainly contributed to this milieu, founding magazines, presses, and aesthetic clusters that encourage and influence each other's experiments. Generally speaking, this time could be characterized as one of great invention and playfulness. Simultaneously, it is also a moment of great aesthetic self-consciousness and emotional removal.

Systematic development is out; obliquity, fracture, and discontinuity are in. Especially among young poets, there is a widespread mistrust of narrative forms and, in fact, a pervasive sense of the inadequacy or exhaustion of all modes other than the associative. Under the label of "narrative," all kinds of poetry currently get lumped misleadingly together, not just story but discursion, argument, even descriptive lyrics. They might better be called the "poetries of continuity."

Let me begin with two poetic examples that I think intriguingly register one aspect of the current temper—mistrust of narrative. The first is by Mark Halliday.

COUPLES

All the young people in their compact cars
He's funny and she's sensible.
The car is going to need some transmission work

soon, but they'll get by alright—
Aunt Louise slips them a hundred dollars
every chance she gets and besides,
both of them are working—
Susan does daycare part time
and Jim finally got some full time work
at Design Future Associates
after those tough nine months as an apprentice.
Or he's in law school
doing amazingly well, he acts so casual
but really he's always pounding the books
and Susan works full time for a market research firm,
she's amazingly sharp about consumer trends
and what between her salary and Aunt Louise
Jim can really afford to concentrate on
his studies. Or he's a journalist and
so is she, and they keep very up
on the news especially state politics.
Plus she does an amazing veal marsala
and he jogs two miles five mornings a week.—
and in June they'll be off to Italy again,
or Mexico; Susan's photographs are
really tasteful, not touristy, she
always reads up on the culture before a trip.
Jim slips in a whacky shot every once in awhile
and everybody laughs, that's old Jim.
. . . They'll get by alright. They have
every one of Linda Ronstadt's albums, and
they're amazingly happy together . . .

The second poem is by Matthea Harvey.

FIRST PERSON FABULOUS

First Person fumed and fizzed under Third Person's tongue while
Third Person slumped at the diner counter, talking, as usual, to no
one. Third Person thought First Person was the toilet paper trailing
from Third Person's shoe, the tiara Third Person once wore in a
dream to a funeral. First Person thought Third Person was a layer of
tar on a gorgeous pink nautilus, a foot on a fountain, a tin hiding
the macaroons, & First person was that nautilus, that fountain, that
pile of macaroons. Sometimes First Person broke free on first dates
(with a Second Person) & then there was the delicious rush of "I
this" and "I that" but then no phone calls & for weeks Third Person wouldn't let First Person near anyone. Poor First Person. Cur-

rently she was exiled to the world of postcards (having a lovely time)—and even then that beast of a Third Person used the implied "I" just to drive First Person crazy. She felt like a television staring at the remote, begging to be turned on. She had so many things she wanted to say. If only she could survive on her own, she'd make Third Person choke on herself & when the detectives arrived & all eyes were on her she'd cry out, "I did it! I did it! Yes, dahlings it was me!"

These two ingenious poems, written by poets of different generations and styles,[1] have something strikingly in common: their intention to hold narrative up for our inspection, at arm's length, without being caught inside its sticky web. Rather than narratives themselves, both poems offer commentaries about narrative, story "samples," safely told by a narrator who operates at an altitude above plot, narrating from a supervisory position. You could truly say that these poems serve to sharpen awareness of our narrative habits, but you could also say they contain a warning about how generic, how overfamiliar, our storytelling is.

Halliday's poem "Couples" seems to make the point that our most precious personal narratives, despite our tender feelings for them, are generic—that human beings (yuppie couples, at least) are reducible to socio-economic-historic clichés—no matter that we cling to the idea of our uniqueness and individuality. These stories of the self, the poem makes clear, are an exhausted resource.

Harvey's ingenious, funny poem trumps the problem by translating the plot into a drama between signifiers, transposing drama into grammar. Her poststructural poem implies that most storytelling (and maybe psychology itself) is structured by grammar. The ironic title, "First Person Fabulous," suggests the essential egotism of all first-person narratives. Tender and witty though the poem is about its "characters," a real involvement by the reader is prevented by the latex condom of self-consciousness. Harvey's poem is representative of the strategic ingenuity of the new poetry, but "First Person Fabulous" is a poem, we are never allowed to forget, about pronouns.

It seems important to point out that both of these poems, though intrinsically skeptical, are also markedly playful. In their inventiveness of detail, in their teasing, in-and-out, back-and-forth development, in their pleasure in idiom, they are not cold in their detachment but imaginatively frolicsome. In fact, the self-consciousness of the poems creates the verbal dimension in which that playground area is situated at a great distance from experience. It is distinctly externalized. *Distance* is as much the distinctive feature of the poems as play—distance, which might be seen as antithetical to that other enterprise of poetry—strong feeling.

What aspect of narrative, with which these poems flirt, in their ironical skeptical ways, is so to be guarded against? A number of familiar explanations present themselves. To start with, it seems likely that narrative poetry in America has been tainted by its overuse in thousands of confessional poems. Not confessionalism itself, but the inadvert sentimentality and narcissism of many such poems have imparted the odor of indulgence to narrative. Our vision of narrative possibilities has been narrowed by so many first-person autobiographical stories, then drowned in a flood of pathos-poems. Psychology itself, probably the most widely shared narrative of the last several generations of American culture, has lost its charisma as a system if not its currency.

Second, many persons think that ours is simply not a narrative age, that contemporary experience is too multitracked, too visual, too manifold and simultaneous to be confined to the linearity of narrative no matter how well done. As Carolyn Forche says, "Our age lacks the structure of a story. Or perhaps it would be closer to say that narrative implies progress and completion. The history of our time does not allow for any of the bromides of progress, nor for the promise of successful closure." Forche herself is an aesthetic convert from narrative poetry to a poetry of lyric-associative fragment.

Not only is organized narration considered inadequate to contemporary experience; its use is felt by some to be oppressive, overcontrolling, suspiciously "authoritarian." Because narrative imposes a story upon experience, because—the argument goes—that story implicitly presents itself as the *whole* story, some readers object to the smugness and presumption of the narration. "Whose narrative is this?" they cry, "Not mine!"

Put more bluntly, the new resistance to conventions of order represents a boredom with, and generalized suspicion of, straightforwardness and orchestration. Systematic development and continuity are considered simplistic, claustrophobic, even unimaginative. In the contemporary arena of the moment, charisma belongs to the erratic and subversive.

There may be yet another, more hidden and less conscious anxiety behind the contemporary mistrust of narrative: a fear of submersion or enclosure. Narrative, after all, and other poetries of sustained development seduce and contain. One signature feature of story is the loss of self-consciousness; in the sequential "grip" of narrative, the reader is "swept away," loses, not consciousness perhaps, but self-consciousness. The speedy conceptuality that characterizes much contemporary poetry prefers the dance of multiple perspectives to sustained participation. It hesitates to enter a point of view that cannot easily be altered or quickly escaped from. It would prefer to remain skeptical, and in that sense, too, one might say that it prefers knowing to feeling.

I offer these two initial poem examples as manifestations of one kind of hip contemporary skittishness. But Harvey and Halliday, though subversive in their ways, are too reader friendly, too lucid and inclusive, to truly represent the poetic fashion of the moment. "Couples" and "First Person Fabulous" are not the epicenter poems of the moment. The predominant Poem of Our Moment is actually a more lyric and disassociative thing. Here is one example by the poet Rachel M. Simon—snappy, jump-cutting, witty, and abstract.

IMPROVISATION

One thing about human nature is that nobody
wants to know the exact dimensions of their small talk.
I can't imagine good advice.
If every human being has skin
how come I can see all of your veins?
Clicks and drips target my skull.
Important voices miss their target.
Some cities are ill-suited for feet.
I'd never buy a door smaller than a tuba, you never know
what sort of friends you'll make.
In the future there will be less to remember.
In the past I have only my body and shoes.
The gut and the throat are two entirely different animals.
My hands don't make good shoelaces, but I'm going to stay
in this lane, even if its slower.
The trick was done with saltwater and smoke
and an ingredient you can only find in an
out of business ethnic food store.
It all comes down to hand-eye coordination.
Once it took all of my energy to get you out of the tub
we had converted from an indoor pool to a house.
I ended up on snorkeling spam lists inadvertently.
It is all inadvertent.
If you don't believe me ask your mom.

"Improvisation" is a quintessential poem of the moment: fast-moving and declarative, wobbling on the balance beam between associative and dissociative, somewhat absurdist, and, indeed, cerebral. Much talent and skill are evident in its making, in its pacing and management of gaps, the hints and sound bites that keep the reader reaching forward for the lynchpin of coherence. The formal stability of serial declaration, for example, is countered by the disjunctness of those declarations. "Improvisation" even contains its own self-description: "It is all inadvertent" is the process metaphor of the poem, describing itself and the modern consciousness the poem embodies. One admirable aspect of the poem is the way it seems capable of incorporating anything, yet the correlative theme of the poem is that all this motley data—that is, experience—*doesn't* add up to a story. Even as the poem implies a world without sequence, the poem itself has no consequence, no center of gravity, no body, no assertion of emotional value.

If we ask what *is* the subject of "Improvisation," the answer would be the dissociated self, and the aspect of self such poems most forcefully represent is its quicksilver uncatchability, its flittering, quicksilver transience. Poems like "Improvisation" showcase personality in the persona of their chatty, free-associating, nutty-smart narrators. It is a self that does not stand still, that implies a kind of spectral, anxious insubstantiality. The voice is plenty sharp in tone, and sometimes observant in its detail, but it is skittery. Elusiveness is the speaker's central characteristic. Speed, wit, and absurdity are its attractive qualities. The last thing such poems are going to do is risk their detachment, their distance, their freedom from accountability. The one thing they are not going to do is commit themselves to the sweaty enclosures of subject matter and the potential embarrassment of sincerity.

I don't wish to base a case on one example, so I will offer a few others. Here are the opening stanzas of two other recent poems, which could be characterized by their speed, wit, dislocation, and self-conscious oddity. The first is by G. C. Waldrep.

WATERCOOLER TARMAC

My harvest has engineered a sanctioned nectary.
The transmission of each apple squeals when I apply the compress.
All my obsequities have finished their summer reading,
they are diligent students,
they understand the difference between precision and Kansas.
This was before I had pried up the floorboard to see what was ticking
underneath.
I keep busy, every plane that flies through my sky requires help, sign
language for the commercial vector.
My octave's intact so this may be working. . . .

The second is by Kevin McFadden.

VARIATIONS AS THE FELL OF THE FALL

Oily fellows, earthmen. Spell
freeway, spell monolith, sell
me a fossil. Wholly repellent.
Malls, only relief. Post. Wheel
wells, the atmosphere (lolly-
lolly) honest, simple welfare,
topsoil anywhere—fell smell,
fell smell. Weaponry, hostile
fish, watermelon peels (lolly-
lolly) parentheses, mile, wolf,
fearsome whelp. Listen (lolly-
lolly) stolen female whisper. . . .

Sure, these styles have discernable origins and different, respectable aesthetic precedents. In "Watercooler Tarmac" and "Improvisation," we might see the cartoony goofiness of James Tate or the unmoored rhetoric of John Ashbery. In the more radical "Variations of the Fell of the Fall," one senses an aleatory nonsense-language system at work. On inspection, it turns out that every line in "Variations" is built from the same identical letters. Although these styles differ, they share an aesthetic principle of verbal-psychic dislocation. Likewise, they all move with a manic swiftness. What is also striking, and representative of the aesthetic moment, is how these poems are committed to a sort of pushy exteriority; they may entertain, but they do not admit the reader.

Of course, dissociative doesn't necessarily mean detached or empty or even hyperintellectual. "Prufrock" is one example of a dissociated yet passionate poem. In various poetic hands, the dissociated-improvisatory mode can represent vivaciousness of self or uncontainable passion or the fractured wash of modernity or an aesthetic allegiance to randomness. The spirit of the poem—if we can recognize what it is— makes all the difference.

What are the intentions of the current version of "difficult" poetry? Some of the stated, advertised intentions of "elusive" poetics are to playfully distort or dismantle established systems of meaning, to recover mystery in poetry, to offer multiple simultaneous interpretive possibilities for the energetic and willing reader to "participate" in. The critic Stephen Burt describes some of the traits of this poetic style, for which he offers the term *elliptical poetry*.

Elliptical poets are always hinting, punning, or swerving away from a never quite unfolded backstory; they are easier to process in parts than in wholes. They believe provisionally in identities but they suspect the Is they invoke; they admire disjunction and confrontation, but they know how little can go a long way. Ellipticists seek the authority of the rebellious; they want to challenge their readers, violate decorum, or explode assumptions about what belongs in a poem, or what matters in life, while meeting traditional lyric goals.

Burt's definition is quite general—it has to be in order to encompass the mélange of poetry he champions—but he gets the mania and the declarativeness right. Also the relentless dodging or obstruction of expectation. Avant-gardes of the past have surely rejected linearity and conventions of coherence, but some of them did so with the motive of asserting worlds of feeling—amazement or distress—which could not be expressed within conventions of order. Consider the surrealism of García Lorca, or Vallejo, which embraced both arbitrariness and passion with radical subjectivity. Yet surrealism operates out of a faith in psychic veracity, and surrealism has a heroic aspect to it. As Louis Aragon says, "[T]he marvelous is born of the refusal of one reality, yet also the development of a new relationship, of a brand new reality this refusal has liberated." Here is Aragon's "pop tune," performed in a style quite congruent to "Improvisation" but with a larger, quite different motive.

CLOUD

A white horse stands up
and that's the small hotel at dawn where he who is always
        first-come-first-served awakes in palatial comfort
Are you going to spend your entire life in this same world?
Half dead
Half asleep
Haven't you had enough of commonplaces yet
People actually look at you without laughter
They have glass eyes
You pass them by you waste your time you pass away and go away
        You count up to a hundred during which you cheat to kill an extra
            ten seconds
You hold up your hand suddenly to volunteer for death.
Fear not
Some day
There will be just one day left and then one day more after that

That will be that No more need to look at men nor their companion
animals their Good Lord provides
And that they make love to now and then
No more need to go on speaking to yourself out loud at night in order
to drown out
The heating units lament No need to lift my own eyelids
Nor to fling my blood around like some discus
Nor to breathe despite my inclination to
Yet despite this I don't want to die
In low tones the bell of my heart sings out its ancient hope
That music I know it so well but the words
Just what were those words saying
        "Idiot"

Aragon's bold, clownish poem, typical of this strain of French surrealism, is an exhortation to wonder. Its leaping, erratic movements are
meant to assert the urgency of the speaker, the range of human nature,
and the volatile resourcefulness of imagination.

The mention of death, the progressive intimacy of the voice, the
arrival at self-examination and tonal sincerity all mark this as a poem
that combines rhetorical performance with interiority. "Life is hard,"
the poem suggests, and "Time is unendurable and absurd, the sleep of
consciousness is oppressive, but it is still important to try to live."
Aragon's poem, for all its whimsy and dishevelment, is finally human-
ist, asserting values.

Narrated and associative poems are *not* each other's aesthetic opposites or sworn enemies. Obviously these modes don't necessarily
exclude each other. They overlap, coexist, and often cross-pollinate.
Nevertheless, one might truly say that the two modes call on fundamentally different resources in reader and writer. Narration and its systematic relatives implicitly honor memory; the disassociative mode primarily values invention. "Continuity poetry" in some way aims to
frame and capture experience; dissociative poetry verifies itself by eluding structures. Their distinct priorities result in different poetries. A
poetry that values clarity and continuity is obligated to develop and
deliver information in ways that are hierarchical and sequential, ways
that accommodate and orchestrate the capacities of human memory. In
contrast, a dissociative poetry is always shuffling the deck in order to
evade knowability.

The Polish poet Czeslaw Milosz, whose well-known phrase "the
pursuit of the real" declares his allegiance in this matter, has something
to say about organization in poems.

[A] poet discovers a secret, namely that he can be faithful to real things only by arranging them hierarchically. Otherwise, as often occurs in contemporary prose poetry, one finds a "heap of broken images, where the sun beats," fragments enjoying perfect equality and hinting at the reluctance of the poet to make a choice.

Would it be so very inaccurate or unfair to say that poems such as "Improvisation" or "Watercooler Tarmac," in the charming "democracy" of their dissociation, have a passive-aggressive relation to meaning? To say that, despite a certain charm, the coy ellipticism of these poems signifies a skepticism about the possibilities for poetic depth, earnestness, even about feeling itself?

These may seem like disproportionately heavy judgments to apply to a few playful butterfly poems fluttering by in the aesthetic breeze, but isn't their self-conscious lack of consequence part of the problem? Perhaps in their deliberate intention to escape the confinement of one system they have also accidentally escaped another. Perhaps in their effort to circumvent linearity or logic or obviousness they have eluded representing anything but attitude—one of the familiar tendencies of modern American culture.

In contrast, to tell a story effectively, or to craft a persuasion, you have to decide what is important and arrange it so that the listener will grasp the grammar of the experience. In other words, you must orchestrate continuities, hierarchies, and transitions. Might we ask, finally—because it's good to remember as well as to go forward—what we lose when we jettison cohesion and continuity from our poetry? Perhaps as readers we lose the pleasure of security, the feeling of being seated deeply inside the poem, of progressing through a dramatic structure that accumulates and deepens, delays and delivers. Likewise, in reading a dissociative poem, we may also miss a kind of recognition, the resonance between experience and art that verifies them both. "The Geraniums," written fifty years ago by a forgotten poet, Genevieve Taggard, offers some of the pleasures of such habitation.

THE GERANIUMS

Even if the geraniums are artificial,
Just the same
In the rear of the Italian café
Under the nimbus of electric light
They are red, no less red
for how they were made. Above

the mirror and the napkins
in the little white pots.
in the semi-clean café
where they have good lasagne . . .
The red is a wonderful joy
really, and so are the people
who like and ignore it. In this place
they also have good bread.

A simple poem, it would seem, "The Geraniums" quietly drama-
tizes a scene that is particular, complex, and finely balanced. It is recognizably modern as well. Here the man-made and the natural are
confusingly bred into each other, pleasure is qualified but real, human
beings are inattentive. Consider, in the opening sentence, the four-line
grammatical delay between the named subject (geraniums) and object
(red) and the way the subsequent clause ("no less red / for how they
were made") then lyrically reiterates and reverses the two paradoxical
qualities of the flowers—their falseness and their beauty. The next sentence contains a similarly extended delay and arrival, which, when it
comes, deepens and widens the speaker's conviction and her affection,
emotionally emphasized by the modifiers "wonderful" and "really."
Taggard's speaker is modest, quietly observant, engaged yet also edito-
rial, measuring and asserting. This organized, hierarchical poem itself is
a quiet joy. Its tone of speculative persuasion, its deepening conviction,
and even its ambivalence are partly possible because of its stability, its
grammar of relativity, its continuity. Is it oppressive for its closure or
boring for its clarity? Not to me. Instead, with lyrical dexterity, it manages both completeness and openness.

I keep wondering if we can identify a broader cultural explanation
for the contemporary attraction to dissociation. Perhaps one reason is
in our current, deeply ambivalent relation to knowledge itself.

We have yielded so much authority to so many agencies, in so
many directions, that we are nauseous. When we go to a doctor, we
entrust ourselves to his or her care blindly. When we see bombs falling
on television, we assume someone else is supervising. We allow
"experts" and "leaders" to make decisions for us because (1) we already
possess more data than we can manage, and (2) at the same time we are
aware that we don't know enough to make smart choices. Forced by
circumstances into this yielding of control, we are deeply anxious
about our ignorance and vulnerability. It is no wonder that we have a
passive-aggressive, somewhat resentful relation to meaning itself. In
this light, the refusal to cooperate with conventions of sense making

seems like—and is—an authentic act of political, even metaphysical protest—the refusal to conform to a grammar of experience that is being debased by all-powerful public systems. This refusal was, we recall, one of the original premises of L-A-N-G-U-A-G-E poetry.

But when we push order away, when we celebrate its unattainability, when our only subject matter becomes instability itself, when we consider artful dyslexia and disarrangement as a self-gratifying end in itself, we give away one of poetry's most fundamental reasons for existing: the individual power to locate and assert value.

In one of the Lannan Foundation interviews, the poet Robert Hass says, "It is wrong to have an elegiac attitude toward reality." Hass, in the context of that conversation, suggests that it is unethical to consider reality decisively outside the reach of language. To exclusively practice an art of which this is a premise and implication—that language is inadequate, that the word cannot reach the world—is a bad idea, one with a price tag attached.

This is a truly pluralistic moment in American poetry, one full of vitality as well as withdrawal. The palpable excitement in new poetry right now, obviously, answers a felt need and provides its own brand of nourishment. The sheer inventiveness abounding is extraordinary. But this might not be the wrong occasion to pronounce the word *fashion.* Fashion is not in itself a negative force but rather a perennial part of the vitality of culture. Fashion is the way that taste changes and then spreads in a kind of swell or wave of admiration. "The Wasteland" was fashionable, and sideburns and Hemingway and war bonds and Sylvia Plath, and existentialism, and bell-bottoms. The danger in fashion is its lack of perspective, that it doesn't always recognize the deep structure of whatever manners it is adopting. Almost by definition, fashion also can gather thoughtless followers. In his preface to the *Norton Postmodern Poetry Anthology,* Paul Hoover acknowledges the potential for this trouble: "The risk is that the avant-garde will become an institution with its own self-protective rituals, powerless to trace or affect the curve of history."

One can understand how dissociative poetry has become fashionable, celebrated, taught, and learned—it is a poetry equal, in its velocity, to the speed and disruptions of contemporary culture. It responds to the postmodern situation with a joyful crookedness. And one can also see why poetics that assert sensible order (which, admittedly, *can* be predictable and reductive) have fallen a bit from fashion; after all, the pretense of order is, in some way, laughable. Art has to play, it has to break rules, to turn against its obligations, to be irresponsible, to recast convention. Some wildness is essential to its freedom. Yet every style has its shadowy limitation, its blind eye, its narcissistic cul-de-sac. There is a moment when a charming enactment of disorientation becomes an homage to dissociation. And there is a moment when the poetic pleasure of elusiveness, inadvertently, commits itself to triviality.

NOTE

1. Halliday is fifty-something, Harvey thirty-something.

DANIEL TOBIN

Ancient Salt, American Grains

Since Ralph Waldo Emerson in "The Poet" declared that America needed to begin mining its own poetic resources instead of deriving the raw materials and methods of its art from England, and Walt Whitman heeded Emerson's call and largely reinvented American poetry in his own expansive image, poetry in America has succeeded in building an indigenous tradition on the foundation of Emerson and Whitman's essentially futurist vision of the poetic imagination. America is an "open road," and the democratic and geographical vistas it surveys require an equally open art. In contrast, it is tempting to invoke Emily Dickinson as the avatar of a contrary poetic, one that while being distinctly American nonetheless preserves its formal and, in particular, metrical ties to the past. That, at least, is Timothy Steele's view in *Missing Measures*. In his scenario, Whitman, Eliot, Pound, Williams, Olson, and their contemporary inheritors compose a dominant experimental lineage alongside that of Dickinson, Robinson, Frost, Bogan, Wilbur, Hecht, and the newer practitioners of the earlier dispensation of meter and form.

If American poetry's double inheritance seems overly pat and polarized in this particular narrative, one need only turn to the recent special American issue of the European journal *Metre* for confirmation of the rift from both sides of the chasm. "American poetry, as such, began with two geniuses" who cut "the Anglo–nostalgic umbilical tube with impertinence, impenitence," so Calvin Bedient writes. In his sweeping condemnation, "a lot of current American poetry is . . . not American, but still English" (26–27). Michael Donaghy, the expatriate American poet who died tragically in his adopted London at the age of fifty, counters Bedient's claim by denouncing the "two party system" of American poetry. Far from muzzling Dickinson's explosive silences under Whitman's impertinent yawp, Donaghy places her work centrally within a metaphysical tradition going back to Herbert and Donne. Another salvo finds Robert Mezey answering what he calls Diane Wakoski's "foolish rant" that she heard the devil in the poetry of John Hollander, as well as her endorsement of the simplistic notions that rhyme and meter underwrite political conservatism and that

Robert Frost is "a bad European influence" (73). For Mezey, Diane Wakoski doesn't have "the faintest idea what she is talking about," and as such she represents the zeitgeist "in one of its cruder and more mindless aspects" (74). Although I agree with Mezey in his condemnation of Wakoski's glib remarks, in such exchanges legitimate questions of technique, aesthetic orientation, tradition, and period style devolve into the memorable skittishness of a *Saturday Night Live* routine: *"Robert, you impotent prig." "Diane, you ignorant slut."* Yet it seems to me a poet inevitably writes at least in part out of the faith that genuinely good poetry—and certainly great poetry—transcends even the limits of its maker's stylistic assumptions as one of the necessary conditions for its being able to last beyond its own narrow historical moment. Out of the quarrel with others, one makes rhetoric, so Yeats claimed, and out of the quarrel with self poetry. To what extent can American poets shift the locus of the conflict between the "closed" forms of traditional poetics and the "open" forms of a long-established avant-garde from the contentious realm of rhetoric to the combustible arena of the individual imagination?

As if implicitly to answer this question, Robert Hass, in his essay "Listening and Making," shifts the conflict between closed and open form to a productive, though similar, binary opposition. In poetry, Hass observes, "repetition makes us feel secure and variation makes us feel free" (115). In this formula, the *metron,* or "measure," with its natural insistence on the closed system of reiterated feet, becomes a vehicle for speech when it is freed, so to speak, by variation. Although one might argue that mere variation at best creates a limited opening for speech within the strict framework of meter, it might also be answered that nonmetrical poetry depends on the metrical system as a ghost in the poetic machine. Free verse is variation writ large, hardly playing tennis without the net (to recall Frost's pithy condemnation), since the net is skirting the iamb. As Hass observes, "freedom from pattern offers us at first an openness, a field of identity, room to move" (116–17). At the same time, however, "it contains the threat of chaos, rudderlessness, vacuity." Or, one may add, the mere flatness of much contemporary poetry. In contrast, for Hass the "reverse face" or shadow side of repetition is claustrophobia, a kind of neurotic nostalgia for the safety of the metrical system. One hears faint nostalgic whispers when Timothy Steele claims (excessively it seems to me) that the free verse poems of Pound and Eliot in both their more experimental and less strident manifestations "undermine the norm [of measure] itself" (62). I greatly admire Steele's mastery of the history of meter, but his stance here verges on nostalgia because (as Hass rightly observes) the perfect iamb is akin to a Platonic abstraction (67). As such, the norm is not the grid or temporal lattice of measure but the poet's living speech—heightened, dramatized—by its transfiguration into the poem. The norm in the sense I intend is Shakespeare: "When in disgrace with fortune and men's eyes." The last two feet of the opening line of this famous sonnet are pushed toward iambic by the metrical expectation, though "men's eyes" by any account of the line's spoken quality is a spondaic foot. In short, the iambic regularity of the line is brought under the rule of the voice through syntax, which—thankfully—avoids making the iamb a metronome. Of course, it would be wrong to discount Steele's more incisive claim that at its best "conventional versification accommodates personally distinctive rhythm" (62), and, indeed, Shakespeare's line exemplifies Steele's claim perfectly.

In modern poetry, surely the paradigmatic example of this truth is the poetry of William Butler Yeats. Yeats, it goes without saying, is a poet for whom the closure of meter and form is emphatically necessary, and his antipathy to more open modes (not to mention his politics) would be strident enough in our day to incite Diane Wakoski's anticonservative tirades. Here is his classic statement on the matter.

> All that is personal soon rots. . . . If I wrote of personal love or sorrow in free verse, or any rhythm that left it unchanged, I would be full of self-contempt because of my egotism and indiscretion, and foresee the boredom of the reader. I must choose a traditional stanza, even what I alter must seem traditional. . . . Talk to me of originality and I will turn on you with rage. I am a crowd. I am a lonely man. I am nothing. Ancient salt is the best packing. (*Essays and Introductions* 522)

Isolated in this way, I imagine that to most contemporary American practitioners of the poet's art for whom the norm is free verse and not meter (inheritors of a confessional aesthetic and inhabitants of a climate that often praises and rewards a poet's message and affiliation—what Yeats called "the literature of the point of view"—over the mastery of their medium) Yeats's observations on craft could hardly seem more antiquated and curmudgeonly. "American poets learn your trade," he might say. Indeed, Yeats's way of working flies in the face of the American poetic ideal as framed by the Whitman tradition of openness and the worship of originality. His own rage for order, "to hammer his thoughts into unity," more often required him to fashion his traditional stanzas out of loose paragraphs and fragments—the very stuff of some modern and postmodern poetry: heaps of broken images, fragments shored against ruins. From the vantage of a century of experimentation, and the triumph of free verse as a mode seemingly consubstantial with the American idiom, it would seem that Yeats's need to pack the personal in the "ancient salt" of traditional form bears little if any relevance to writing, as Williams suggested, in "the American grain." Or, if it does, it would seem to place itself within the context of a polemical aside rigid in its understanding of the art and contrary to the real force and scope of the American experience.

Yeats's appeal to the ancient salt of tradition represents the technical application of his Platonic ideal. Although, as he remarks, "a poet writes always of his personal life," at the same time "he is never the bundle of accident and incoherence that sits down to breakfast; he has been reborn as an idea, something intended, complete" (509). The closure Yeats seeks is not only technical and historical but, as implied here, metaphysical. The formal qualities of compression and closure that Yeats requires of his art are the artistic manifestations of ethical and ultimately spiritual needs. But Yeats by his own lights also cries "in Plato's teeth." The desire to be reborn into a Platonic idea complete and intended, and therefore secure in the safe but claustrophobic neatness of the poem, is countered in the work by the answering gravity of the heart's "foul rag and bone shop"—the very accidence he seeks to escape. Plato's launch into formal idealism is rebutted by Aristotle's plunge into accident, into the disruptive but freeing processes of life. For Yeats, vivid speech is the embodiment of this counterforce within the poem.

> It was a long time before I had made a music to my liking; I began to make it when I discovered some twenty years ago that I must seek, not as Wordsworth thought, words in common use, but a powerful and passionate syntax for passionate subject matter. (*Essays and Introductions* 521)

Although Yeats further states that he compels himself "to accept these traditional metres that have developed in the language," the measure of his lines never reifies into the mere mechanics of verse, as though they were the imitation of some ideal form; rather, measure in Yeats's poetry realizes a personal though distinctive rhythm through the way passionate syntax fuses with the *metron,* creating rhythm, combining itself with other textures of sound.

> That is no country for old men. The young
> In one another's arms, birds in the trees

—Those dying generations at their song,
The salmon-falls, the mackerel crowded seas,
Fish, flesh or fowl, commend all summer long
Whatever is begotten born and dies.
Caught in that sensual music all neglect
Monuments of unaging intellect.

Thematically these famous opening lines from "Sailing to Byzantium" embody the fundamental tension in Yeats's work, the conflict between flesh and spirit, the Platonic idea and the Aristotelean attention to process. Thematically Plato has the upper hand, for Yeats clearly favors the monumental endurance of art over the passing pleasures of the dying generations. By the end of the poem, he transmutes himself into a golden bird, abstracted from life but nonetheless able to bear witness to it. He has become the ideal transfigured from mere accidence. However, if we look even momentarily at the dynamic rhythm of Yeats's lines—rhythm created by the pressure of his syntax—we realize that in fact the sensual music of the poet's own impossible longing passionately shapes his declamation of the ideal. To my ear, only three of these eight lines—3, 4, and 6—can be read as purely iambic, and all of them evoke some attribute of the passing fleshly world rather than the ideal realm of art. The second line is also iambic, with a trochaic substitution in the fourth position, and likewise evokes the passing world with its doomed lovers. In lines 1, 5, 7, and 8, however, Yeats's syntax alters the percussive iamb according to the designs of the speaker's passion, his disgust with age, his muted jealousy of the young, his anger at impending death, his raging need for an eternity intuited paradoxically by the intellect alone. The greatest departure from the iambic backbeat occurs in the fifth line where the rhythm becomes positively sprung, the added stresses—"Fish, Flesh, or fowl, commend all summer long"—combined with the textures of the three initial fricatives modulating into the quieter, liquid double ems and els—communicate the poet's almost speechless combination of fury and longing. The result of this yoking of meter and syntax here is energy, tension, and intensity while the last three feet of the stanza's final line return the poem to an iambic equilibrium. Scoring into the poem Yeats's unrelieved quarrel between flesh and spirit, this interplay between traditional meter and passionate syntax continues throughout the poem with tonal variations until it reaches its final equilibrium in the last line with the straight iambic pentameter of "of what is past, or passing, or to come."

One could have continued the analysis, enjoining Yeats's management of enjambment, caesura, and octava rima, but the essential point is that in a great poet such as Yeats the seemingly closed system of meter and form becomes a vehicle in which passion is freed into the poem. "How can we know the dancer from the dance?" Yeats asks at the end of "Among School Children," knowing well that even improvisational dance requires a sense of form in order to liberate emotion. Nevertheless, given the American tradition of formal experimentation, do poets working in traditional meter and form comprise only a minor company within the American mainstream? Is the ancient salt really anathema to the American grain? The aesthetic claims that prompt such questions seem strained and are finally a matter of polemics instead of practice. Neither Robinson nor Frost nor Wilbur nor Nemerov nor Hecht—regardless of what one might think of their poetry—are "English" poets because they write in traditional meter and form, no more than are David Jones and Basil Bunting "American" poets because they followed the example of Pound in a British context that has remained closer to the grain of an indigenous tradition in which meter and form figure largely. Richard Wilbur's formalism, in turn, suggests nothing new except that it is a squarely American incarnation of historically long-standing traditions. Not unlike Yeats, at his best he appeals to ceremony without devolving into the ceremonious. And, of course, the formalism in English-language poetry is in fact multinational. Sonnets traveled from Italy to England during the Renaissance. sestinas and villanelle came into the language from the French. Pantoums are a Malaysian form. Ghazals, a burgeoning form in contemporary American poetry through the work of Agha Shahid Ali, find their origin in Persian culture. It is simply absurd to say that nonmetrical poetry is the only legitimate mode for American poets and that to work otherwise is to engage in a marginal art or at worst an un-American activity. Pound, the most vigorous advocate of the free verse revolution ("Compose in sequence of the musical phrase, not in sequence of metronome") was a fascist. There is no inherent correlation between politics and style, and indeed the most liberal art can become dogmatic under the pressure of polemics.

Putting aside such prejudices, it is possible to explore, for example, how Yeats's ideas about passionate syntax might reverberate in an American context with Frost's theory of sentence sounds. "A dramatic necessity," Frost observed, "goes deep into the nature of the sentence. Sentences are not different enough to hold the attention unless they are dramatic. . . . All that can save them is the speaking tone of voice somehow entangled in the words and fastened to the page for the ear of the imagination" (675). In essence, this is Frost's theory of the sound of

sense or sentence sounds. His claims for speech and the dramatic organization of the sentence reiterate in an American context Yeats's
enthusiasm for passionate syntax. Even the blank verse of an essentially
meditative poem such as "Directive" manifests dramatic energy
through its sentence sounds.

> Back out of all this now too much for us,
> Back in a time made simple by the loss
> Of detail, burned, dissolved, and broken off
> Like graveyard marble sculpture in the weather,
> There is a house that is no more a house
> Upon a farm that is no more a farm
> And in a town that is no more a town.

Far from organizing itself according to some iambic drum
machine, the first line is both syntactically and metrically disruptive.
Though still within the contours of an indigenous speech, the line is
speech that "makes strange" in a manner that—even more strangely—
anticipates the contortions of Charles Olson's work. The second line
intensifies the poem's energy through anaphora, the repetition of *back*
placing the reader like the speaker in a kind of time warp. This is real
retrospective movement and not nostalgia, a backward thrust and not
merely a backward look. Were we to closely analyze Frost's metrical
pyrotechnics here, we would find very few regular feet through the
poem's first four lines while the last three lines that comprise this opening sentence resolve into regular iambics—a sentence sound that shifts
dramatically from a jarringly propulsive beginning to its soft landing, as
it were, in the past. Though constructed word by word, the sound
experienced in these lines is the entire sentence woven through the
temporal grid of Frost's blank verse, and so to place the burden of
Frost's music entirely on measure, as though each note were greater
than the symphony, is to miss Frost's fundamental insight about the
nature of working in traditional meter. The net is important, but the
play is more important. As is so often the case in Frost's greatest work,
the sound of sense is both serious and ironic at the same time. There is
no safety in the past, though there may be the illusion of safety—or a
momentary stay against confusion—which the poet at once requires
and keeps from hardening into finality. "Here are your waters and your
watering place. / Drink and be whole again beyond confusion" epito-
mizes the paradox of closure with an opening, since the poem gives us
no real faith that finding even a toy Holy Grail is at all within our
power, though our better angels would believe that finding it must be
possible.

One might say that for Frost the form of a poem emerges from the evolving shape of its sentence sounds with the provision that Frost saw meter as the necessary skeletal frame that had already established itself in the greater body of the art. Something similar might be said of Yeats. Finding his paradigm in organic theories of form extending back at least as far as the romantics, Robert Hass, in "One Body: Some Notes on Form," locates the formal sense literally and not just metaphorically in a human biological necessity. "Maybe our first experience of form is the experience of our own formation," Hass remarks (57). Not surprisingly, for Hass this intuition of the organic sources of form extends to poetry generally and not just free verse.

> We speak of the sonnet as a form when no two sonnets, however similar their structures, have the same form. . . . The form of a poem exists in the relation between its music and its seeing; form is not the number or kind of restrictions, many or few, with which a piece of writing begins. A sonnet imposes one set of restrictions and a poem by Robert Creeley with relatively short lines and three- or four-line stanzas another. There are always restrictions because, as Creeley says, quoting Pound, "Verse consists of a constant and a variant." (65)

It is easy to misconstrue organicism in poetry as advocating a kind of free-flowing, intuitive profusion as if nature gave no restrictions to its apparently limitless productions. But variation is not formlessness. Coleridge, following Schelling, envisioned a poetry coincident with the *naturans*—the "organic form" shaping itself "as it develops from within" (173)—rather than the *naturata,* nature's particular manifestations. Yet Coleridge wrote in meter and form and disputed Wordsworth's claim, in his "Preface to the *Lyrical Ballads,"* that poetry should be written in the common speech of ordinary people. On the contrary, like Yeats after him, he believed it should be dramatized, heightened from life, but not antiquated or artificial. For Coleridge, there was no inherent contradiction between organic form and the inherited conventions of poetry. In our own time, Hass's biological understanding of poetic form grows out of Coleridge's organic conception, and yet Hass himself remarks that "now, I think, free verse has lost its edge, become neutral, the given instrument" (70). How extraordinary to find so eloquent an advocate of organic form in agreement with one of the basic tenets of the New Formalism, that the "official art of free verse" has become ineffectual, even decadent (Steele, 283). Conversely, when Timothy Steele laments the Victorian tendency to read "poems in a sing song way to bring out their metrical identity" as an unfortunate practice that obliterated "natural degrees of relative speech stress within lines" (59–60), he essentially brings meter under the governance of speech. As such, he is in essential agreement with Hass's claim that "the pure iamb can't be rendered; it only exists as a felt principle of order, beneath all possible embodiments, in the mind of the listener. It exists in silence, is invisible, unspeakable. An imagination of order. A music of the spheres" (67). If scansion is not meter, then meter comes to life only in speech. The remote godhead of the *metron* cannot exist without the body of the living word.

The idea of meter as some outmoded deity relevant to only a few remnant disciples is an exaggeration, of course, but from the standpoint of some of the twentieth century's more radical declarations of poetic independence the likening of traditional meter and form to an antiquated and soon to be extinct faith is not entirely inaccurate. In his essay "The Poem as a Field of Action," William Carlos Williams proposes "sweeping changes from top to bottom on the poetic structure. . . . I say we are through with the iambic pentameter as presently conceived, at least of dramatic verse; through with the measured quatrain, the staid concatenations of sound in the usual stanza, the sonnet" (281). If Pound, for all his revolutionary fervor, saw rhythm as a "form cut in time," then Williams, in announcing that poetry is through with the measured quatrain and usual stanza, shifts the locus of form from time to space. The poem is a field of action or energy, and if the temporal unfolding of passionate speech or sentence sounds exists it is registered more in the spatial display of the page than in the temporal interplay of meter and line. The ramifications of this shift, so significant for some postmodern poetry, are even more emphatically articulated in Charles Olson's polemical treatise "Projective Verse." In Olson's diatribe against traditional poetics, the tension within the "closed" and "open" attributes of poetry becomes a gulf between seemingly mutually exclusive approaches to the art.

The primary source of Olson's complaint against closed or nonprojective verse is that, he claims, poetry since Shakespeare has gradually lost its grounding in the voice and has become "print bred" (239). It therefore has ceased to be a "reproducer of the voice" since rhyme and measure have outlived their necessity as aids to memory (245). In contrast, projective or open verse eschews the inherited line, stanza, and overall form in favor of "composition by field" in order to restore "a point by point vividness" to the speech of poetry. For Olson, the locus of vivid speech lies initially in the syllable and then in the line understood as a kind of inscription of the poet's breath. "The line comes . . . from the breath," Olson writes, "from the breath of the man who writes," though everything "starts from the syllable" (242). From this core idea, Olson elaborates his program for revolutionizing modern poetry.

> It is by their syllables that words juxtapose in beauty, by partaking of sound, the minimum source of speech. . . . It would do no harm, as an correction to both prose and verse as now written, if both rime and meter, and, in the quantity of words, both sense and sound, were less in the forefront of the mind than the syllable, if the syllable, that fine creature, were more allowed to lead the harmony on. (241)

The field of Olson's projective verse is essentially a field of the voice, but it is voice operating at a register of sound before sense rather than the sentence sound, as in Frost's poetry. Here is an excerpt from "I, Maximus of Gloucester, to You."

> in! in! the bowspirit, bird, the beak
> in, the bend is, in, goes in, the form
> that which you make, what holds, which is
> the law of object, strut after strut, what you are, what you
>   must be, what
> the force can throw up, can, right now hereinafter erect,
> the mast, the mast, the tender
> mast!

As should be clear from these lines, the speech of Olson's poem intends to affect "the listener" in a manner that, initially at least, short-circuits any rush to comprehension. The syntax of this speech likewise intends to be passionate but in a manner that elides the personal voice entirely, as we find it in Yeats's poetry. It is intensely "disruptive" and "fragmentary," as David Perkins observes, as well as "kinetic" (495). What we hear instead is the voice as medium in which, to use Olson's words, syntax is "kicked around" for the purpose of generating a different kind of kinesis. The lines read like either the words of a person gradually losing consciousness or those of a person overtaken by an oracle whose meaning cannot be fully expressed in completed thoughts. The emphasis finally is on process rather than closure since in Olson's understanding of poetry every line break constitutes a new turn of breath that carries with it a possibility for furthering the voice's projection and therefore the poet's need to pursue every worthy impulse. As they stand, the lines compress the action and thus the metaphor of the boat's bowspirit plunging into the waves like the beak of a bird and then pressing beyond that first sense to the matter of the poetic process itself, the boat as seagoing craft transforming itself into the craft of making "the form / that which you make, what holds. . . ." Although the point is that the craft of poetry should refuse holding, refuse closure for the sake of what the force of breath itself "can throw up" in the process of discovery instead of being content to remain harbored (to push the metaphor perhaps too far) within vessels of received form.

In addition to exemplifying his own practice, Charles Olson's program of projective verse is particularly significant because it both gathers into itself many of the innovations advocated earlier in the century by Pound, Eliot, Williams, and others and sets the table for the more experimental postmodern poetries that have followed us into the new century. For example, it is possible to foresee Susan Howe's linguistic montages in Charles Olson's claim that the new technology of the typewriter can indicate "exactly the breath, the pauses, the suspensions even of syllables, the juxtaposition of even parts of phrases" and so for the first time "without the convention of rime and meter, record the listening [the poet] has done" and so further "indicate how he would want any reader . . . to voice his work" (245). How much more would Olson see the computer developing this potential even further? Notice, however, that Olson's concern is with the breath, with speech, and that the page—the typewriter's field of action—suggests a spatial orientation exclusive of those oral traditions that have shaped traditional meter and form. Of course, stanzas by definition are "little rooms," but the spatial metaphor in the word's etymology does nothing to diminish the oral and therefore temporal dimension of poetry. People on the street do not speak in octava rima or blank verse, but Yeats's and Frost's use of these conventions on the page has less of a visual appeal than the deconstruction of traditional form into atomized, "nontraditional" parts on the page whether by pauses, syllables, or juxtapositions of phrase. The phrase "composition by field" clearly suggests as much, and visual poems such as George Herbert's "Easter Wings" and "The Altar" and John Hollander's "Swan and Shadow" are exceptions that prove the rule. So, by a strange reversal of original intent, Olson's program might be said to more deeply entrench the poet in the print-bred culture from which he sought to liberate it, as well as the burgeoning digital culture, precisely because the freedom brought by scrapping traditional meter and form makes positioning on the page even more integral to indicating how the reader ought to listen to the moves the poem makes.

A second problem, suggested earlier, concerns the issue of what Charles Olson's friend Robert Creeley called restriction. Because projective verse (and potentially all free verse) calls for a radical adherence to openness, to a furtherance of the poet's impulse to discover, there is nothing to stop the poem from not stopping. The obvious result is shapelessness, which is one of the reasons why Hass fears that free verse has run its course. Pound's *Cantos,* Williams's *Paterson,* and Olson's own *Maximus Poems* all lose in formal integrity because, in the final analysis, they have no closure. In contrast, a long sequence such as Berryman's *Dream Songs,* though clearly open in its articulation of Henry's angst-ridden musings, nevertheless obtains an accrued sense of closure through Berryman's elongation and reformalization of the sonnet. Likewise, though multifarious in the formal expression of its parts, the Irish poet John Montague's *The Rough Field* obtains closure through the leitmotif of the journey and the sequence's overall circular structure. It almost goes without saying that if the great pitfall of traditional verse is a staid satisfaction in filling out the form to the letter of convention, then the great pitfall of nontraditional verse is to make convention out of originality. The result is verse that reads like the proverbial chopped prose or, as seems more and more the case, verse that runs like words in spate in lines that confuse excess with passion. At the far side of the gulf between open and closed poetries, lies mannerism: on the one hand, an idolatry of tradition and form that mistakes security for achievement; on the other, a pretentiousness that mistakes the fashion for sophistication.

Whether Olson's is a program for a more sophisticated poetry or not, if the literary historian David Perkins is right in observing that he "writes in a language that was never spoken anywhere" (519), then the irony of "Projective Verse" is that it reminds us that poetry ought to have the strength and vigor of speech that the best poetry has never lost, and it does so with practical acknowledgment that speech is not merely a recording of what might be heard in conversation but is speech shaped by the ear of the poet. To redouble the irony, despite his desire to escape the metrical straitjacket, the last run-over line from "Maximus," quoted earlier, is pure iambic tetrameter ("the mast, the mast, the tender / mast"), which perhaps only suggests that measure does exist in the rhythms of speech, however "kicked around" that speech might become, and it is one of the poet's essential jobs to listen for it. Despite Olson's objection to traditional meter and form, some of the ancient salt gets into the American grain. Moreover, in instances in which attentive listening shapes the process of composition, I would argue that the gulf between closed and open modes collapses and does so regardless of the individual poet's particular aesthetic or polemical program.

A. R. Ammons's "Corson's Inlet" is undoubtedly a poem shaped by the poet's embrace of open poetics and his refusal to be limited by what he called in *Garbage* "the tidy boxes" of conventional stanzaic structure. I know of no other poem that locates itself and its poet more steadfastly within the tradition of organic verse. Indeed, "the "field of action" envisioned in "Corson's Inlet" translates the biological metaphor underlying organicism into an overall poetic structure derived from contemporary physics. Like any shoreline, the size of Corson's Inlet depends on the scale of measurement. On the scale of maps a given shoreline might be ten miles long, but even if one were to measure the inlet with a straightedge the minute curves and juttings of the shoreline would be missed. To obtain the "actual" length of the shoreline you would need a still more subtle device, though the smaller and presumably more intimate the scale of measurement the more intricately formed the shoreline reveals itself to be. Corson's Inlet is a fractal shore, and, as fractal geometry demonstrates, its ever finer edges can be measured infinitely. Ammons's walk is an encounter with infinity, with the ultimate openness of form that finally composes all of nature, indeed all of physical reality, and the poem is not only shaped by the poet's recognition of that openness but becomes a self-reflexive model for it.

> I allow myself eddies of meaning:
> yield to a direction of significance
> running
> like a stream through the geography of my work:
> you can find
> in my sayings
> swerves of action
> like the inlet's cutting edge:
> there are dunes of motion,
> organizations of grass, white sandy paths of remembrance
> in the overall wandering of mirroring mind. . . .

As these lines suggest, Ammons's poem intends to be an ars poetica mimetic of the inlet's own structure and organization and not merely an objective meditation on the scene. As such, the ultimately open form of physical reality guides the poet's reflections. "I have reached no conclusions," he continues, "I have erected no boundaries / shutting out and shutting in, separating inside / from outside: I have drawn no lines. . . ." The poet's whole effort is to follow the motion forward, continually breaking beyond the boundaries of line and stanza into wider, more rarified "fields of order." The poem is therefore a model of projective verse, its ideal "an order held / in constant change" without "finality of vision." In keeping with this open ideal, "Corson's Inlet" is a single sentence held together by thresholds of colons. As such, the poem's self-reflexive liminality extends to grammar and syntax. What would Frost make of this sentence sound? Is Ammons just playing tennis without the net? And if, to borrow Yeats's phrase, any poem looks "out of shape from toe to top" it seems to be this one.

Yet, as in any successful poem, whether open or closed, "Corson's Inlet" exhibits a perfect coincidence between content and form. At the same time, it would be easy to justify the arbitrary management of lines in a poem simply by appealing to the ephemeral nature of the world: "I make / no form / of formlessness." In this scenario, a single line might read "as," as it does in Ammons' poem, a line arguably as far from any rhythmic vitality, as from any metrical validity, as one could possibly write. Arguably, however, the success of Ammons's poem, even in the matter of this single-word line, springs from the poem's orchestration of texture and structure in achieving its overall form. In her essay "The Flexible Lyric," Ellen Bryant Voigt describes the relationship among these three elements of a poem—texture, structure, and form—in the following way.

> To say a building has a sound structure means that the foundation and frame are adequate for the shape and weight. . . . By extension, structure in poems seems neither "paraphrasable" content . . . nor "achieved harmony" . . . but rather the support for both content and its embodiment in the words chosen and arranged in harmony or tension. That is, structure is the way all the poem's materials are organized, whether they are abstract or concrete, precise or suggestive, denoted or connoted, sensory or referential, singular or recurring. Since almost all poems in English are linear—read left to right down the page—structure is also the purposeful order in which materials are released to the reader, whereas form creates pattern in these materials, to establish pleasing proportion, balance, unity—"a single effect"—in an otherwise overwhelmingly various texture. (124–25)

Given Voigt's insight, the questions to ask of a free verse poem such as "Corson's Inlet" is whether and where "texture has been used in the service of structure" and where it has been used to achieve "a formal arrangement" (150). While one could trace how the poem successively and successfully builds structure and formal integrity from the textural substructures of Ammons's swerving lines, the poem's most achieved scale of measurement is precisely what Ammons says eludes him in the poem: the overall. Although "Corson's Inlet" portrays a manifold and elusive order, the poem's formal achievement—the "shape of its understanding"—rests in its ability to attain a suitable and pleasing closure despite textures that easily could have dispersed into overwhelming variety: "not chaos." The overall pattern or form of the poem is circular: "I went for a walk over the dunes again this morning . . . tomorrow a new walk is a new walk." Across the span of its single sentence the circular movement of the poem is dynamic because it speaks to the deep reality of recurrence, not just the poet's personal habit of taking walks. "Corson's Inlet," to borrow the subtitle of Ammons's book-length poem *Sphere,* has "the form of a motion." Recurrence is an open circle. It is the poem's overall formal organization, realized through its textures and structural "fields of action," that finally lends even a one-word line like "as" credibility since the line finds its true measure on a different order of scale—not the syllable, not the *metron,* not the line but the overall. And "as" as a line also makes sense we can paraphrase since the word embodies in microcosm the ambitious mimetic intentions of the poem, the coterminus spaces of the poet's "mirroring mind" and the equally mind-mirroring reality of the world.

Underlying Ammons's use of open poetics in "Corson's Inlet" is an idea of order that presumes a deep formal correspondence between the poem and reality. Unlike the seashore encountered by the singer of Wallace Stevens's "The Idea of Order at Key West," the inlet on which Ammons's walker meditates offers a version of the sublime that need not be "mastered" or "portioned out" because the poem and the world on which the poem reflects are finally all a part of one flow. The "blessed rage for order" has resolved into a blessed acceptance of organic and even subatomic form. The conflict between one poet's desire to impose order on reality by means of what Olson called "closed verse" and another poet's desire to discern in reality a more rarified and open conception of form originates in the apparent gap between two seemingly contrary ontologies. Do poems master or receive the world? But the opposition is false since the world is rife with formal symmetries and mathematical structures, rhythms, recurrent measures, all manifesting themselves both within and as the natural expression of the flow. Perhaps, given the mainstream tradition of American poetry and the fragmented nature of our postmodern world, the traditional formal poem seems for many too tame, too tended within the present historical and cultural context, while for those across the divide open verse appears to be a culpable indulgence in formlessness—a hypermimetic reiteration of chaotic life.

Steering her own craft beyond the contentious seas between these clashing rocks, Elizabeth Bishop offers a model art gratefully above polemics in which fixed ideas of order give way to the patient practice of the repertoire. Equally masterful at couplets, quatrains, ballads, sestinas, the villanella—"The Prodigal" is formally a double sonnet!—and free verse, Bishop's work has risen to such universally high regard precisely because her poems manifest an openness to the world's variety and the poet's own contrary impulses without losing artistic control, intelligence, and their unique brand of restrained but unmistakable passion. Written in free verse, "At the Fishhouses" manifests Bishop's genius for showing us a world, for pacing us through that world with measured attention to the right detail given at just the right time, until, by the poem's end, textures that might have seemed random have fallen together with explosive continuity:

> Although it is a cold evening,
> down by one of the fishhouses
> an old man sits netting,
> his net, in the gloaming almost invisible,
> a dark purple brown,
> and his shuttle worn and polished.

As the opening of her poem demonstrates, the acuity of Bishop's visual attention is fine almost beyond comparison, but what gives the scene its subtle intensity is the audible pacing of the lines. Each is a complete phrase that gradually releases and concentrates the poem's dramatic focus. Moreover, it contains the most delicate of alterations— the comma after netting and the subsequent line break that place's the old man's net in clear juxtaposition to the gloaming, which renders it nearly invisible. This blending of the human landscape with the surrounding nonhuman atmosphere will become crucial to the poem, and the net as a tool that permits access to the sea's otherworld resonates with the apparently frail but secure device of the poem itself as it lowers the reader ever more deeply into the liminal world of the fishhouses. Of course, the consonance and assonance of the lines do their work as well—"although," "cold," "old," "gloaming," "almost," "invisible," "purple," "shuttle," "polished." The poem's sonic textures, filled with plosives and liquids announce the sea's "heavy surface" as well as its unbearable depths before it even appears in the

poem's thirteenth line, its opacity a muted contrast to the silver translucence of the dock area with its gangplanks, gables, wheelbarrows, and
fish tubs. But for the emerald moss of the shoreward houses and the
rust on the old capstan, like "dried blood," the world of the poem is
nearly monochromatic.

Beyond Bishop's vivid description, the significance of these details
derives from the pacing. After the opening five lines, Bishop departs
from her focus on the old man and spends the next twenty-five
describing the indigenous surroundings. In short, she slows the pace
even further in order to widen the aperture of the poem's focus. The
details and textures throughout these lines compose a living map and
not merely a random survey of the scene. She is defining the space of
the poem in a way that inevitably returns us to the old man, who now
ceases to be part of a painterly setting and is revealed as a friend of the
poet's grandfather. How many lesser poets would have cut the preceding twenty-five lines, or condensed them and restructured the poem
around this personal detail, thereby marring the vivid surfaces—"the
principal beauty"—that the poem regards so patiently, so lovingly? But
neither is this personal detail superfluous, for it introduces the past, and
therefore time, into the poem, a crucial move at this juncture, for it is
between time and timelessness that the poem's spaces hover. This
becomes apparent in the short strophe that follows with its interplay of
verticals, "down" and "up" balancing each other on the water's edge
until the brief scene comes to rest on the horizontal tree trunks—again
silver and a threshold between the historical human world and the
timeless world of the sea. Here, as it were, is the poem's spirit level, it's
balance point between alternate universes.

> Cold dark deep and absolutely clear,
> element bearable to no mortal,
> to fish and to seals. . . .

Rhetorically these lines constitute a dramatic shift in tone in which
the world's fleeting principal beauties, unlike the iridescent scales of
fishes taken up from this otherworld, encounter an impenetrable limit.
The arrival of the seal in the poem, to which the poet, with marvelous
good humor, sings Baptist hymns, suggests the possibility of mediating
these worlds, the absolute world of the sea and the ephemeral human
world. One might hear, even in a good workshop, someone suggest
that this detail is distracting, an unnecessary redirection in a poem that
directs us all too often, before us and behind us, up and down. But the
seal is a mediator, like the hymns to which it appears to listen and shrug

off, a mediator between worlds. Likewise, the second redirection, to the tall firs, a million Christmas trees, underscores the restrained religious sense that has entered the poem. The poet, like the seal, is a believer in "total immersion," though so extreme a baptism in this context represents a loss of identity rather than a fulfillment of religious promise. Bishop, as always, moves by margins and reversals to the center, though none of those margins, reversals, or redirections are extraneous to the shape of the poem's understanding. The icy freedom of the water above the stones and then "above the world" is a perceptual trick, an illusion that reveals the truth of the sea as a kind of radioactive subspace, a metaphor not for the ground of being but for an ontological flow that finally permeates Bishop's shore as well, and that resists full translation into human terms.

> If you should dip your hand in,
> your wrist would ache immediately,
> your bones would begin to ache and your hand would burn
> as if the water were a transmutation of fire
> that feeds on stones and burns with a dark gray flame. (66)

The water *is* a transmutation of fire, like all things a metamorphosis from primal energy. At this point, Bishop's lines lengthen to accommodate the increase in the poem's intellectual and emotional resonance. One would think the ontological nature of the world would be enough for one poem to tackle, let alone do so in utterly concrete terms that allow for remnant old men as well as comical seals, but as its final move "At the Fishhouses" redirects us again, from ontology now to epistemology, and so to the historically conditioned nature of all knowledge, and therefore all talk about what beyond the sea represents. As in "Corson's Inlet," the overall transcends the poem's widening scope, but, whereas Ammons's poem confidently models the poet's work on a subliminal, primal, and recurrent flow, Bishop's poem offers a more circumspect vantage. In "At the Fishhouses," to drink from the sea is not the same as drinking from Frost's imaginary grail to become "whole again beyond confusion" or lifted like Yeats's bird out of the sensual music. The world resists us, and knowledge of it is often bitter and briny and is certainly fleeting. With this final realization, Bishop's resolutely paced and tightly controlled free verse in "At the Fishhouses" offers a closure more free than the circular path of "Corson's Inlet" for at the poem's end she launches us expressly into the open. Tomorrow a new walk might be a new walk by the fishhouses. Though flowing eventually, our knowledge of the world will be "flown." From the perspective of Bishop's poem, Ammons's faith in scientific knowledge as a model for poetic form is merely one more conditioned way to envision the world and the poems that seek to derive order from it. Despite his preference for open form, I doubt whether Ammons would deny Bishop's insight. In the final analysis, the two poems offer overlapping rather than contrary visions of the world and the formal approaches poems might employ to respond to the world.

"Everything only connected by 'and' and by 'and'," so Elizabeth Bishop observes in "Over 2000 Illustrations and a Complete Concordance," a phrase that could have been incorporated by Charles Olson in "Projective Verse." And yet within her poems a world defined by contiguity and resistant to metaphor progressively gains in metaphorical intensity and revelatory power. In turn, the world of her poems resists neat closure while still embodying formal necessity and retains its openness to new impulses while securing its textures within the larger order of the whole. Whether she is writing a villanella or a free verse meditation, her forms are always actively engaged with the world she encounters and imagines, never slack or intransigent or merely imposed on the elusive conditions of life, which finally is characteristic of all good poems whether packed in the ancient salt or orchestrated in the American grain. Regardless of school, program, or ideology, good poets are scavengers who somehow manage to find what they need, and good poems of any formal orientation embody the desire to clarify life out of the welter of experience. In such poems, the walker becomes a dancer whose mastery we know by the choreography of the dance, the world another dance we are called to join again and again in its passing and in our passing to know with ever greater intimacy and integrity.

NOTE

First appeared in *Marlboro Review* 10 (summer-fall 2000), reprinted in *Irish Pages* 1 (summer 2002).

WORKS CITED

Ammons, A. R. *Collected Poems*. New York: Norton, 1972.
Bedient, Calvin. "Five Notes on American Poetry." *Metre* 7–8 (fall 2000): 26–29.
Bishop, Elizabeth. *The Complete Poems, 1927–1979*. New York: Farrar, Straus and Giroux, 1984.

Coleridge, Samuel Taylor. *Selected Prose*. New York: Random House, 1951.

Donaghy, Michael. "The Exile's Accent." *Metre* 7–8 (fall 2000): 183–88.

Frost, Robert. *Robert Frost: Complete Poems, Prose, and Plays*. New York: Library of America, 1995.

Hass, Robert. *Twentieth Century Pleasures*. New York: Ecco, 1984.

Mezey, Robert. "On Form." *Metre* 7–8 (fall 2000): 65–66.

Olson, Charles. *Collected Poems*. Berkeley: University of California Press, 1987.

Olson, Charles. "Projective Verse." In *Collected Prose*. Berkeley: University of California Press, 1997.

Perkins, David. *A History of Modern Poetry: Modernism and After*. Cambridge: Harvard University Press, 1987.

Steele, Timothy. *Missing Measures: Modern Poetry and the Revolt against Meter*. Fayetteville: University of Arkansas Press, 1990.

Voigt, Ellen Bryant. *The Flexible Lyric*. Athens: University of Georgia Press, 1999.

Williams, William Carlos. *Selected Prose*. New York: New Directions, 1969.

Yeats, W. B. *The Collected Poems of W. B. Yeats*. New York: Macmillan, 1989.

Yeats, W. B. *Essays and Introductions*. New York: Macmillan, 1961.

PART 3   *Elements Visible*

Icebergs behoove the soul
(both being self-made from elements least visible)
to see them so: fleshed, fair, erected indivisible.
                    —Elizabeth Bishop, "The Imaginary Iceberg"

STEPHEN DOBYNS

Aspects of the Syllable

Since the first anthologies of English poetry were printed in the sixteenth century, a mild disagreement has persisted as to where the poem exists: in the air as a sound; on the page as a text; or, third, in the reader's or listener's mind, that a poem isn't a poem until it is perceived. For the purposes of what follows, I would like to define the poem both as a sound and as something fixed to the page since the third alternative—that it isn't a poem until it is perceived—would seem to be suggested by the other two.

Literature and music are sequential arts with their information coming to us incrementally out of the future. We in turn anticipate what is going to happen by using our experience of the world and our experience of the particular art form. Literature can also create the illusion of time by presenting a narrative and then often using suspense to make us care about the narrative. We become invested in the question of what is going to happen. We anticipate the possible turnings, and the writer uses our anticipation as energy, sometimes rewarding it, sometimes frustrating it.

When confronted with the poem on the page, our anticipation begins before we read a word. The very shape of the poem leads us to make certain assumptions. Does the poem have symmetrical stanzas, asymmetrical stanzas, no stanzas, short lines, long lines, both short and long, are there unexplained gaps, spaces, and dropped lines? The presence of symmetrical stanzas can create a reassuring sense of control. We feel that nothing can go too wrong with such an imposition of order. Wallace Stevens consistently used a three-line stanza to create the impression of orderliness, to give the impression that someone was in charge, on material that used constant surprise and a wide range of diction. Traditionally, a poem without stanzas suggests a narrative and a stanzaic poem suggests a lyric, though there are many exceptions.

When we hear a poem read, we usually can't tell if it is stichic or stanzaic, while unless the poem is written in a traditional form it can be difficult to have a sense of the lines if the reader doesn't pause at the line breaks or if there isn't end-rhyme. We begin our anticipating with the title, which may offer us a great deal of material, such as James

Wright's "In Response to a Rumor That the Oldest Whorehouse in Wheeling, West Virginia, Has Been Condemned," or very little. Bill Knott has dozens of poems called simply "Poem."

Our main tool in anticipating what comes next is the basic order of the English sentence: subject-verb-object. When we hear the subject, we anticipate the verb; when we hear the verb, we anticipate the direct object. Even if the sentence begins with something else, such as a prepositional phrase, we know that the subject and verb are coming. So, if I begin a sentence with the words "The lion," you anticipate what the lion is going to do. If I follow the subject with a verb such as "leaps," then tension is created that is based on knowledge. Lions are dangerous. If I said, "The kitten leaps," there would be little or no tension. Likewise, little tension would exist if I said the lion "sleeps" or "eats." But with the verb "leaps" you become more engaged. Now you wait for the direct object. Will the lion leap "on the red rubber ball" or "on the little girl running through the grass"? If it is the latter, the tension continues to increase. You want to know what happens to the girl. And here is the second tool that we have in anticipating what will happen next, which, very simply, is our sense of cause and effect. What is the effect of a lion leaping on a little girl? Nothing nice, I expect.

Our experience of the world—both direct and indirect experience, like reading or seeing films—has the ability to educate our sense of cause and effect. We are not born with this. A baby is impelled to learn it through discomfort, that feelings of discomfort—hunger, pain, sadness—lead the baby to do something about it, which is cry, and ideally someone will show up to alleviate the problem.

So in the written arts we deal with this information coming to us out of the future with our knowledge of the Subject-verb-object order of the English sentence and by our sense of cause and effect. A poet or fiction writer must make his or her audience care about what comes next. What influences that caring is not just the subject matter but also the ordering of the information and the language selected to convey that ordering. And it isn't just the language but the individual words and the qualities revealed by those words—not only in terms of meaning but also in terms of sound, which in many cases affects our sense of the meaning.

Paul Valéry wrote, "Ordinary spoken language is a practical tool. It is constantly resolving immediate problems. . . . On the other hand, poetic usage is dominated by *personal* conditions, by a conscious, continuous and sustained musical feeling. . . . Here language is no longer a transitive act. On the contrary, *it has its own value*" (170–71).

As English speakers, we are blessed in our synonyms. Due to the Norman Conquest of 1066, thousands of French words were added to Old English with the result that English has more synonyms than other Western language. Another effect of the conquest was the gradual loss of English inflections—all those word endings that one must memorize when learning other languages, which govern our sense of the subject, verb, and object by giving us information about gender, number, case, tense, and person. As Old English evolved into Middle English, these inflections began to disappear. Middle English was the language of the conquered people. It was spoken rather than written down, and the word endings, the inflections, were gradually lopped off. The aristocracy spoke French, and until the Statute of Pleading in 1362 all court proceedings were written in Latin. After that date, they were written in English: Chaucer's English. Actually, in England in 1066 four major dialects were in use: Northumbrian and Mercian, which were linked as Anglian dialects; Kentish, which was spoken in southeastern England; and West Saxon, which was spoken in southwestern and southern England. West Saxon was the dialect of the court of King Alfred in the ninth century, and it was the dialect of London, which was the seat of power. The English that we use derives mostly from West Saxon, but those who spoke it after 1066 were the underclass, and how it was spoken or spelled or arranged was not governed by established rules like the rules governing Latin and French.

The effect of the loss of inflections is the unadorned syllable and the fact that English has more word endings than other Western languages. Because the presence of inflections means fewer word endings, it is easier to rhyme in languages such as French, Spanish, and Italian than in English. This was quickly made apparent to Thomas Wyatt and Henry Howard, the earl of Surrey, early in the sixteenth century when they began to adapt the Petrarchan sonnet to English use. In the Petrarchan sonnet, the rhyme scheme is the same in the first two quatrains, so the author has to come up with eight words to fit two rhymes. In the English sonnet, as it developed, the first two quatrains didn't use the same rhymes and the poet could use four rhymes with eight words. What is ABBA-ABBA in Petrarch, became ABAB-CDCD in the English sonnet. This creates different expectations.

When we hear a poem, it comes to us in a string of mostly uninflected syllables. The third-person singular verb adds an s and the past tenses will add an *ed* or *en,* but this means little in the vast warehouse of possible word endings.

When we read the first sentence of a poem on the page, rather than hearing it out loud, we have a more accurate idea of what might lie ahead because of the shape of the poem and because we might have noticed certain words farther on, but our basic experience is still syllable by syllable and we ready ourselves for what is coming with our knowledge of word order and our sense of cause and effect.

If you imagine a stream of sound coming from a person's mouth, then syllables are junctures within that stream. The stream becomes segmented. Our word "word" derives from the proto-Indo-European for breaking off or biting off something. It goes back to the idea that we have a steady stream of preexisting sound and we bite chunks out of it to make individual words. Well, what do we do with these chunks? We speak. The word "speak" derives from the proto-Indo-European for strew, sprinkle, scatter, which have the same root. We scatter words as we might scatter straw or sparks. To speak, then, is to bite off pieces of sound from a stream of sound and scatter them in front of other people.

As you may recall, neurolinguists use the word "chunking" to describe what happens when we process syntax. The term was coined by George A. Miller in his 1956 essay "The Magical Number Seven, Plus or Minus Two: Some Limits on Our Capacity for Processing Information," in which Miller wrote that our immediate or short-term memory has a capacity of "seven, plus or minus two, chunks" of information, a number that drops to about five when English monosyllabic words are used. Hearing words coming at us, we tend to process them in groups of five syllables, although we can teach ourselves to increase that number (Miller, 81–97).

A syllable can have up to three parts, which, as *The New Princeton Encyclopedia of Poetry and Poetics* will tell you, are "onset," "nucleus" or "peak," and "coda." In a three-part syllable, the "nucleus" or "peak" is the vowel and the "onset" and "coda" "are consonants or consonant clusters." Obviously a monosyllabic word is a syllable, while a polysyllabic word is made up of syllables that by themselves may or may not be words. A three-part syllable can be as different as the words "bit" and "through," "known" or "cat." A two-part syllable will have a consonant and a vowel in either order, such as "an" and "to." A one-part syllable is the single vowel: "a" or "I," for instance (*New Princeton,* 1249–50).

A syllable may be closed or open. If it ends with a vowel sound, the syllable is open—one can sound it indefinitely—but that vowel sound need not be a vowel, as is the case with the word/syllable "through." "Bit," "peak," and "root" are all closed syllables. We can't keep sounding them. There is also an in-between group of syllables ending in consonants that are neither completely open nor closed. These are syllables ending in labials, nasals, and sibilants. The words "hill," "shown," and "bits" can continue to be sounded even though they end in consonants, though not as long, perhaps, as syllables ending in vowel sounds.

Although there are other aspects to syllables and their range of sounds, at the moment I wish to consider the effects created by being open or closed. Here is a poem, "The Hill-Shade," by the Dorset poet William Barnes, who lived from 1801 to 1886. The designation "Dorset" is of consequence because his poems were mostly written in the dialect of that region, although this is not one of them.

> At such a time, of year and day,
>   In ages gone, that steep hill-brow
> Cast down an evening shade, that lay
>   In shape the same as lies there now:
> Though then no shadows wheel'd around
> The things that now are on the ground.
>
> The hill's high shape may long outstand
>   The house, of slowly-wasting stone;
> The house may longer shade the land
>   Than man's on-gliding shade is shown;
> The man himself may longer stay
> Than stands the summer's rick of hay.
>
> The trees that rise, with boughs o'er boughs,
>   To me for trees long-fall'n may pass;
> And I could take these red hair'd cows
>   For those that pull'd my first-known grass;
> Our flow'rs seem yet on ground and spray,
> But, oh, our people; where are they?
>   —(*Oxford,* 413)

Written in iambic tetrameter, the three six-line stanzas have a rhyme scheme that runs A-B-A-B-C-C. In the second stanza, the rhymes of the first four lines—"outstand," stone," "land," and "shown"—are off-rhymes of the C rhymes in stanza one—"around" and "ground"—while the C rhymes of stanza two—"stay" and "hay"—are full rhymes of the A rhymes of stanza one. In stanza three, the A rhymes—"boughs" and "cows"—are plural forms of the B rhymes in stanza one—"brow" and "now." The B rhymes in stanza three—"pass" and "grass"—link with the sibilants of the A rhymes and are echoed by seven internal words in the first four lines of stanza three, some being royal rhymes—"trees," "rise," "boughs," "trees," "these," "those," and "first." Finally, the C rhymes of stanza three are the same as the C rhymes of stanza two and the A rhymes of stanza one.

The subject of the poem is simple: things pass away and pass away at different speeds—hills very slowly, houses more quickly, people very quickly, a rick of hay even faster. But in the third stanza Barnes makes a slight change: these things that pass away faster than human beings have no real specificity, and this year's flower or cow is much like last year's. Human beings, on the other hand, are irreplaceable: "But, oh, our people; where are they?"

Barnes uses his open and closed syllables, as well as the rhymes that emphasize them, to create a metaphor for this transience. Within the body of the poem are dozens of full and half rhymes of his end-rhymes, while if you compare the first parts of his eighteen lines to the last parts you see that in the first parts of his lines there are many closed syllables and in the very last parts there are none—as in lines three and four, "Cast down an evening shade, that lay / In shape the same as lies there now." The nasals and sibilants fall into that in-between area and can continue to be sounded. So the syllables in each of the eighteen lines either move from closed to open or stay open all the way through a particular line.

The open syllable that receives increasing emphasis is the A rhyme of stanza one—a long *A*—which is also used for the C rhymes of stanzas two and three. This is heightened by the O sound of the B rhymes of stanza one—"brow" and "now." That O appears often in the poem, setting us up for the "Oh" in the last line—an outcry of grief. Barnes first uses what is called a short O in phonics, then he mixes short and long Os as he prepares for the dramatic long O in the last line. Of course, how he pronounced these vowels in his Dorset accent is hard to tell, though some sense of it may be found in his dialect poems. In the poem "The Maid of Newton," the word "hay" is written to sound like "high" and "maid" to sound like "mide." In another poem, "Neighbor Playmates," Barnes inserts a *W* before the O in the words "rope," "more," and "stone" to give a sense of the pronunciation: "rwope," "mwore," and "stwone."

In "The Hill-Shade," Barnes's open syllables come to signify our mortality, our transience. They form the poem's dominant noise. Their effect is also influenced by the pacing of the poem and how Barnes uses stress, duration, pitch, and timbre, but at this point we are just concerned with open and closed syllables. The open syllable ending the poem becomes a sound without closure. Its long cry is still going on. It is the speaker's articulation of our fate. At the beginning of the poem, we have no idea of how Barnes is using open and closed syllables. But when we come to think about what, in the sound, makes the last line so strong we understand.

Four features influence our sense of the syllable and consequently the word. These are stress, duration, pitch, and timbre. The first three are called the intonational features of sounds, while the fourth, timbre, is a sort of poor cousin often added to the list. Timbre is perhaps a weak label, and a better would be "quality," but "quality" has sometimes been used to describe stress, so that would be confusing. Timbre concerns the texture of the sound, its coloration, "the sonorous quality of a sound," whether it is rough or smooth, something in between or something else altogether (*New Princeton,* 1291–92).

The three primary intonational features form the basis for three different metrical systems throughout the world. The Germanic languages use a prosody based on a stress system; the Romance languages use a prosody based on duration, as does Arabic poetry; while two thousand of the world's four thousand languages, many of them Asian, use a system based on pitch. As far as I know, there is no prosodic system based on timbre, but one can be imagined.

A syllable by itself is nothing. It lacks stress, duration, pitch, and perhaps timbre. Separately all syllables are equal. But put two syllables together and we see differences in their intonational features. The exception is when the two syllables seem to be about the same. For instance, two syllables might have the same degree of stress, such as "of the" and "rat pack." At times, it take a third or fourth syllable before we see the contrast, as in "of the rat pack" or "of the rat." When syllables occur in a line of poetry or prose—when they occur in a syllabic environment—then we quickly see that some are stressed and some unstressed. Every sentence—whether in poetry or prose, whether written in traditional verse or free verse—can be scanned and broken into feet. Traditional verse has repeating feet—iambic pentameter is five repeating iambs, while a free verse line may have any number of feet and none of them might repeat. But they can still be scanned. In poetry written in English, whether formal or free, one always deals with the relationship of stressed and unstressed syllables. One can't avoid it; it's built into the language. Indeed, English denotation can depend exactly on stressed and unstressed syllables. Consider, for instance, the examples "conTRACT" and "CONtract," "minUTE" and "MINute." And the relationship between stressed and unstressed syllables can have an emotional dynamic—in a stream of syllables, the accented syllables tend to be more affective than unaccented syllables.

Now the idea of meter, even a particular meter, is an abstraction, and to impose the abstraction on the living poem can cause problems. In 1900, the Danish linguist Otto Jespersen argued in favor of what he called "the relative stress principle," that is, that the degree of stress is influenced by a syllable's surroundings. He wrote, "The metrical value of a syllable depends on what comes before and what follows after it" (*New Princeton,* 1019–20). As a result, syllables we might think of as strong will become weak if placed between two stronger syllables and syllables that are weak will become strong if placed between two weaker syllables. In addition, the rhythm of a line might accent syllables that would not ordinarily be accented. Many volumes have been written on this subject, but for our purposes it is enough to paraphrase Jespersen and say that it is the relative stress that counts. His argument is also taken as evidence that there can be no such thing as a pure pyrrhic or pure spondee, which in fact may be true, but what is important is the poet's intention and not the critic's quibble.

Often a difference may exist between metrical stress and speech stress. Metrical stress is the meter—an iambic pentameter line has ten syllables alternating between unstressed and stressed syllables. Speech stress, on the other hand, is how we might phrase the line in normal speech. The two need not be the same. Clearly they are the same in the first line of Milton's sonnet on his blindness: "When I consider how my light is spent." When we speak the line in a normal voice, it falls easily into iambic pentameter. The same is true of the first line of Philip Larkin's "Aubade": "I work all day and get half drunk at night." But the first two lines of Donald Justice's sonnet "The Poet at Seven" begin to emphasize the speech stress: "And on the porch across the upturned chair, / The boy would spread a dingy counterpane . . ." You can sound out the iambic pentameter, but it creates a sense of artificiality. This is even truer of Phillip Larkin's "The Explosion," the first three lines of which read "On the day of the explosion / Shadows pointed from the pithead. / In the sun the slagheap slept." Those lines and the entire poem are written in trochaic tetrameter, the same meter as "Hiawatha," and those first lines are exactly trochaic—ON the DAY of THE ex-PLO-sion—but to read the lines emphasizing the meter creates an artificial, not to say comic, effect.

This indicates that a plain binary opposition of unstressed/stressed, short/long, high/low, and rough/smooth may work in prosodic analysis, but it is a simplification that can lead us to misread a poem. There are more than two degrees of stress. Machines have shown that there can be hundreds. But in discussing syllables I want to use the Trager-Smith system, which argues for four degrees of stress—primary, secondary, tertiary, and weak—which are noted 1–2–3–4 with 1 being the primary stress. This system is also an abstraction, and we could instead use three or five or ten degrees of stress, but four degrees will suit us for now.

As you may imagine, a syllable combination of weak and primary, 4–1, creates a lot of emphasis, though not as much as the double stress we call a spondee, while if the 4–1 pattern is repeated it creates a casual or comic tone. Phillip Larkin's "This Be the Verse" uses 4–1 iambic stress to heighten the comic effect.

> They fuck you *up* your mum and dad,
>   They may not mean to but they do
> They pass on all the faults they had
>   And add some extra just for you.
>
> But they were fucked *up* **in** their turn
>   By fools **in** old-style hats and coats,
> Who half the time were soppy-stern
>   And half at one another's throats.
>   —(Larkin, *High Windows*, 30)

The iambic tetrameter and short syllables combined with the 4–1 iambic stress create a speed suggestive of the jazzy Sidney Bechet dance steps that Larkin loved. Also, as an example of the relative stress principle at work, one sees that in the two appearances of the word "up"— in line one of the first stanza and line one of the second—in the first instance "up" is stressed and in the second it is unstressed. Also, looking at the two instances of the word "in" in the first and second lines of the second stanza, the first time it is stressed and the second it is unstressed.

In contrast, consider at the first stanza of Larkin's "At Grass," also written in iambic tetrameter, for how he uses stress ratio.

> The eye can hardly pick them out
> From the cold shade they shelter in
> Till wind distresses tail and mane;
> Then one crops grass, and moves about
> —The other seeming to look on—
> And stands anonymous again.
>   —(Larkin, *The Less Deceived*, 45)

The difference in tone between the two poems is also influenced by the presence, in the second example, of syllables of longer duration, but look at the difference in the iambs. The first line, instead of being 4-1, 4-1, 4-1, 4-1, is perhaps 4-2, 3-2, 4-1, 3-2. In the second line, Larkin uses substitutions, replacing the two initial iambs with a pyrrhic and a spondee because he wants to give special emphasis to "cold shade." The fourth line is perhaps 4-2, 3-2, 4-2, 4-2.

The use of these four gradations of stress is one way a poet can modulate his or her meaning. Looking again at Barnes's "The Hill-Shade," you see that the iambic tetrameter of stanza one is nearly all 4-1, moving from weak to primary stress. This creates a casual tone. The speaker is making a rather offhand remark. But this 4-1 ratio changes in the next stanza, as the speaker begins to see a deeper meaning. So the first line of the second stanza is perhaps 4-1, 2-1, 2-1, 3-1. And this closer relationship between the stresses continues, although the last two lines of stanza two go back to 4–1 again.

But in the last stanza the speaker surprises in himself an even deeper meaning. I say "surprises" because the nature of the formal change makes it seem that a psychological change is taking place in front of us. It creates an illusion of immediacy and spontaneity. The deeper meaning and increased meditative quality of the last stanza is reflected in the stress ratios between the syllables. The third and fourth lines seem to be 4-1, 2-1, 2-1, 2-1 / 4-1, 3-2, 4-1, 3-2, while the last line becomes 3-1, 2-1, 4-1, 3-2. Others might see it a little differently, but the point is that one finds a clear difference in the stress ratios between the first and third stanzas, and this appears to be an incremental change indicative of the poem's growing seriousness. The change is used to modulate meaning.

Another way in which stressed and unstressed syllables can modulate meaning is in the use of substitutions, replacing an anticipated foot with another to create a slight surprise, as Larkin did in the second line of "At Grass": "from the cold shade." Look at the first two stanzas of a poem by Thomas Wyatt, "They fle from me that sometyme."

> They fle from me that sometyme did me seke
> With naked fote stalking in my chambre.
> I have sene theim gentill tame and meke
> That nowe are wyld and do not remembre
> That sometyme they put theimself in daunger
> To take bred at my hand; and now they raunge
> Besely seking with a continuell chaunge.
>
> Thancked be fortune, it hath ben othrewise
> Twenty tymes better; but ons in speciall,
> In thyn arraye after a pleasaunt gyse,
> When her lose gowne from her shoulders did fall,
> And she me caught in her armes long and small;
> Therewithall swetely did me kysse,
> And softely saide, *dere hert, howe like you this?*
> —(*Oxford*, 29)

Written nearly five hundred years ago, the poem uses an English that is very clear to us, although Wyatt's pronunciation would have been more French, with "chambre," "daunger," and "remembre" stressed on their last syllables, and "speciall," meaning one time in particular, given three syllables. "Besely," the first word of the seventh line, is a spelling of "busily" but also puns on "basely." A courtier in the court of Henry VIII, Wyatt was imprisoned several times for brawling and sexual misconduct and was also accused of treason. He died at the age of thirty-nine in 1542. The poem is written in iambic pentameter, and the metrical substitutions are used to heighten the drama. Since Chaucer, 150 years before, the five-foot decasyllabic line had emerged in English as the line of choice, although it didn't come to be called iambic pentameter until the end of sixteenth century.

Wyatt's first substitution appears in line two, where we find the trochee "stalking" instead of an iamb. This creates a little sonic metaphor enacting the tiptoe movement of the woman's foot: "With naked fote stalking in my chambre," as Wyatt describes the occasional nighttime activities in Henry VIII's palace. In the second stanza, Wyatt shifts to a specific woman, who enters his chamber dressed in her nightgown. The substitutions in the last four lines enact this scene. In line four, we have an iamb, spondee, pyrrhic, trochee, and a final iamb: "When her lose gowne from her shoulders did fall." In the next line, Wyatt rather brilliantly puts the direct object "me" before the verb "caught," so this line, too, begins with an iamb and a spondee, then a pyrrhic, another spondee, and an iamb: "And she me caught in her armes long and small." The effect of these substitutions is to create sonic metaphors that show the nightgown slowly sliding from the woman's shoulders, and then, naked as a jaybird, she steps forward to embrace Sir Thomas. Well, if you read the lines as he intended, they can take your breath. The next substitutions are the trochee "swetely" in line six and the spondee "dere hert" in line seven, with a pun on "hart," meaning deer. These substitutions also modulate meaning by using stress-unstress relationships to give the impression of physical movement.

Although duration as an intonational feature lacks the drama of stress, it is still useful in controlling meaning. Duration isn't necessarily affected by the length or brevity of the word but by the length of the syllables, the hardness or softness of the consonants, and whether the syllables are open or closed. Here is the poem "Girl Help" by Janet Lewis.

Mild and slow and young,
She moves about the room,
And stirs the summer dust
With her wide broom.

In the warm, lofted air,
Soft lips together pressed,
Soft wispy hair,
She stops to rest,

And stops to breathe,
Among the summer hum,
The great white lilacs bloom
Scented with days to come.
—(*American Poetry*, 251)

This is primarily iambic trimeter with a number of substitutions and exceptions. While the meter, rhyme, and open syllables affect the poem's slowness, it is primarily the duration of the syllables that creates a sense of lethargy and near stupor. The poem describes an adolescent girl dreaming of her future while supposedly cleaning the house, and the long-duration *O*s—"slow," "young," "move," "room," "broom," "soft," "among," "bloom," "come"—along with all the nasals make the twelve short lines seem very protracted. You will notice that the pattern changes somewhat in the second stanza, where there are fewer long-duration *O*s and nasals, and then Lewis returns to them in the last stanza. The effect is to create a further surprise while making sure we don't become exhausted by the poem's method too soon.

In Janet Lewis's poem, we see the comic possibilities of duration, but the opposite effect is created in the last two lines of W. B. Yeats's "The Second Coming."

And what rough beast, its hour come round at last,
Slouches toward Bethlehem to be born.
—(Yeats, 200)

Written in loose iambic pentameter, the poem's long-duration *O*s and nasals in the last two lines enact the slouching movement of the beast. In addition, with "slouches" Yeats substitutes a trochee where we expect an iamb, using the same effect that Wyatt used with the word "stalking" centuries before. But Yeats's creature slouches, it doesn't stalk, and so he heightens our sense of the movement with syllables of long duration.

To return again to Barnes's "The Hill-Shade," we see that he gradually uses an increasing number of long-duration syllables per line throughout his eighteen-line poem, ending with "But, oh, our people; where are they?" The words of short duration in the first stanza, including "such," "steep," "hill," "cast," and "shape," are replaced in the last stanza with "bough," "long," "cows," "known," "ground," and so on, all leading to the outcry, "oh," in the last line. Clearly, the syllables of short duration are not all the same length. "Steep" may be longer than "shape," but both are considerably shorter than "bough" and "cow."

Pitch is a subtler feature of the syllable. Simply put, we have fifteen degrees of vowel pitch ranging from low *OO* to high *EE*. By "pitch," I mean frequency. The speed of sound is of course constant; it comes to us in waves. The shorter the waves the more waves occur in each second, consequently the higher the frequency and the higher the pitch. The highest pitch—*EE*—has the most sound waves per second. The lowest—*OO*—has the least. The fifteen vowel sounds may also be divided into bass, tenor, and alto vowels.

Vowel sounds can have psychological effect, as will be seen in the low-pitched words "calm," "cool," and soothe" as opposed to the high-pitched "scream," and "shriek," but the effect may be nearly subliminal. Halfway up the scale of vowel pitch is a short *U* sound: "Uh." In his book *Western Wind,* John Frederick Nims refers to this as "the shudder vowel," as in "ugh" or "mud," "blunder," "bungle," "chump," "clumsy," "crummy," "runt," "pus," and "repugnant." But these are imprecise areas with many exceptions. For instance, "summer" and "comfort" also use the shudder vowel. And some of our fifteen sounds, such as "boy" and "buy," are diphthongs, in which the second vowel raises the pitch. However, as Nims goes on to say, the fact that this is not an exact science doesn't keep it from being a useful tool in our study of poetry (151–72).

Look at Keats's "When I Have Fears."

> When I have fears that I may cease to be
>   Before my pen has gleaned my teeming brain,
> Before high-piled books, in charact'ry,
>   Hold like rich garners the full-ripened grain;
> When I behold, upon the night's starred face,
>   Huge cloudy symbols of a high romance,
> And think that I may never live to trace
>   Their shadows, with the magic hand of chance;
> And when I feel, fair creature of the hour,
>   That I shall never look upon thee more,

> Never have relish in the faery power
>   Of unreflecting love!—then on the shore
> Of the wide world I stand alone, and think
> Till Love and Fame to nothingness do sink.
>   —(Keats, 237)

It is appropriate that Keats chose the Shakespearean sonnet to discuss his ambition, each with its own subject and beginning with "when" and then a concluding couplet. We also see examples of how he uses duration and stress to control modulation. For instance, the importance of the image in line six—"Huge cloudy symbols of a high romance"—is indicated by the syllables of long duration, while the anxiety that the image creates in the speaker leads to the 4–1, weak-primary stress ratios in line seven: "And think that I may never live to trace." In any poem, all four of these features—stress, duration, pitch, and timbre—will appear, but one may be stronger than the others.

In the first line of the sonnet, Keats uses three syllables of the highest pitch: "fears," "cease," and "be," while the two pronouns "I" are only two levels below them. Indeed, the first quatrain has many high-pitched syllables: "pen," "glean," "teem," "piled," "tree" in "charact'ry" "rich," and "ripe." Keats is afraid he will die of the same disease that killed his brother, Tom, before he gets a chance to write the poems that he wants to write. His hope of writing these poems is weakened by his despair. It is the latter feeling that comes to dominate the poem, and it is enacted by the slow change from high-frequency to low-frequency syllables.

For in the second quatrain we have none of the high *EE* sounds. He almost entirely abandons the alto range for the tenor range. Although he uses four *I*s, the dominant pitch is created by tenor range *A*s and *O*s: "behold," "face," "cloudy," "symbols," "romance," "trace," "shadows," "chance." The anxiety that is indicated in the already mentioned metrical ratios of the seventh line heightens this despair, while in the first line of the third quatrain—"And when I feel, fair creature of the hour"—we see the whole range of pitch enacted from alto to bass. Then it stays low, and the dominating syllables are "look," "on," "more," "power," "love," and "shore." This pitch change not only reflects Keats's despair but also his analysis, his very reasoning process, while his concluding couplet presents us with the lowest examples of pitch—"Of the wide world I stand alone, and think / Till Love and Fame to nothingness do sink"—a despair that is also affected by syllables of long duration. The very last word—"sink"—sounds low, despite the *I*, because it comes at the end of a low-pitched line. In addition, the final *K* drags down the higher *I,* as you can see if you compare "thin" and "think," "sin" and "sink," "win" and "wink." The short *I* of "sink" is the fourth vowel sound from the top in terms of frequency; it is the highest tenor vowel. The *K,* however, creates a small diphthong, adding a barely voiced "Uh" sound at the end of the word—the shudder vowel again. But even more the word "sink" reflects what Keats has done. The pitch has sunk from high to low, his hope has sunk, his expectations have sunk, and his life will sink. Keats uses the decreasing vowel pitch as a metaphor for his darkening emotional state.

Looking again at Barnes's "The Hill-Shade" one can see that he, too, uses vowel pitch to heighten his meaning. In Barnes's case, however, he uses the higher pitch vowels toward the beginning of the lines and then lowers the pitch so that the end words have the lowest pitch. The first line of the second stanza descends bit by bit right to the last word: "The hill's high shape may long outstand." The same is true of the last line of the third stanza: "The trees that rise, with boughs o'er boughs." Many of the lines are low pitched all the way through, such as line two of stanza two—"The house, of slowly-wasting stone"—and of course the poem's last line—"But, oh, our people; where are they?" In addition, in keeping with the metrical lightness of the first stanza and its use of syllables of shorter duration, it is also in that stanza where you find the most high-pitched vowels.

For any of these sound features to work, there must be contrast, and this is even truer of timbre. We have perhaps a sound of language in our ear, a sound that is modest and somewhat unassuming. This is the norm. It is the sound of daily discourse. For the most part, it is serious, generally good-natured, and courteous. Timbre works best set against that norm so that at the end of Yeats's "The Second Coming"—"And what rough beast, its hour come round at last, / Slouches toward Bethlehem to be born?"—the word "rough" is effective because its texture or timbre is far "rougher" than the other words in those lines.

In discussing timbre, we are somewhat at a disadvantage because words such as "rough," "smooth," "sweet," and "tart" are themselves metaphors for the harmonics, vibrations, and formants found in the resonant frequencies of the vocal tract. Yet we know it when we see it, and we can also often feel it. We can feel the vibration of the *R,* the explosive quality of *B* and *P,* the dental pop of *D* and *T,* the liquid *L*s, the buzz of the nasals and hiss of the sibilants, the slight whistle of the fricatives such as "fie" and "thigh." Any language, and especially a Germanic language, activates the mouth.

These elements of texture are all, to some extent, suggestive of emotion. In the sounds themselves, we can hear what we might imagine to be anger or melancholy or joy. Consequently, one's use of timbre must be consistent with the emotional content of the poem. Indeed, it helps the writer modulate that emotion. This is a complicated way of saying that the sound must be consistent with the sense. But look at the first stanza of Robert Lowell's "The Quaker Graveyard in Nantucket."

> A brackish reach of shoal off Madaket
> The sea was still breaking violently and night
> Had steamed into our North Atlantic Fleet,
> When the drowned sailor clutched the drag-net. Light
> Flashed from his matted head and marble feet,
> He grappled at the net
> With the coiled, hurdling muscles of his thighs:
> The corpse was bloodless, a botch of reds and whites,
> Its open, staring eyes
> Were lusterless dead lights
> Or cabin windows on a stranded hulk
> Heavy with sand. We weight the body, close
> Its eyes and heave it seaward whence it came
> Where the heel-headed dogfish barks its nose
> On Ahab's void and forehead; and the name
> Is blocked in yellow chalk.
> Sailors, who pitch this portent at the sea
> Where dreadnaughts shall confess
> Its hell-bent deity,
> When you are powerless
> To sand-bag this Atlantic bulwark, faced
> By the earth-shaker, green, unwearied, chaste
> In his steel scales: ask for no Orphean lute
> To pluck life back. The guns of the steeled fleet
> Recoil and then repeat
> The hoarse salute.
>
> —(Lowell, 14)

This is not the voice of daily discourse, and we ask ourselves why. The beginning lines are dominated by a large number of harsh sounds: "brack," "reach," "Madaket," "break," "lent," "night," "Atlantic," "Fleet," "clutch," "net," "light," "mat," "feet," "grap," and "net," which Lowell keeps up all the way through the stanza then heightens again in the last three lines—"pluck," "back," "fleet," "repeat," "salute." The harshness of these sounds is also increased by the fact that they are all closed syllables of short duration.

We can describe the sound quality of "ack" in various ways, all of which would be metaphors and examples of synesthesia unless we moved into the area of phonetics and psychoacoustics. But we immediately recognize the harsh quality of "ack," and we see how Lowell is carefully repeating that sound or sounds similar to it. There is also the associative aspect of the sound emotionally, psychologically, and intellectually. It is not a peaceful sound; it is violent and disruptive. The question is whether the sound is appropriate to the subject matter. For instance, it wouldn't be useful in a lullaby. You don't sing a baby to sleep at night going "Ack-ack-ack." The poem, first published in 1946, is an elegy for Lowell's cousin, who died at sea during the war. The timbre of the dominating syllables is meant to reflect, on the simplest level, the writer's anger and grief and the violence of death while describing the retrieval and subsequent sea burial of a drowned sailor. You will also remember that Lowell was a conscientious objector during the war.

Lowell emphasizes timbre while also making great use of stress, duration, and pitch. He wants extreme contrasts, which reflect the turbulent sea and the emotion of the scene. In the first three pentameter lines, the iambs move from weak to primary stress with such violence that Lowell is forced to insert a useless word, "still," in the second line to keep the rhythm from getting out of control and becoming exaggerated. Then at the start of the fourth line he breaks that movement with a pyrrhic and a spondee, while the violent enjambment of "Light / flashed" is meant to enact what it describes. Throughout the stanza, Lowell uses a weak to primary stress ratio, breaking it with spondees and violent enjambments so that the meter seems about to break apart. And if you look at pitch you can see that nearly every line uses both high and low, as in lines eight through ten: "The corpse was bloodless, a botch of reds and whites, / Its open, staring eyes / Were lusterless dead lights." He uses duration similarly; that is, to create jarring contrast. In the first two lines, we may stumble over "shoal" and "still" because they are of longer duration than the syllables in their immediate environment. Lowell wants to begin the stanza with great speed, which he complicates with a series of tongue-twisting sounds achieved by the harsh quality of the timbre. All of this is in keeping with his intention and his meaning.

The tone coloration of Barnes's "The Hill-Shade" is simpler and governed by low-pitch O and A sounds along with nasals and sibilants.

After the jaunty beginning, the poem grows increasingly sonorous and the pitch descends. Barnes uses few plosive consonants, preferring fricatives and softer sounds. There is none of Lowell's harsh "Ack-ack-ack." This affects the tone, creating softness, gloominess, and melancholy, which is in keeping with his intended meaning and how he also uses stress, duration, and pitch.

A final point about Barnes is the meaning of his title, "The Hill-Shade." The word "shade" appears in the first two stanzas in its more conventional meaning: the relative darkness created by the interception of rays of light. But by the end of the poem, the meaning evoked is that of a disembodied spirit. This changes our sense of the title, expanding it to include the two meanings, with the greater emphasis being on the dead. It also answers the question posed by the last line: "But, oh, our people; where are they?" The shades of our people are all around us, whether literally, as ghosts, or as memories. So Barnes takes the word/syllable "shade" and accustoms us to one of its meanings and then surprises us at the end by changing his focus to a more powerful meaning, at which point we see that it existed in his title all along.

The real subject behind an analysis of the sonic features of syllables is modulation. How does a poet modulate his or her meaning? If you read a poem out loud, you use your own voice to modulate meaning. Your voice becomes like the band that gives life to the sappy song lyric. But on the page one of the ways to modulate meaning is by the sound features inherent in the syllable. Another is by the line break.

These four sonic features all have different degrees of associative meaning or suggestion. If the poet doesn't pay attention to these features, then his or her poem will modulate meaning regardless, and it may not be the meaning the poet wants. It has been argued by formalists that if a poet abandons traditional meter then he or she also abandons the ability to modulate. But this is incorrect. Surely, it affects that ability, but, as I say, whether in free or traditional verse, one is always dealing with the relationship between stressed and unstressed syllables. With free verse, however, it will be harder to modulate meaning, which is why the free verse poet must pay special attention to these other aspects of the syllable, to learn the ways it can be used to manipulate nuance. If not, the poet's expression becomes so generalized that it opens itself up to misreading.

That misreading, unluckily, is where the poem might exist. If a poem isn't a poem until it is perceived, that perception is left open to a large number of misinterpretations if the poet doesn't control his or her meaning. Thousands of poems fail because the poet hasn't closed the road to alternative readings. By learning how to use the intonational features available to the syllable, the poet is able to become more certain that his or her intended meaning will be the one perceived by the reader.

NOTE

First appeared in *Writer's Chronicle* 38, no. 4 (February 2006): 56–64.

WORKS CITED

American Poetry: The Twentieth Century. Vol. 2: *E. E. Cummings to Meg Swenson.* New York: Library of America, 2000.

Barnes, William. *The Selected Poems of William Barnes.* Edited by Thomas Hardy. London: Henry P. Froude, 1908.

Keats, John. *The Complete Poems of John Keats.* New York: Modern Library, 1994.

Larkin, Philip. *High Windows.* New York: Faber and Faber, 1976.

Larkin, Philip. *The Less Deceived.* Hessle, East Yorkshire: Marvell, 1962.

Lowell, Robert. *Collected Poems.* Edited by Frank Bidart and David Gewanter. New York: Farrar, Straus and Giroux, 2003.

Miller, George A. "The Magical Number Seven, Plus or Minus Two: Some Limits on Our Capacity for Processing Information." *Psychological Review* 63 (1956): 63, 81–97.

The New Princeton Encyclopedia of Poetry and Poetics. Edited by Alex Preminger and T. F. V. Brogan. Princeton: Princeton University Press, 1993.

Nims, John Frederick. *Western Wind.* 4th ed. New York: McGraw Hill, 2000.

The Oxford Book of English Verse. Edited by Christopher Ricks. Oxford: Oxford University Press, 1999.

Valéry, Paul. "The Art of Poetry." In *The Collected Works of Paul Valéry.* Edited by Jackson Matthews, translated by Denise Follijot. Bollingen series 45, vol. 7. Princeton: Princeton University Press, 1989.

Yeats, William Butler. *The Collected Works of William Butler Yeats.* Edited by Richard Finneran, Vol. 1. New York: Scribners, 1989.

ELLEN BRYANT VOIGT

On and Off the Grid: Syntax, Part II

"Vocal" rhythm (phrasing), which "organizes musical time . . . on the large scale," and "instrumental" rhythm (meter), which organizes it on the small scale: this is how the musicologist Robert Jourdain describes the two rhythmic systems at work in music.

> Meter . . . organizes small groups of notes, and sometimes larger ones, and thereby provides a sort of grid upon which music is drawn. On the other hand, phrasing imparts a kind of narrative to music. It is the mechanism by which a composition can play out a grand drama. . . . Phrasing is nothing like meter. For one thing, its markers are more subtle. Where meter presents a regular, mostly predictable succession of emphasized notes, phrasing constantly varies. (*Music, The Brain, and Ecstasy,* 123–24, 130)

Robert Frost made a remarkably similar distinction when articulating his own prosody. "A sentence," he said,

> is not interesting merely in conveying a meaning of words. It must do something more: it must convey a meaning by sound.

He called these "sentence sounds" "the sound of sense," out of which "I . . . consciously set myself to make music." "Dramatic tones of meaning" came from phrasing, from "vital sentences" (as opposed to "grammatical sentences") apprehended by the ear, which are "struck across a limited meter" to create "endless possibilities for tune."

> [I]t's a tune of the blend of those two things [rhythm and meter]. Something rises—it's neither one of these things. It's neither the meter nor the rhythm; it's a tune arising from the stress on these, same as your fingers on the strings, you know. The twang!

In other words, as Jourdain says of music, "The two kinds of rhythm are not entirely at peace with one another" (124). For Frost, a fixed grid in poetry was paramount.

All I ask is iambic. . . . The crossed swords are always the same. The sword dancer varies his position between them.

Which shows the temperament behind his famous put-down: that free verse is like playing tennis without a net. Less well known is Charles Wright's rejoinder: that free verse is actually "the high wire act without the net." Frost worried he would "be lost in the air with just cutting loose"—cutting loose, that is, from iambic "as rigid as two crossed swords in the Sword Dance." But the high-wire walker, far from "cutting loose," depends entirely, thrillingly, on the thin line along which he inches his slippered feet. One should not infer from Wright's felicitous figure that in open-form, or "free verse," poems something is *missing:* instead, the issues of pattern and variation, tension and release, shape and energy—matters of form—remain the same, to be negotiated poet by poet, poem by poem, within the strictures of individual temperament and aesthetic.

In part I of this essay (published in 2003), I examined open verse poems by Stanley Kunitz and D. H. Lawrence in which only a barely discernible "grid" had been established, not by "predictable" measure in the line but by strict consonance between the line and what the linguists call syntactical "chunks," what Frost calls "the sound of sense." Stanley Kunitz and D.H. Lawrence would no doubt agree with Frost that "the living part of a poem is in the intonation entangled somehow in the syntax idiom and meaning of a sentence," even though neither thought strict meter was the only way to create "the other thing— something . . . for me to put a strain on." Instead of Frost's rigid "crossed swords," both "King of the River" and "The Man Who Has Come Through" rely on a faithful coincidence between the rhythms available in the syntax and the rhythm created by the line—what I call "consonant" lineation. Here are the opening sentences of both poems.

> If the water were clear enough,
> if the water were still,
> but the water is not clear,
> the water is not still,
> you would see yourself,
> slipped out of your skin,
> nosing upstream,
> slapping, thrashing,
> tumbling
> over the rocks
> till you paint them

with your belly's blood:
Finned Ego,
yard of muscle that coils,
uncoils.
—Kunitz, "King of the River"

Not I, not I, but the wind that blows through me!
A fine wind is blowing the new direction of Time.
If only I let it bear me, carry me, if only it carry me!
If only I am sensitive, subtle, oh, delicate, a winged gift!
If only, most lovely of all, I yield myself and am borrowed
By the fine, fine wind that takes its course through the chaos of the world
Like a fine, an exquisite chisel, a wedge-blade inserted;
If only I am keen and hard like the sheer tip of a wedge
Driven by invisible blows,
The rock will split, we shall come at the wonder, we shall find the
Hesperides.
—Lawrence, "Song of the Man Who Has Come Through"

In the Lawrence poem, the long line, making its own "sound of sense," usually combines ("chunks together," as the linguists would say) pieces of syntax that are often overlapping or synonymous and then divides the resulting musical phrase from its long sentence. Because the line lengths vary wildly, pattern must derive from syntax—the similarities in sentence structure—and from lexical repetition, both of which are absorbed and managed by chunking, end-stop, and anaphora. As in a Whitman poem, the formal choices emphasize what Robert Jourdain calls the "narrative" of the composition, its "grand drama"—an effect essentially removed from the poem if it is recast into Kunitz's short line:

If only I let it bear me, carry me,
if only it carry me!
If only I am sensitive, subtle,
oh, delicate, a winged gift!
If only, most lovely of all,
I yield myself
and am borrowed
by the fine, fine wind
that takes its course
through the chaos of the world. . . .

Isolated this way, the repetitions become tedious and self-indulgent, the text static and overwritten, struggling within a nonfunctional form.

The short consonant line works well in the Kunitz poem because, as in Frost, large-scale musical phrasing is managed there not by the line but by syntax—the highly complex, highly repetitious syntax, emphasized by stanzas, that structures the poem. While Lawrence's lines drive us past markers and combine distinct grammatical units into sweeping musical phrases, Kunitz uses the line for stability and clarity, parsing out the composite pieces of his long hypotactic sentences and exaggerating the directness of his short declaratives. This deflects some of the grand syntactical drama and slows us down, bringing to the poem a stateliness of tone, a studied persuasion not possible with Lawrence's rushing tempo. Marked—doubly punctuated—by the lineation, Kunitz's smaller chunks take on a rough grammatical equivalence, making syntactical hierarchy, among the pieces of the sentence, secondary to the formal arrangement of the poem. It is only obliquely that this arrangement is faithful enough to a rudimentary pattern, in the length and syntactical integrity of the lines, to suggest a sort of "grid upon which the music is played."

Meanwhile, it is important to emphasize that even when the grid is more pronounced, more regular, and overt and predictable—even in Frost's own heavily iambic verse or Pope's unvarying pentameter—poetry in English can only approximate the quantifiable, numerical meter of music. While musical meter controls the duration of individual notes, the language comprises syllables of hugely variable weight and worth due to its blend of polysyllabic Latinate words and Teutonic monosyllables, its irregular verbs and Greek prefixes, its pace-slowing clusters of consonants and its *sustenuto* long vowels, its dependence on lexical stress (**con**-tent vs. con-**tent, pro**-test vs. pro-**test)** or rhetorical stress (bring me **that** book) to indicate grammatical function and meaning. With poetic roots not in quantitative poetries such as Greek or French but in the accentual verse of Anglo-Saxon, much of the great accentual syllabic poetry in English offers, in its meter, only a very flexible grid indeed, a sort of palimpsest behind the rhythmic phrasing of syntax, as the following traditional sonnet will demonstrate.

29

When, in disgrace with fortune and men's eyes,
I all alone beweep my outcast state,
And trouble deaf heaven with my bootless cries,
And look upon myself, and curse my fate. . . .
Wishing me like to one more rich in hope,
Featured like him, like him with friends possessed,
Desiring this man's art and that man's scope,

With what I most enjoy contented least;
Yet in these thoughts myself almost despising
Haply I think on thee—and then my state,
Like to the lark at break of day arising
From sullen earth, sings hymns at heaven's gate;
For thy sweet love remembered such wealth brings
That then I scorn to change my state with kings.

An untortured reading of the first quatrain produces something like this:

> **When,** in dis-**grace** with **for-**tune and **men's eyes,**
> I **all** a-**lone** be-**weep** my **out-cast state,**
> And **troub-**le **deaf heav'n** with my **boot-**less **cries,**
> And **look** upon my**self,** and **curse** my **fate,**

Although the iambic foot (u /) is the most prominent, no line here consists only of iambs. One can of course assign variant feet to ensure the pentameter "count" for each decasyllabic line, but the "accentual" part is rather slippery: line 2 seems to have six speech stresses, while line 4 may have only four—lexically, "upon" carries more emphasis on the second syllable than on the first, but prepositions are merely function words, essentially unheard (and often literally missing in other, inflected languages). Although the stanza hints at metrical pattern, what dominates is not a regular, "instrumental" rhythm but "vocal" phrasing, determined by the syntax—an introductory phrase (line 1), and then four dependent clauses, the first two, roughly the same in length, presented in the unbroken or unpunctuated lines 2 and 3, the last two, shorter, chunked together by a single mid-stopped line. What the brain "hears" as it works rapidly to decode the language is not four equivalent lines but a sequence of rhythmic units that swell and then diminish, drawn by transitive verbs.

> When,
> in disgrace with fortune and men's eyes,
> I all alone beweep my outcast state,
> And trouble deaf heaven with my bootless cries,
> And look upon myself,
> and curse my fate. . . .

At stanza's end, although the second hard rhyme signals resolution, the brain knows otherwise: the poem's initial conjunction (*when*) has "marked" what follows as a subordinate clause: we keep reading to find the subject and verb. But that fundament is further delayed by syntax even less grammatically significant, phrases made from parallel present participles bracketed by rhyme.

> **Wishing** me like to one more rich in hope,
> **Desiring** this man's art and that man's scope . . .

—and each in turn modified by past participles that lead, right-branching, to a final, subordinate clause.

> **Featured** like him,
> **Possessed** like him with friends,
> **Contented** least with *what I most enjoy.* . . .

We become aware of the "grid" for this music only gradually. The first two lines begin with falling rhythm

> **Wish-**ing me **like** . . .
> **Fea-**tured like **him** . . .

before the stanza settles into initial iambs.

> De-**sir-**ing **this** . . .
> With **what** I **most.** . . .

The quatrain continues to pack the lines with additional stresses—and uses syntax to do so, adding rhetorical stress to monosyllabic words.

> Wish-ing me **like** to **one more rich** in **hope,**
> **Fea-**tured like **him,** *like* **him** with **friends** po-**ssess'd,**
> De-**sir-**ing **this man's art** and **that man's scope.** . . ,

In the "chunking" line 2, with its caesura, normal syntax is rearranged for close repetition (*like him, like him*) that complicates the smooth iambs easily available ("featured like him, possessed like him with friends"), even as the stanza's final modifying syntax is rearranged in order to *achieve* it, closing the eight-line-long dependent clause (and the strikingly Petrarchan octave) on the poem's first exactly iambic pentameter line.

> With **what** I **most** en-**joy** con-**tent-**ed **least.** . . .

The two stanzas have an architecture, in which line 8 becomes a syntactical and metrical resolution.

Shakespeare, however, is not finished with his variations. What opens the third stanza is one more delay of the fundament, one more reversed initial foot, and an extra syllable: only then will he deliver the syntactical and metrical goods.

> **Yet** in these **thoughts** my-**self** al-**most** [alt., **al**-most] de-**spis**-ing,
> **Hap**-ly I **think** on **thee**—and **then** my **state**. . . .

The feminine ending at line 9, the poem's first, tumbles us into the initial stress of another reversed foot before alliteration ("**th**ese **th**oughts . . . **th**ink . . . **th**ee . . . **th**en") pounds the iambs like stakes into the ground as the poem delivers its first independent clause (*I think*). The formal music of the poem now arm wrestles the syntax for control of the poem, and this tension will enact the most ecstatic, and musically interesting, moment. After the double conjunction (*and then),* the second subject-noun (*state*) is left suspended on the end-stopped line, divided from its predicate by interruptive modification.

> **Like** to the **lark** at **break** of **day** a-**ris**-ing. . . .

As in the previous line, Shakespeare uses music to reinforce the rising thrust from the reversed foot: a dense collaboration of alliteration (Like-Lark), half-rhyme (liKe-larK-breaK) and long vowels (I-AH-AY-AY-I) gathers momentum, spills past the decasyllabic limit, delivers a triple rhyme, and this time is not contained by a punctuated end-stop. Instead, the right branching syntax pours down through the series of prepositions (to-at-of), their rising rhythm highlighting each monosyllabic noun (lark-break-day) in an irresistible extension past the line.

> **Like** to the **lark** at **break** of **day** a-**ris**-ing / from **sull**-en **earth**. . . .

The contract with the reader—that each line will be coincident to, consonant with, syntactical rhythm—has been broken, just as the simile provides the last delay, holding the reader off from the second predicate in the compound. Everything in the poem—the consistent end-stops, the emerging meter, the thickening texture of vowels and consonants, the sudden enjambment, and most particularly the long periodic sentence with its parallel and then interruptive modification—has conspired to deliver the strongest possible stress on the long-awaited verb and its object: *sings hymns.*

> **Like** to the **lark** at **break** of **day** a-**ris**-ing
> from **sull**-en **earth, sings hymns** at **Heav**-en's **gate**;

Aside from the formal resolution provided by the rhyme, return to end-stop, and now audible pattern of iambic pentameter, with its two characteristic variations (inverted initial foot and spondaic substitution), there is also great structural pleasure here, the rightness of closure provided by completion of the sentence at argument's end and fortune's reversal.

The couplet, then, its tag-rhymes echoing that last important (and rhymed) predicate (*sings-brings-kings*), serves as a kind of envoi, gathering all the previous effects into its right-branching subordinate syntax.

> For **thy sweet love** re-**mem**-ber'd **such wealth brings,**
> That **then** I **scorn** to **change** my **state** with **kings.**

Line 13 is characteristically Shakespearean, its two spondees balancing the line on the natural amphibrach (re-**mem**-ber'd), the first slowed by the two long vowels (**thy sweet love**), the second by mouth-gumming consonants **such wealth brings.** Again, variations yield to pattern, tension to resolution: line 14, with its perfectly exact iambic pentameter and perfectly idiomatic phrasing, is built with monosyllables, the stresses falling naturally on the key words of the clause, the negligible function words tossed to the side, in an ideal précis.

> **then scorn change state kings.**

According to Robert Frost:

> The surest way to reach the heart [of the reader] is through the ear. The visual images thrown up by a poem are important, but it is more important still to choose and arrange words in a sequence so as virtually to control the intonations and pauses of the reader's voice. By arrangement and choice of words on the part of the poet, the effects of humor, pathos, hysteria, anger, and in fact, all effects, can be indicated or obtained.

As a skilled dramatist, Shakespeare was a master of what Frost calls "sentence sound;" in Sonnet 29, it dominates meter and sweeps past the lineation exactly at the place in the poem where the speaker "Haply" thinks "on thee" and is swept into joy—the climactic moment in both the dramatic situation of this lyric and the "grand drama" of its composition. But other emotional "effects" can also be obtained when the line resists the rhythm of "the speaking voice" and sounds a counterpoint to it, as in the following poem by Donald Justice. Again, syntax structures the poem and gives it forward momentum—but within rhymed couplets closer to Frost's "crossed swords" than to Shakespeare's palimpsest, not a strict iambic or any other metrical foot but five syllables per line arranged into pairings of every metrical foot known to mankind and a two-line stanza most often consonant with the syntax but sometimes syncopated by it. The effect is something like jazz improvisation: predictability is foreclosed without loss of coherence.

TO THE HAWKS

McNamara, Rusk, Bundy

Farewell is the bell
Beginning to ring.

The children singing
Do not yet hear it.

The sun is shining
In their song. The sun

Is in fact shining
Upon the schoolyard,

On children swinging
Like tongues of a bell

Swung out on the long
Arc of a silence

That will not seem to
Have been a silence

Till it is broken
As it is breaking.

There is a sun now
Louder than the sun

Of which the children
Are singing, brighter,

Too, than that other
Against whose brightness

Their eyes seem caught in
The act of shutting.

The young schoolteacher,
Waving one arm in

Time to the music,
Is waving farewell.

> Her mouth is open
> To sound the alarm.
>
> The mouth of the world
> Grows round with the sound.
> —Justice

Competing patterns of music dominate this poem. It opens with a closed couplet, one line end-paused, one line end-stopped. The two dimeter lines have exactly matched metrical feet (iamb then anapest), and the halving of the line is reinforced by internal rhyme.

> Fare-**well** is the **bell**
> Be-gin-**ning** to **ring.**

This little marvel is followed by another closed, consonant, dimeter couplet.

> The **chil**-dren **sing**-ing
> Do **not** *yet* **hear** it.

In these two lines, also end-paused and then end-stopped, a slightly different metric is cloned by the use of feminine (unstressed) endings. Meanwhile, the two quite independent couplets have been linked, in lines 2 and 3, with end-rhyme and internal rhyme and linked to the next couplet as well.

> Begin**ning** to **ring** . . . The children **singing.** . . .
> The sun is shin**ing**
> In their song. The sun. . . .

But this new couplet is substantially different from the others and not only because it is open, not self-enclosed by sentence-end. This time, the metrical match is also linking, not self-enclosed: line 5, end-paused, is the same iamb and amphibrach of lines 3 and 4, but line 6 has an initial anapest and a caesura. The caesura creates the first midline pause in the poem, isolates one more key word, *sun,* and then lets the rhyming syllables loose into a startling mitosis, generating couplet after linked couplet down the page.

> sun is shining In song sun is in shining Upon school On children swinging tongues bell Swung on long silence will been silence Till is broken As is breaking.

There is an enormous amount of lexical repetition and rhyme in the rest of the poem, too. Of the poem's thirty-two lines, all but six end with a repeating or rhymed word; or, if we allow a liberal definition of rhyme for effects such as *seem to/music, brighter/brightness* and *schoolyard/ schoolteacher*, all but two: *hear it,* and *the world.* When we also factor in the internal rhyme, repeating words and alliteration (s, sh, sk, sw, b, br), it's hard to imagine a texture of consonants cohering more completely than this one, unless it's Hopkins.

So much formal pattern can paralyze a poem, but something else begins to happen with that anomalous third couplet. The wonderful initial symmetry is like those famous short opening phrases in Beethoven's Fifth. And you remember what happens there—the short chunks continue, but they are swept up into a bigger chunk, an overarching, longer phrase. So, too, in this poem. After his two perfectly matched declarative sentences, each two lines long, Justice double stitches with direct repetition (*The sun is shining, The sun is in fact shining*), ignores the syntactical integrity of both the line and the stanza, and follows the poem's shortest sentence (eight syllables) with the poem's longest (fifty-two syllables).

The sun is (in fact) shining [shining where?].
            Upon the schoolyard,
           On children [which children?]
                  Swinging like tongues [what kind of tongues?]
                  Of a bell [which bell?]
                      Swung out [swung out
where?]
                  On the long arc [which arc?]
                    Of a
silence . . .

Right-branching, unstoppable, alternating prepositional and participial phrases, the sentence barrels through the short lines, conscripts the small-scale rhythm as it wishes, creates at line 10 another open (though end-paused) couplet (*Like tongues of a bell*), and, at line 11, spills into the poem's first initial stress (*Swung*) and the first of two clear and violent enjambments (*the long / Arc of a silence, That will not seem to / Have been broken*).

Like Beethoven's exposition of his opening theme, this is a kind of runaway horse, the syntax right branching toward the poem's first restrictive clause (*That will not seem to / Have been broken*) and coming to rest on the poem's first compound: another subordinate clause, this one a closed couplet tightly "rhymed" by syntax, meter, direct repetition, and alliteration and placed exactly at the poem's halfway mark.

Till it is broken
As it is breaking.

Justice is also a composer of music and knows full well the arc created when a piece, as Jourdain says,

> wanders into unfamiliar territory then returns to momentary repose. Upon hearing this resolution, a brain groups the preceding notes, then readies itself to perceive the next progression. Lesser resolutions create lesser phrases that can be built into hierarchies of larger ones. (130–31)

This tight couplet is a "lesser resolution," a place to pause after that asymmetrical, hypotactic fourth sentence, completing the rushing repetition of the original key words (*sun, children, singing*) and metaphor (*bell, ring, singing, hear, song, tongues, bell, silence* and now *louder, singing*). Then the poem pushes off again into the secondary imagery (*shining, brighter, brightness, eyes*) in another rhyming set (*Louder, brighter, other, schoolteacher*). This happens in a new long right-branching sentence, and just think how many paratactic declaratives would be required for its literal translation.

> The children are singing about a sun. The children's eyes are shutting against its brightness. They seem caught in the act of doing so. Another sun [has appeared]. It is louder. It is brighter.

Instead, prepositions (*than, of, against*) introduce relative pronouns (*which, whose*) and subordinate clauses (*children are singing, their eyes seem caught*) in an elaborate mobile strung from the truly weak little bar of our common inversion, the expletive (*There is a sun*). This is fearless hypotaxis and compression. The sentence also wreaks several even more forceful variations in the line as it goes: most notably, the caesuras in lines 20 and 21 (*are singing, brighter, // too, than that other . . .*), and the enjambment of line 23, which violates the natural chunking of the idiom: *caught in // the act.*

But we've made the significant turn back to the barn—Justice is not interested, here, in an open-ended structure. Sentence 5 is forty syllables, shorter than the one preceding it, and will be halved by sentence 6 and then halved again. And sentence 6 will cause only one significant disturbance in the formal arrangements—after the clustered stresses, three of them now (*The **young schoolteach**-er, **Wa**-ving **one arm*** *in*), there is another violent enjambment, another idiomatic grammatical chunk (*in time*) divided across both line and stanza, the couplet awkwardly forced open, creating tension, which is resolved by the end of the sentence, the closing of the couplet, and the reintroduction of the poem's first word.

> The **young schoolteach**-er,
> Wa-ving **one arm** in
>
> **Time** to the **mu**-sic,
> Is **wa**-ving fare-**well**.

But even this degree of formal asymmetry is too much for Justice's classicism. Itself a bell, that word becomes a pivot in the final run of direct repetition and connective rhyme, as dense as the opening: waving / arm / waving / mouth /open /sound / alarm / mouth / grows round / sound. Closure then gets hammered down with tremendous finality in two closed couplets, two ten-syllable declarative sentences, four perfectly consonant lines that seem to reproduce—and rearrange—the poem's opening meter, syntactical chunks and balanced internal rhyme.

> Her mouth is o-pen
> To sound the a-larm.
>
> The mouth of the world
> Grows round with the sound.

The poem forms an enclosed loop, like the Greek symbol for infinity, an apt emblem for the lyric that stops time, the children, the teacher and the world all *caught in / the act* of one incomprehensible, world-destroying moment.

Meanwhile, it seems entirely accurate to say that in this poem its "two kinds of rhythm are not entirely at peace with one another" (Jourdain, 124), and therein lies its primary source of energetic formal tension. Justice avoids Frost's "crossed swords" of iambic, keeping instead a mathematically fixed but musically flexible grid: the pentasyllabic line length never varies, but within its constraint the dimeter possibilities are explored to their fullest. The objective seems to be pattern without boredom, asymmetry without incoherence—as was the case in a poetics from early last century, the "verse libere" that preceded "verse libre" (for a clear account, see Stephen Dobyns's essay in *Best Words, Best Order*): accentual-syllabic meter was not foresworn but subverted, no longer stable but among the moving parts, a fixed number of scannable feet (or, alternatively, accents or syllables) without predictable placement of stresses among unstressed syllables (as in "To the Hawks"). Or, in a simple alternative, a prominent foot without the predictable number of feet in the line, which one can find in Phillip Larkin's poem "Cut Grass." What Larkin does is establish a grid, or pulse, not with rigid meter but with iambs, spondees, and consonance between the line and the syntactical chunks. This divides the burden of cohesion between form and structure and allows an overall musical arc or phrasing: as the poem unfolds, what is encompassed by the line moves from independent clause to subordinate, from clause to prepositional phrase, from prepositional phrase to participial, from central syntactical significance to lesser.

> Cut Grass
> Cut grass lies frail:
> Brief is the breath
> Mown stalks exhale.
> Long, long the death
>
> It dies in the white hours
> Of young-leafed June
> With chestnut flowers,
> With hedges snowlike strewn,
>
> White lilac bowed,
> Lost lanes of Queen Anne's lace,
> And that high-builded cloud
> Moving at summer's pace.
> —Larkin

There are only two sentences in this Larkin poem. The first is made of paired independent clauses yoked by a colon. The first of those, one line long, is four syllables, a compressed simple declarative sentence, two adjectives (*cut* and *frail*) flanking the fundament, *grass* (subject) *lies* (predicate). The second clause also uses the same copula, or "linking" verb, *is,* but with its attached modification, line 3, it's twice as long. And this time, instead of the so-called normal or natural syntactical order, which puts the subject first in the sentence, it is "inverted": the subject of the sentence is actually *breath*.

Why would Larkin want to do this, other than for the pleasure of that small-scale variation, a way to make line 2 a little different from line 1, just as good musicians never play repeated notes at exactly the same dynamic? Perhaps he is thinking about his *next* move. His two sentences will be vastly different in length. In order to tether that centrifugal energy, he needs pattern, some similarities between the two, a centripetal force to help the rhyme scheme hold this small lyric together. But those similarities cannot be obvious (since Larkin is never obvious) or boring (Larkin is never boring). And short, simple, declarative sentences in normal order carry both the great advantage of extreme clarity and the great risk of boring predictability. By inverting the fundamental subject and its predicate adjective in the second and third independent clauses (lines 2 and 4), he creates a subtle similarity, which is then reinforced formally, by the lineation: all four lines in the first stanza can begin with an adjective.

And those adjectives are exactly syntactically parallel in lines 1 and 3 (*cut grass, mown stalks*) and lines 2 and 4 (*brief* and *long*), "rhyming" the lines syntactically at their heads, as well as literally at their ends. Meanwhile, too, lines 1 and 3 are end-stopped by punctuation. Line 2 isn't punctuated, but it's what I call end-paused: the line "break" appears at a natural division in the syntax between the independent and the restrictive clauses. And this is just a temporary stay: the sentence completes itself in the very next line within the rhymed and metered stanza.

Which brings us back to a better reason for the inversion at line 2: it allows an even more radical inversion in its parallel line, line 4, a clause that not only reverses subject and linked modifier but leaves the link out altogether. So syntactically weak, the little copula, so unworthy of utterance. And the pattern implies it clearly enough. Unbeknownst to you, your brain is inferring this actual grammatical clause, with its curiously transitive subordinate verb: *The death that cut grass dies is long.* Larkin is free to repeat the adjective, delay the subject, elide the predicate, and supply modification far too long and elaborate—the rest of the poem—ever to have been jammed in between subject and weak verb in normal order.

These particular syntactical choices—parallelism, inversion, and elision—have helped to make what seems to me one of the most perfect stanzas in the English language. In a mere sixteen syllables, he gives us four clauses, the syntactical unit of greatest integrity, all of them matched by adjective placement, all of them exactly the same length (four syllables); three of them independent, thus syntactically powerful; two of those paired by inversion. Meanwhile, there is masterful small-scale music: the fabric of monosyllables, the full, masculine rhyme, the dense alliteration of *L* and *S* and *B* sounds, and the meter, which is both steady and subtly varied. That compressed opening line encloses four stresses in a row.

Cut grass lies frail. . . .

In other words, two spondees. Line 2 is framed by alliterated stresses.

Brief is the **breath.** . . .

Falling and then rising, a trochee and an iamb. Line 3 is akin to both.

Mown stalks ex-**hale**

has the initial spondee of line one, but the closing iamb of line 4. And this arrangement is then repeated,

Long, long the **death** . . . ,

to form the default position: torqued iambic, each line front-loaded. Pattern, then, in the strict four-syllable, two-foot line, but subtle variation to the pattern, too, in how the stresses are distributed.

But here's what makes the stanza perfect in my mind: all that pattern, embedded in the syntax, dimeter, and rhyme, is overturned by an enormous asymmetry: the tightly unified stanza itself is incomplete, open-ended, unbalanced. A restrictive clause makes its noun specific, "restricts" its meaning. The death in line 4 is a particular death, the one that "cut grass" dies, but we have to go across the stanzaic divide to fetch up that limiting modification. This move is a syntactical match to what immediately preceded it, the first sentence, which also ended on a restrictive clause, but, whereas that first restrictive clause encompassed a mere four syllables—*mown stalks exhale*—this one will span two stanzas and forty-four syllables. Nothing in the symmetrical, balanced, patterned, compressed first three lines has prepared us for this second sentence, which is going to blow dimeter right out of the water.

The linguistic principle at work is a common one in English: what the linguists call right branching (for a clear, accessible account, see Steven Pinker, *The Language Instinct*). That image of a gravity-defying tree is borne out here in Larkin's highly asymmetrical second sentence. Its precariousness becomes even more apparent if you think of right-branching syntax as a mobile: the fundament, subject and predicate, provides the bar from which is hung a modifier, a word or a phrase, and from that modifier another and another and so on. Larkin's is an especially precarious mobile because it hangs not from the fundament (which has, after all, an elided predicate) but one rung down, from that restrictive (i.e., subordinate) clause, and combines right branching with more of the parallelism that opened the poem.

> The death [that] it dies
> *In* the white hours
> *Of* young-leafed June,
> *with* chestnut flowers,
> *with* hedges snowlike strewn,
> [with] white lilac bowed,
> [with] lost lanes of Queen Anne's lace,
> and [with] that high-builded cloud
> moving *at* summer's pace.

Larkin is terribly sly here. With so many prepositions tethered to different spots in the restrictive clause, and some of them placed at the head of the line, some of them elided, each of their phrases punctuated, literally or by end-pause, and the last of them dangling not from the subordinate predicate but from a participle (*moving*), it's easy to misperceive the referents. The five "withs" belong not to the proximate noun (June), even though the return to dimeter for two lines would have us think so (Of **young-leaf**'d **June** / With **chest**nut **flow**ers). Rather, these parallel phrases are adverbial, attached to the verb: *chestnut flowers, hedges, lilac, Queen Anne's lace,* and *cloud* are all also dying alongside the *mown stalks.*

He didn't leave out those "withs" to confuse us. We're not confused: again, parallelism in the syntax and in the lines implies what is missing. And elision has allowed him to correct the potential boredom of that list, a small-scale variation. It also gives him, in stanza 3, some stabilizing similarities to stanza 1: adjective-noun at the head of the line (*Cut grass, mown stalks, white lilac, lost lanes*); a return to the default metrical pattern, spondee and iamb (*White lilac bowed*); and another initial spondee, *Lost lanes,* "rhymed" by alliteration to the earlier *Long, long.* These echoes restore pattern, though not enough, even with the rhyme scheme, to overtake the galloping syntax. Syntax stays in charge of what musicologists call large-scale phrasing, conscripting the line to parse the chunks and the stanza to organize them, hurtling toward the final elaboration of the cloud, the "briefest" (shortest-lived) item in the list.

This arrangement—this architecture—is the essential drama of the poem's composition, as well as the source of the dynamic shift in tone from the clipped disinterest of the opening to the final notes of ennui: syntax orchestrates that inexorable movement. Larkin knows this: he is willing to loosen his meter, alternating dimeter and trimeter lines, but

he consistently reinforces the syntax by keeping the lines consonant
with it, helping us parse the sentence as it opens out. Or, rather, opens
UP: the camera that had focused down at the beginning of the poem,
onto the grass at our feet, now points upward, accusingly it seems to
me, at the sky.

Syntax in charge: the influence of the great dramatist on our poetry
has been indelible. Despite historic periods and individual aesthetics
that would keep metrical patterns strict and primary, syntax-driven
enjambment increased and prospered from Milton forward and
increasingly led to uncommon strategies in order to maintain a
dynamic relationship between poetry's two rhythmic systems, syntax
and line. What disorients us in "Cut Grass" is how one metrical pattern
is so quickly crowded out by another pattern, the poet sowing discord
within the formal arrangement, casting iamb against spondee, two-foot
against three-foot line.

But Larkin's arrangement is hardly revolutionary: if one seeks a
complicated syntax, then an iambic pulse set in consonant lines of varying length proved a useful choice, "freeing" the line from small-scale
musical phrasing in order that it parse or punctuate the sentences. The
opening of Eliot's "Ash-Wednesday" provides a fine example, accompanied here by Donald Davie's persuasive commentary.

1. Because I do not hope to turn again
2. Because I do not hope
3. Because I do not hope to turn
4. Desiring this man's gift and that man's scope
5. I no longer strive to strive towards such things
6. (Why should the aged eagle stretch its wings?)
7. Why should I mourn
8. The vanished power of the usual reign?
9. Because I do not hope to know again
10. The infirm glory of the positive hour
11. Because I do not think
12. Because I know I shall not know
13. The one veritable transitory power
14. Because I cannot drink
15. There, where trees flower, and springs flow, for there is
    nothing again.
    Now if we compare lines 8, 10 and 13, it will be
    observed that 10 and 13 are tied together by an end-
    rhyme, but that 8 and 10 are tied together no less closely
    by similarity of grammar. What we have here, in fact, is a

sort of parity of esteem between rhyme and metre and grammar or syntax. Every line in the second section, except for the last of all, "rhymes" with some one or more lines in the first section. Thus 9 is linked with 8 by end-rhyme, but . . . 10 no less "rhymes" with 8 by virtue of grammar. 11 rhymes by syntax with 2. 12 rhymes with 3 by virtue of metre and a certain syntactical similarity, but also by syntax with 5 ("Know I shall not know" echoing "strive to strive"). 13 rhymes through 10 with 8. And 14 rhymes, by meter and syntax, with 2. (*Articulate Energy*, 91)

Eliot's use of iambs should be strict enough to satisfy even Frost, more constant in these fifteen lines than in the fourteen lines of Shakespeare's Sonnet 29. It is the *number* of iambic feet in a given line that shifts, allowing or resisting or flirting with the expected pentameter, even as markers (here, end-stop, end-pause, and anaphora) chunk what Jourdain would call a "torrent of notes" in the periodic sentence and sentence fragment, enabling our perception of the "complex hierarchies" Davie has analyzed. The "ghost of meter" is no more apparent than the time signature—the musical meter, the "measured rhythm"— in one of Debussy's Preludes.

With lines so consonant with the syntax, so thoroughly end-paused if not end-stopped, Eliot's poem seems a close cousin to the open-form Lawrence and Kunitz poems I discussed earlier—there is the same "parity of esteem" among syntactical chunks, ample lexical repetition and anaphora, varying line lengths. The chief formal difference between them is that Lawrence and Kunitz avoid altogether any sort of metrical pulse in the line, any recurrent placement of stress among unstressed syllables, and avoid even its "ghost." But "breaking the back of the iamb," as Pound had it, to open the way for more variable rhythms, employed a weapon with a distinguished history in English-language poetry: syntactical rhythm more powerful than the smaller-scale pattern of the line. The new, open-form prosody simply looked with greater and greater boldness toward ways in which large-scale rhythm could be released entirely from a "grid," from "repetitive, evenly paced accentuations of measured rhythm," and, like vocal phrasing in music, build a succession of irregular sonic shapes that combine in various ways like the parts of a painting, sometimes hanging in exquisite balance, sometimes joining forces to gyrate or plunge or swirl (Jourdain, 122–23).

NOTE

This essay continues the examination of syntax in English-language poetry begun in "Rhythm of Thought, Rhythm of Song," published in the *Kenyon Review* 25, no. 1 (winter 2003).

CARL DENNIS

The Temporal Lyric

Although we often contrast the lyric with the narrative poem, within the lyric itself one may distinguish two kinds of structure, one temporal, one not. Both kinds of poems may be said to be plotted, with a rationale for the sequence of parts, but the nontemporal plot involves the amplification and intensification of a single state of mind while the temporal plot presents a psychological development in which the speaker reaches a position by the end of the poem different from the one he or she occupies in the beginning. Readers and writers need to keep these two kinds of lyrics distinct. Writing out of a romantic or postromantic position, we are likely to view all poems as the history of a poet's experience in "the vale of soul-making" and so are liable to force temporal readings on poems that are essentially exclamatory or argumentative. We tend to assume that all movement has to be psychological, that the speaker, like the main character in a novel, has to change in order to be convincing. But this is to disparage a rhetorical focus that concentrates on defining or persuading, a focus that includes most of the lyrics that have been written, including, in all likelihood, most of our own. The point of dwelling on the distinction is not to suggest that the two forms are antagonistic, for they often overlap, but to be in a better position to appreciate the tension that is created when the two modes are brought into dialogue.

Although lyrics are more likely to be organized rhetorically, especially those that present arguments, are much more common than those that present psychological narratives, discussion of the lyric has suffered from the fact that the oldest and most influential piece of criticism of poetry in the West, Aristotle's *Poetics,* is formulated with specific reference not to lyric poetry but to drama and to epic and so presents temporal plotting as the central element of the poem. The poem relates to the world to the extent that it performs a mimesis, or imitation, and what is imitated is a temporal action. Tragedy (Aristotle contends) is an imitation not of men, as such, but of action and life, of happiness and misery. And happiness and misery are not states of being but forms of activity.

In response to this formulation, the writer of poems that are not narratives must either reject the notion of imitation, and leave uncertain the connection between the poem and the world, or enlarge the notion of plot to include other definitions than a causal sequence of events over time. One of the most successful contemporary attempts in the direction of expansion comes out of speech-act theory. Here the poem is regarded as a dramatic event in which a fictive speaker performs a speech act that gives specific embodiment, in a particular context, to one or more of the basic tasks that we ask ordinary language to perform—explaining, questioning, demanding, promising, apologizing, praising, castigating, pleading, and the like. Each one of these acts has its particular plot if we use the term to refer not to a sequence of temporal events but to a sequence of rhetorical moves that carry out the task that the specific function requires. Such a completed action possesses the wholeness that Aristotle demands of a poem: it possesses a proper beginning, middle, and an end, the order of incidents being such that transposing or removing any one of them will disorder the whole.

I want first to examine a poem in terms of this rhetorical notion of plot and then look at some nonnarrative poems in which time seems to play a more significant role. For my example of the poem as speech act, I choose one familiar to most students of the lyric in English, Marvell's "To His Coy Mistress."

Had we but world enough, and time,
This coyness, lady, were no crime.
We would sit down, and think which way
To walk, and pass our long love's day.
Thou by the Indian Ganges' side
Should'st rubies find; I by the tide
Of Humber would complain. I would
Love you ten years before the flood,
And you should, if you please, refuse
Till the conversion of the Jews.
My vegetable love should grow
Vaster than empires and more slow;
An hundred years should go to praise
Thine eyes, and on thy forehead gaze;
Two hundred to adore each breast,
But thirty thousand to the rest;
An age at least to every part,
And the last age should show your heart.
For, lady, you deserve this state
Nor would I love at lower rate.

But at my back I always hear
Time's winged chariot hurrying near;
And yonder all before us lie
Deserts of vast eternity.
Thy beauty shall no more be found
Nor, in thy marble vault, shall sound
My echoing song; then worms shall try
That long-preserved virginity,
And your quaint honor turn to dust,
And into ashes all my lust.
The grave's a fine and private place
But none, I think, do there embrace.

Now therefore, while the youthful hue
Sits on thy skin like morning dew,
And while thy willing soul transpires
At every pore with instant fires,
Now let us sport us while we may,
And now, like amorous birds of prey,
Rather at once our time devour
Than languages in his slow-chapped power.
Let us roll all our strength and all
Our sweetness up into one ball,
And tear our pleasures with rough strife
Thorough the iron gates of life:
Thus, though we cannot make our sun
Stand still, yet we will make him run.

The speech act that is dramatized here is a plea, an appeal to the lady to give up her coyness, which is structured obviously not as a narrative but as an argument, as a syllogism, with a major premise, a minor premise, and a conclusion.

If we had world enough and time
This coyness were no crime.
We don't have world enough and time.
This coyness is a crime.

This sequence of propositions is unsound, of course, in terms of formal logic, because denying the truth of the first premise does not necessarily prove the conclusion false. There may be other reasons for the lady's coyness besides the presumption of unlimited time. But the argument does have the force and feel of logic because is exposes as inaccurate what may be the lady's chief objection to yielding to the speaker. The poem is successful because it gives its conventional carpe-diem movement a fresh, dramatic enactment, with a distinctive richness of tone and range of reference. With respect to tone, we can trace a shifting mixture of tenderness and mockery, wittiness and earnestness, as the argument advances. These shifts are intrinsic to what we may call the plot of the poem if we regard the plot not as a narrative of shifting states of feeling but as the unfolding of a fixed rhetorical strategy. So in the first stanza, which presents the unthreatened realm of wish, the tone is playfully tender. The witty exaggeration gently mocks the lady's reserve, but the mockery is directed less to her wish for formal courtship that to her expectation that this wish can be embodied in the actual world where love must find expression. The lady does deserve the ceremony, and the lover would be willing to provide it if he lived in a timeless, golden world, and this willingness is exemplified in the very elaborateness of his description of the courtship that he can't offer. If the world offered itself as a stage set for the play of love, he would have no trouble extending the play for millennia, not to humor the lady's wishes but to do justice to her worth and the feelings within him that her worth inspires. When the lover turns in the second stanza to describing the hostile, devouring world that their love must actually face, his tone becomes harsher. Dropping any attempt to spare her delicacy, he offers the brutal comparison of the feasting of worms on the lady's body to the violation of a multiple rape. And in the third stanza, when the lover presents the possibility of satisfying a more limited courtship in the moment, the tone becomes realistically encouraging, as he speaks of a love that makes up in intensity what it loses in ceremony. Although the wish for a leisurely ideal can't be fulfilled, the lovers have a chance to fashion a plainer and harsher beauty if they realize they must fight for their joys rather than expecting time to provide them. The amorous birds of prey are both beautiful and aggressive as they tear their pleasures through the bars of their cage.

The same point about the tonal shifts here can be made about the shifts in frame of reference. They are not meant to suggest a shift in perspective on the part of the speaker, merely a shift in strategy as the argument develops. The golden age courtship of the first stanza is associated not only with images of the pastoral and the classical golden age but with the Christian scheme of time extending from Genesis to the Second Coming so that the denial of endless time and space in the second stanza implies a denial of the validity of religious belief. The lovers in the world of time must live unsustained by any faith that might make time purposeful and redemptive. They have nothing to look forward to but "deserts of vast eternity," a crushing emptiness that turns values into dust and annihilates the spirit. And the chariot of the sun, in the last stanza, while more mythically exalted than the empty desert, still suggests that much of the human wish for meaning and purpose will never be realized. This evoking and dismissal of traditions is clearly not a temporal one. The speaker does not move through them and find them wanting as he gropes toward some final limited affirmation. He knows at the beginning of the poem what hopes are foolish and what are realistic, what systems of belief are available and what are superannuated, and is trying through his argument to bring the lady into agreement with his position about the necessity of giving time a run for its money.

Marvell's poem, then, is example of a speech act. It has a plot but not a temporal narrative. Its overtly argumentative structure is part of a post-Elizabethan inheritance that attempts to give the love lyric more vigor and personality. But in the same era we find poems that are focused inward, not outward, which turn from argument to the juxtaposition of opposed feeling states, and in this kind of poem the question of temporal development is more difficult to answer. Consider this well-known Holy Sonnet by John Donne.

> At the round earth's imagined corners, blow
> Your trumpets, angels; and arise, arise
> From death, you numberless infinities
> Of souls, and to your scattered bodies go;
> All whom the flood did, and fire shall, o'erthrow,
> All whom war, dearth, age, agues, tyrannies,
> Despair, law, chance hath slain, and you whose eyes
> Shall behold God, and never taste death's woe.
> But let them sleep, Lord, and me mourn a space;
> For, if above all these, my sins abound,
> T' late to ask abundance of Thy grace
> When we are there. Here on this lowly ground,
> Tech me how to repent; for that's as good
> As if Thou had'st sealed my pardon with Thy blood.

Approaching the poem as we did Marvell's, as the performance of a speech act, we can call it a double prayer that expresses contradictory wishes, the wish for immediate contact expressed in the octet of the sonnet, calling for the last judgment to come at once, and the canceling of that wish in the sestet by the speaker's request for more time to prepare his soul before he meets his maker face to face. We can say that the poem enacts the double feelings of the Christian believer, eagerness for contact with God and hesitation about the state of his or her own worthiness. And we can give names to the parts of the self in conflict.

The press for immediate contact expresses the impulses of the heart, of religious emotions, and the hesitation expresses the prudence of right reason that places emotional needs in a larger context. The contrast between these two voices is insisted on by the prosody. The imperative prayer of the feelings boldly issues commands to the angels and the dead with a kind of breakneck rush that can't be bothered, in its breathlessness, to pause at the ends of lines and bunches its stresses for greater emphasis, as opposed to the calmer speech of right reason with its longer periods and quieter, regular iambics.

In this reading, the structure is rhetorical, not temporal. The double prayer is interpreted not as a sequence in time but as a way of dramatizing the static condition of religious ambivalence. But a post-romantic critic looking for temporal plotting might argue that sequence here is crucial, that the poem is about having second thoughts after first thoughts, how reflection comes to modify impulse. This position has more weight behind it than it does when it is applied to Marvell's poem, for we seem to be witnessing the poet learning something in the course of the poem. Rather than proving a point to a listener, like Marvell's speaker, the speaker in the last part of this poem critiques his initial imperatives as premature, to be postponed until he has gone through a long process of repentance. And the shift is perhaps set in motion by the mention of the word *death* at the end of the octet, allowing us to imagine a momentum of unspoken thought that leads to the shift in the next line. Still, if we focus on the stated not the implied, we have to say that this narrative sequence consists of a beginning and an end but not a middle, that it foregrounds dramatic juxtaposition, not temporal process. And this kind of reversal is built into the notion of the *volta,* or turn, which is inherent in the genre of the poem, the Italian sonnet. To some degree, then, the shift can be anticipated from the beginning rather than understood as discovered only as the poem develops. And this beginning, in particular, suggests by its very extravagance that it's only a half wish, not a full one, an extravagance underscored in the first line by the reference to the "round world's imagined corners," which comments on the fictiveness of the figure even as the speaker issues his commands. All this artfulness makes us feel that we are not so much reading a poem that enacts a change over time as witnessing a ritualistic performance of a religious dialogue.

Now I want to jump ahead about 230 years to a poem by Emily Dickinson that also works on a stark juxtaposition of attitudes, though one in which plot, I would argue, may be thought of in temporal terms as well as rhetorical.

These are the days when Birds come back—
A very few—a Bird or two—
To take a backward look.

These are the days when skies resume
The old—old sophistries of June—
A blue and gold mistake.

Oh fraud that cannot cheat the Bee—
Almost thy plausibility
Induces my belief.

Till ranks of seeds their witness bear—
And softly thro' the altered air
Hurries a timid leaf.

Oh Sacrament of summer days,
Oh Last Communion in the Haze—
Permit a child to join.

Thy sacred emblems to partake—
Thy consecrated bread to take
And thine immortal wine!

The poem takes two very different attitudes toward Indian summer, the sudden, brief spell of summery weather in late fall. The first four stanzas read the season as a misleading omen of the return of spring, a "sophistry" that the return of cold weather soon exposes as false. And the last two read the season symbolically as a final opportunity for contact with the life of the spirit before the natural death that comes with winter. In some ways, this shift is even more radically discontinuous than the shift in Donne's poem. Whereas Donne's speaker presents contrasting phases of a single religious longing, Dickinson's speaker shifts from secular prudence to religious conviction. After dismissing the season as a false promise of summer, it makes a leap of faith that reads it as a true promise of life, endowing it with the potency of the sacrament of the Last Supper. One can't call this sudden assertion of faith conventionally Christian, for it seems to imply that transcendence may be reached through a love of beauty sufficiently intense, not through submission to the God of the Bible. But, to the extent that its bread is consecrated and its wine immortal, this natural sacrament seems to hold out the promise of some super-natural validation.

The discontinuity between the two parts of the poem suggests that it should be read as a speech act, with a rhetorical plot, not a temporal one. The first four stanzas may be read as the foil for the final the two stanzas. The initial enactment of skeptical objections to trusting the season gives credence to speaker's closing assertion of belief. We can't dismiss this assertion as the voice of naive innocence because the poet has already passed through experience and found it wanting. We are made to feel that the conclusion comes not from a failure to consider alternatives but from some deeper level of response. The knowing adult chooses to become a child, not the ignorant natural child but the enlightened spiritual child who embodies the speaker's deepest convictions.

But, if the poem has a rhetorical plot, it may also be argued that it takes place in time, perhaps more fully than Johnson's poem. The sudden shift from the fourth to the fifth stanza is anticipated by a shift from the second stanza to the third, a shift that suggests the poet's deepening emotional engagement. In the first two stanzas, the speaker is detached and dismissive. The returning bird is taken in by the season, but the shrewd poet isn't, and her skepticism applies not simply to the season but the spring that the season imitates. June seemed to claim it would last forever, but it turned out to be only pretending, sophistic in its evidence. But in the second two stanzas the poet drops her distant tone and expresses not critical detachment but pained disappointment, suddenly addressing the season directly in the second person, castigating it for its fraudulent beauty, so piercing that for a moment it caused her to believe in its promise despite all she knows. Now, instead of contrasting her knowing distance to the naïveté of birds, she contrasts her eagerness to be deceived to the shrewdness of the bee, who cannot be taken in, so that she has to be taught again the hard way as the season begins to move off. The poem, then, doesn't simply juxtapose unbelief to belief but moves from neutral disbelief to the frustrated wish to believe, to fulfilled wish. The exclamation "Oh fraud," which seems rhetorically opposed to "Oh Sacrament," turns out to occur midway in an emotional plot in which wish wins out over fact. The leap near the end is still great, but the poem can be seen to have not only a beginning and an end but the makings of a middle. It enacts a resistance to the flow of time by a leap of faith, but that resistance has a plot that can be understood as taking place before us in time in the successive shifts of feeling, from guarded dismissal to hurt accusation to emotional engagement with an Indian summer reconceived as a symbolic promise.

Dickinson's immediate model for the lyric poem that develops temporally was the English romantics, especially Wordsworth and Coleridge, with their many poems that present the poet in a particular setting undergoing an experience that changes his perspective. So in Wordsworth's "Resolution and Independence" the outward plot of an encounter with the leech gatherer is parallel to a psychological plot in which a mood of apprehension gives way to a mood of confidence as the speaker's imagination uses the leech gatherer as a catalyst to activate its own healing powers. In Dickinson's poem, the action is rooted in a particular response to a literal landscape, unlike the poems by Marvell and Donne, but here there is no outward event that triggers the change of perspective. The poet is moved to a different relation to the season simply through the pressure of emotional need. And this sense of pressure is intensified by presenting the change as occurring in the present moment. We can find a model for this present-tense plotting in Coleridge's conversation poems, though in them the mind of the speaker is calm, free to idle and drift as it moves by association from the immediate moment to other scenes and other times and so return by the end with a larger perspective than it had at the outset. Whether the plot is set in the past or present, the romantic poets provide a new model of structure that permits a variety of perspectives to enter the poem not as part of an atemporal dialogue but as successive stages in the mind of a single listener, and they lead to poems in America such as Whitman's "Drum Taps," a grand narrative of psychic change as the poet redefines his relation to the Civil War, as the drumbeating patriot of the opening sections gives way to the wound dresser, a mother substitute for the dying soldiers on both sides of the conflict. But such grand narratives are much less common than the kind of modest and quiet temporal plotting that occurs within more traditional lyrics, providing enough space for the speaker to make some subtle adjustments.

I want to conclude by looking at two poems in which the temporal development is more obvious than it is in Dickinson's poem, one by a younger contemporary of Dickinson, Frederick Goddard Tuckerman, and one by Elizabeth Bishop. Here is a strange and haunting sonnet by Tuckerman.

> An upper chamber in a darkened house,
> Where, ere his footsteps reached ripe manhood's brink,
> Terror and anguish were his lot to drink;
> I cannot rid the thought nor hold it close
> But dimly dream upon the man alone:
> Now though the autumn clouds most softly pass,
> The cricket chides beneath the doorstep stone
> And greener than the season grows the grass.
> Nor can I drop my lids nor shade my brows,
> But there he stands beside the lifted sash;
> And with a swooning of the heart, I think

Where the black shingles slope to meet the boughs,
And, shattered on the roof like smallest snows,
The tiny petals of the mountain ash.

This is mysterious poem about a man who seems to have lived near the speaker but whom the speaker never seems to have met, someone whose misfortunes the speaker has heard about from others. The man's story seems to haunt the speaker. He can't "rid" himself of its power. But he can't "hold it close" because, presumably, the details he knows are so sketchy and the man's experience is so different from his own. In terms of speech-act theory, we can understand the poem as one of definition, the precise description of a complicated feeling, here a midregion of frustrated engagement in which the poet is reduced to "dimly dreaming" of someone he wishes he could have known more clearly. Or at least this formulation describes the poet's position in the first five lines. In the lines that remain, however, he moves from accepting his distance to breaking through it. This movement seems to begin at the end of the octet in the description of the oddity of the weather.

> Now though the autumn clouds most softly pass,
> The cricket chides beneath the doorstep stone
> And greener than the season grows the grass.

These signs of summer in the midst of fall seem to provide a more positive description of the speaker's middle state than the one in the early lines. The summer weather in fall here suggests more of an opportunity for appreciation than simple frustration. And this opportunity is taken advantage of in the lines that follow as the poet's imagination works to close the gap between him and the mysterious tenant. First, he summons the image man of the man he never saw in actual life, making him a living presence.

> Nor can I drop my lids nor shade my brows,
> But there he stands beside the lifted sash.

And then, with a further effort of the imagination, he manages to enter the mind of the dead stranger to look through his eyes at the scene outside his window.

> And with a swooning of the heart, I think
> Where the black shingles slope to meet the boughs,

And, shattered on the roof like smallest snows,
The tiny petals of the mountain ash.

What does the poet imagine the man seeing from his window? A scene
in spring with the petals of the mountain ash sprinkled on the roof, but
which looks to the man, the poet imagines, like snowflakes. Writing in
a fall that feels like summer, the poet uses his imagination to understand
the sad stranger as a man whose spring feels like winter. This haunting
image, which converts beauty into harshness, a shedding of spring blos-
soms into a winter shattering, shows how far the poet has moved from
the opening, how much psychological space he has crossed in a narrative of increasing empathy.

We can see a more complicated example of a descriptive poem
with a narrative development in Elizabeth Bishop's "The Fish."

> I caught a tremendous fish
> and held him beside the boat
> half out of the water, with my hook
> fast in a corner of his mouth.
> He didn't fight.
> He hadn't fought at all.
> He hung a grunting weight,
> battered and venerable
> and homely. Here and there
> his brown skin hung in strips
> like ancient wallpaper,
> and its pattern of darker brown
> was like wallpaper:
> shapes like full-blown roses
> stained and lost through age.
> He was speckled with barnacles,
> fine rosettes of lime,
> and infested
> with tiny white sea-lice,
> and underneath two or three
> rags of green weed hung down.
> While his gills were breathing in
> the terrible oxygen
> —the frightening gill,
> fresh and crisp with blood,
> that can cut so badly—
> I thought of the coarse white flesh
> packed in like feathers,
> the big bones and the little bones,

the dramatic reds and blacks
of his shiny entrails,
and the pink swim-bladder
like a big peony.
I looked into his eyes
which far larger than mine
but shallower, and yellowed,
the irises backed and packed
with tarnished tinfoil,
seen through the lenses
of old scratched isinglass.
They lifted a little, but not
to return my stare.
—It was more like the tipping
of an object toward the light.
I admired his sullen face,
the mechanism of his jaw,
and then I saw
that from his lower lip
—if you could call lit a lip—
grim, wet, and weapon like,
hung five old pieces of fish-line,
or four and a wire leader
with the swivel still attached,
with all their five big hooks
grown firmly in his mouth.
A green line, frayed at the end
when he broke it, two heavier lines,
with a fine black thread
still crimped from the strain and snap
when it broke and he got away.
Like medals with their ribbons
frayed and wavering,
a five-haired beard of wisdom
trailing from his aching jaw.
I stared and stared
and victory filled up
the little rented boat,
from the pool of bilge
where oil had spread a rainbow
around the rusted engine
to the bailer rusted orange,
the sun-cracked thwarts,
the oarlocks on their strings,
the gunnels—until everything

was rainbow, rainbow, rainbow!
And I let the fish go.

Though there is an action at the beginning of this poem, "I caught a tremendous fish," and an action at the end, "I let the fish go," the poem is primarily engaged with description. If we want to find out why the speaker lets the fish go we have to understand the description as a form of activity that has a direction so that the outward action at the end objectifies what has occurred within the mind of the speaker during the act of describing. The proximate cause is the poet's observing, toward the end of the description, the broken fish lines dangling from the fish's mouth, which she reads in human terms first as battle medals and then as "a five-haired beard of wisdom" in a jaw that she imagines sympathetically as still aching. The victory that fills up the boat, it seems, is at least partly the victory represented by the fish's endurance, and the oil rainbow is part of the blessing she wants to confer on the fish, a homely blessing that befits her "little rented boat." But the full plot of the poem doesn't become clear until we ask what is going on in the first forty-five lines of description, which concentrate not on understanding the fish in moral terms but on trying to bring it before us as precisely and objectively as possible. The description is full of figures, but they are not figures that make human connections. They insist on the otherness of the fish, with its wallpaper skin, white flesh like feathers, tinfoil irises, and peony swim bladder. And the details seem chosen, in fact, to insist on its strangeness, not familiarity—skin in strips and speckled with barnacles, gills blood engorged and sharp-edged—a strangeness that intensifies as she looks at the face, at least at first, and focuses on the eyes.

> I looked into his eyes
> which were larger than mine,
> but shallower, and yellowed,
> the irises backed and packed
> with tarnished tinfoil
> seen through the lenses
> of old scratched isinglass.
> They shifted a little, but not
> to return my stare.

Why does the speaker give so much attention to the otherness of the fish before she reads the fish in human terms? I think we can give two answers, depending on whether we see the poem as a speech act or a temporal event. As a speech act, we can say that in order for the final reading to convince us, to feel not like easy personification, a fanciful projection of the poet unto the fish, we have to be made to believe she can see the fish objectively. The initial description establishes the credentials of the speaker as someone who has the time and intention to look at the fish as it really is so that the final description is felt as genuine discovery, not projection. As a temporal event, on the other hand, we can say that there is a causal relation, not only a rhetorical one, between the first seeing and the second. She cannot see the fish in human terms without first seeing the fish as a thing apart. The objective seeing, the patient anatomy that the speaker is willing to carry through, from outside to inside, from head to tail, leads her in the course of the poem to an act of discovery that allows her to see the fish more intimately. Only after she is honest about the difference can the likeness become evident to her.

In this reading, the most important line in the poem is "and then I saw," with the implication not merely of temporal sequence but of causality: "Because I saw all this, I was enabled to see more." And this temporal movement gives added meaning to the victory at the end of the poem. It is not only the fish that is victorious. The poet to achieves a victory in understanding the fish's human significance. Catching the fish was easy. What is harder is catching the implications of the fish, and these she does catch by the end of the poem so that the homely rainbow is an insignia of her own success. In the course of the poem's narrative, the poet wins her own medals. This temporal structure does not override the rhetorical importance of the opening description as a means of establishing the speaker's credibility, but it does add a narrative layer to the speech act of description. The drama of the poem can be best appreciated if we keep the differences between the two kinds of plotting firmly in mind.

CHRIS FORHAN

When I Say "I"

Poets' Use of the First Person

At a writers' conference a few years back, a poet of some repute complained about the habit we have gotten into of referring to a poem's "speaker." "'Speaker' isn't quite right," he argued. "There has to be a better term." If he knew what that term is, he wasn't saying, but many contemporary poets share his discomfort. Is a poem always "speaking," exactly? Might we be more accurate, in some cases, to refer to the poem's "thinker"? Its "feeler"? Its "nervous system"? And is the voice of the poem necessarily a singular, identifiable voice? Maybe we should talk about the poem's "center of attention."

If we are evasive on this matter, however, it is a necessary evasiveness, especially when we are talking about a first-person poem that works—that moves and haunts us. The "I" in such a poem is essentially unknowable or at least incompletely knowable.

When I write a poem that uses the first-person singular, I hardly ever feel that I am referring to myself, exactly. In fact, part of what compels me to finish the poem is that I want to be surprised by what is on the mind of this "I"; I want to try to figure out who this "I" might be. The poem becomes a record of this attempt, and, if the poem is successful, the attempt at least partially fails. Still, whatever self the "I" refers to is real. It exists in the poem but not only in the poem. It is constructed by the language, but I recognize it from elsewhere. I've met it while walking down a darkened, vacant street; I've met it in a restaurant, invisible in the empty seat beside me; I've met it in dreams.

We know what recent language theory would say about this. Deconstruction sees a gap between word and meaning, an imprecise relationship between signifier and signified. Thus, it is questionable whether we can read a lyric poem as the expression of a coherent "I." A poem is not spoken but written, and to write is to give control over to language, which doubles or erases its meanings as it goes, the self's intentions be damned.

But if the self that a poem professes to express is necessarily a product of the poem's language, and if language itself is contingent on various social, historical, and cultural conditions, we nonetheless read poems to be reminded of what it feels like to be human, what it feels like to have a self, whatever that self might be. At least I do. It is useful to question the degree to which poetic language can express an identifiable and coherent self, but it is reductive to conclude that poetic expression is therefore, above all else, suspect.

Language *does* have meanings. It *does* communicate. Let's say that, while attending a dinner party, I announce that I believe I am experiencing a heart attack. On hearing this, the assembled guests might immediately note that the word *heart* is shadowed by the similar-sounding word spelled "*h-a-r-t,*" which refers to a deer, and that in using the word *attack* I have unconsciously alluded to the concept of *tacking* objects to bulletin boards (themselves a kind of text) and that it is a short leap from the notion of the deer to that of other hoofed animals, so my statement is equally an unintended reference to the childhood game of *pinning* (tacking) the tail on the donkey—a subject I didn't have in mind, exactly, when I spoke, but one that is worth pondering, specifically as it represents the willingness of a hegemonic Western culture to domesticate, objectify, and reconstruct for its own ethnocentric purposes the natural world—a willingness, indeed, born of the narrow perspective suggested by the very blindfold traditionally donned by he or she whose task it is to pin the tail on the donkey.

Still, while all this deconstruction is going on, I hope someone at the table calls 911. I am finally not very interested in poems that merely bring me the old news that words mean less or more than we think they do. We live in a poetic age that prizes the fragment, discontinuity, and aggressive indeterminacy—often at the expense of, or even while holding in contempt, lyricism. But, however worthy its desire to reflect the shifting, elusive nature of reality, any aesthetic uninterested in the ways that language embodies feeling is fatally crippled. We still sing amid the rubble.

Some of our better contemporary poets do not pretend to speak directly out of a static, definable self, but they also do not dismiss entirely the capacity of language to communicate subjective human experience. They use the pronoun "I," but the identity of that "I" is often vague—and it is typically not, or at least not merely, the poet. Instead, in using a first-person speaker, these writers interrogate the nature of the self and confront its ultimate mystery. Their poems do not use language merely to remind us that language is insufficient; instead, they employ the ambiguity and indirectness of poetic expression to come as close as possible to conveying the complicated and bewildering quality of subjective experience. These are poets who, in saying "I," know that there is something at stake when they do, who know that to write the poem is to fumble after the "I," following where it leads—and to follow the "eye" where it looks. As Charles Wright says, "The 'I' is the great turnkey for the poem, the great opener. Almost all the 'great' poems—from Sappho to Yeats—are in the 1st person singular. Especially since the Romantics, it's hard to have a 'vision' if you're not in it, and it's not in you."

The "I" of the sort of poem I am thinking of may be born out of autobiography, but it is also half created—recognizable from our experience in the world but quickened into speech only in the realm of the poem because it is the compressed, gestural, musical language of poetry that comes closest to saying what cannot be said. Others, of course, have thought about this. As Marvin Bell puts it, "The I in the poem is not you but someone who knows a lot about you." Rimbaud famously proclaimed in a letter, "It's wrong to say: I think. Better to say: I am thought . . . . I is an *other*" (100). I am reminded, too, of a peculiar statement the actor Anthony Hopkins made once in an interview that, on reflection, suggests nothing so much as the disinterestedness that Keats argued is so important to the true artist. When the interviewer persisted in asking him probing autobiographical questions, Hopkins stumbled, paused, and finally explained, "My life is none of my business."

For poets whose work, in the 1950s and 1960s, was the first described as "confessional"—writers such as Lowell, Plath, Berryman, and Sexton—their lives were very much their business. No matter the (considerable) stylistic differences among them, these writers shared the poetic project of treating intimate, sometimes disturbing autobiographical material in a way that did not shut readers out of the poem's concerns. Their challenge was to transform the private life into public art. The fields cultivated by these poets have continued, in the decades since, to be tilled by writers whose work is energized by the urgent claims of the autobiographical; however, such work also risks—if it focuses on an "I" that seems merely to be the poet, untransformed and unexamined, speaking out of his or her own personal life—being limited in its vision and irrelevant to the reader. A poet working in the confessional mode must be wary of writing, to borrow Stephen Yenser's terms in his criticism of Lowell's late work, "gossip" not "gospel" (qtd. in Hamilton, 432).

Decades before the work of the first generation of confessional poets, William Carlos Williams, in poems employing stripped-down diction and natural speech rhythms, was showing how a poet might convey his intimate life with immediacy and tension and without the enervating effect that can result from the inclusion of private details that seem of import only to the poet, not the poem. In "Danse Russe" and "Waiting," for instance, the "I" of the poems is Williams, but it also could be anyone. Of her own use of first person, Emily Dickinson explained, "When I state myself, as the Representative of the verse—it does not mean—me—but a supposed person" ("To T. W. Higginson," 176). Williams's speakers have the whiff of that supposed person about them. Theirs is the voice of someone—it could be almost anyone—caught in the act of thinking.

DANSE RUSSE

If I when my wife is sleeping
and the baby and Kathleen
are sleeping
and the sun is a flame-white disc
in silken mists
above shining trees,—

if I in my north room
dance naked, grotesquely
before my mirror
waving my shirt round my head
and singing softly to myself:
"I am lonely, lonely,
I was born to be lonely,
I am best so!"
If I admire my arms, my face,
my shoulders, flanks, buttocks
against the yellow drawn shades,—
Who shall say I am not
the happy genius of my household? (86–87)

This poem's speaker is a husband and father; considering the craving for freedom and solitude in the poem, that fact is relevant—but the poem doesn't give us any more information about this particular marriage than we need in order to make that connection. Who, though, we might ask, is Kathleen? It doesn't matter. The man in the poem is, on one level, Williams himself, and Kathleen was a domestic worker who lived with the Williams family for a time. But *not* knowing that fact, I would argue, does not prevent us from understanding the poem. In fact, it *helps*. The poem is a single sentence, a burst of thought, a brief revery; it is the internal musing of someone who doesn't need to explain to himself who is living in his house—and the intensity of that reverie is underscored by the offhand way the poet mentions "Kathleen" without comment and moves along. This light touch, this naturalness, makes the "I" of the poem sound both genuine and appealingly mysterious.

A similar sort of expansive use of the first person occurs in Williams's poem "Waiting."

WAITING

When I am alone I am happy.
The air is cool. The sky is
flecked and splashed and wound
with color. The crimson phalloi
of the sassafras leaves
hang crowded before me
in shoals on the heavy branches.
When I reach my doorstep
I am greeted by
the happy shrieks of my children
and my heart sinks.
I am crushed.
Are not my children as dear to me
as falling leaves or
must one become stupid
to grow older?
It seems much as if Sorrow
had tripped up my heels.
Let us see, let us see!
What did I plan to say to her
when it should happen to me
as it has happened now? (163–64)

Here, again, are Williams and his family; nonetheless, again the poem works no matter who we imagine the speaker to be. The "I" of "Waiting" is characterized by a sort of transparency; although he talks a lot about himself—although he is engaged in a private meditation—the poem never becomes unnecessarily private. In fact, as with "Danse Russe," the moves the poem makes that emphasize the intimacy of the meditation help draw us into the poem, not close us out. It is the poem's last four lines that I am especially interested in. "Let us see, let us see!" Williams writes. We might expect, in such an intimate, meditative poem, that the line would read, "Let *me* see, let *me* see." The shift into the first-person plural is like a change of key; it introduces a bemused, even vaguely comic, note. For a moment, we hear the controlled voice of the doctor who says to the patient, "So how are we today? Let us take a look under that bandage, shall we?" The poem's language has become a little odd, as if the speaker is beginning to put a slight distance between himself and his subject—the oddness coming from the fact that the subject is, of course, himself. Earlier in the poem, the speaker has mentioned his "children"; he has not simply called them "they." In the poem's last sentence, however, he refers, obliquely, to "her." This is a move comparable to the one Williams makes in "Danse Russe" when he mentions "Kathleen." In this case, we understand that "her" means the wife; the simple pronoun is all we need, and the entrance of the wife into the poem so suddenly and so late and in only that small word *her* makes the poem feel even more intimate and intense, more like something overheard, not explained. By these last four lines of the poem, the language has become unsettled; one can hear it even in the rhythm, with the predominance of mono-syllables and the stilted syntax. By the time the speaker refers to what has happened "to me," we can't be blamed for wondering just what that "me" is. This is a poem that does not presume to understand the self, but it does record what it is like to have one.

Two more recent poets, Charles Simic and Anne Carson, often center their poems around an "I," but they use distinctive strategies to suggest that this self is somehow a projected and impersonal one—if not always completely fictional, at least insufficiently knowable. Their first-person speakers can therefore seem strangely veiled. Details in Simic's work can sometimes be connected to specific experiences in his life—for instance, his childhood in Yugoslavia during World War II, his emigration to the United States, his experiences in New York City as a young adult, and his marriage—but it is usually a mistake not to distinguish between Simic and the first-person speakers of his poems. His "I" is typically a shadowy self, a possible self, a stranger—a self that exists somehow in the middle ground between language and the inef-fable. As Simic put it in an interview, "[F]or me there is no *one* 'I.' 'I' is many. 'I' is an organizing principle, a necessary fiction, etc. Actually, I'd put more emphasis on consciousness, that which witnesses but has no need of a pronoun" (*The Uncertain Certainty*, 67). The use of an almost cipherlike first-person speaker is in accord with Simic's notion that poetry isn't so much about the poet's self as about all selves, or about some essential selfness (however cryptic or absurd) that is shared by all humans. "Poetry is the archeology of the self," he has said. "The bits and pieces one keeps digging up belong to the world—everybody's world. It's a paradox that has always amused me. Just when you think you're most subjective, you meet everybody else" (Weigl, 210).

The poem "Cameo Appearance" is about the anonymous human

self: the self either without a meaningful, knowable identity or with an identity that has been blotted out by powerful, impersonal forces.

CAMEO APPEARANCE

I had a small, nonspeaking part
In a bloody epic. I was one of the
Bombed and fleeing humanity.
In the distance our great leader
Crowed like a rooster from a balcony,
Or was it a great actor
Impersonating our great leader?

That's me there, I said to the kiddies.
I'm squeezed between the man
With two bandaged hands raised
And the old woman with her mouth open
As if she were showing us a tooth

That hurts badly. The hundred times
I rewound the tape, not once
Could they catch sight of me
In that huge gray crowd,
That was like any other gray crowd.

Trot off to bed, I said finally.
I know I was there. One take
Is all they had time for.
We ran, and the planes grazed our hair,
And then they were no more
As we stood dazed in the burning city,
But, of course, they didn't film that.

"That's me there," the speaker says to "the kiddies" as he watches the film of a wartime scene. Who is this "me," though? This is one of the many instances in Simic's work of a recurring theme that he refers to in another poem as "the great secret which kept eluding me: / knowing who I am" ("The Initiate," 59). The speaker in "Cameo Appearance" knows he "was there" and is intent on proving it to the children with visual evidence, as if his relevance and identity will be assured if he can do so. However, he can't find himself. He has been erased—and what has been erased was of little value to begin with; as the poem announces in its opening line, "I had a small, non-speaking part." The speaker is important not as a distinctive character so much as a representative of all humans, and humans in this poem are irrelevant and disposable; all of "[b]ombed and fleeing humanity" implicitly has a "small, non-speaking part." The questioning of the meaning and truth of identity continues with the lines "In the distance our great leader / Crowed like a rooster from a balcony. / Or was it a great actor / Impersonating our great leader?" The only thing that seems certain in this poem, the only fact that can be recorded, is the suffering of humans who are impotent to protect themselves against modern, impersonal weapons of brutality. Tellingly, it is this suffering and these weapons, certainties that they are—not the poem's speaker—that are depicted with precise images.:

> . . . the man
> With two bandaged hands raised
> And the old woman with her mouth open
> As if she were showing us a tooth
> That hurts badly. . . .
> We ran, and the planes grazed our hair.

Were it not for the one mention of the planes and the film, this could be a war in almost any place and any century. Typical of the images in a Simic poem, the descriptions of the man and woman here are specific in their visual detail yet also generic, even archetypal, in their feel, as if these two humans are recurring characters in a story that has been told for ages. One male and one female representative of the bombed and fleeing masses, they might be what became of Adam and Eve long after they were kicked out of Paradise. It is not, then, finally the speaker of the poem who is the central character; the central character is any of us—anyone who might be fleetingly glimpsed among the "gray crowd / That was like any other gray crowd."

The speaker of "Cameo Appearance" is a victim of forces larger than himself, whether forces of the state or of the cosmos; he is absent from official history. His is a familiar voice in Simic's poetry—the voice of a self that lacks definition and coherence, the voice of a floating, questioning, bemused consciousness. In what can be read as an ars poetica—one that has as its basis a suspicion of ultimate claims about individual identity—Simic once wrote, "Others pray to God; I pray to chance to show me the way out of this prison I call myself" (*Orphan Factory*, 46).

The self-professed subject for Simic is, as he has said, "always 'truth,' but not the literal one" (Weigl, 222). This leads to poems with a surreal and mythic bent. One would be hard-pressed to call Anne Carson a surrealist, but she, like Simic, is not content with a conventional realistic approach. Her lyrics and narratives tend to be fragmented, even collagelike, in their mixing of various genres and modes of discourse, which contributes to the sense that the poems' speakers have uncertain knowledge of themselves and the significance of their experience.

And who are Carson's speakers? Whose consciousness is it that the poems record? It is not much help to our understanding of Carson's poems to read their speakers as being simply the poet herself. As Carson has said:

> I've often, while [using the first person], wondered, "Who is this *I*?" It's not identical with me. It's continuous but yet constructed. I don't exactly know how to define that quality that's in *I*. It's all mixed up with autobiography, but it's not the same . . . because I don't simply want to tell what is. I want to tell what is with all the radiations around it of what could be. So it's not simply a transcription of anything that actually happened but what actually happened, plus all the thoughts that one could think about it if one could walk around it, stop time and walk around the moment. And once you add in all that gradation of the moment it's no longer the event. The event is just the raw material that goes into your observation of what you see when you walk around it. It could be any subject matter. (Gannon, 29–30)

Carson, then, is a poet who prizes fidelity to truth and the imagination (and perhaps does not see those two things as being in opposition). She is interested in probing the subject of the self and circling around it without reaching for tidy explanations. Her poems, as a result, are, at least on the surface, formally messy. Her long poem *The Glass Essay* is an example. In telling the story of a failed love affair and her response to it, the poem's speaker mixes that narrative with several other tales, primarily the stories of a visit to her mother and of the life and work of Emily Brontë, but also briefer subplots involving her dreams, her psychotherapy sessions, and a visit to her ailing father in the hospital. She shifts abruptly from one narrative thread to another and from one mode of discourse to another; the general sense of disjunction is also contributed to by her tendency to employ clipped, declarative sentences, a technique that often leaves ambiguous the connection between thoughts. In its gaps and veerings, the poem refuses the temptation to construct an easily comprehensible and coherent version of the self. It is an illustration of Hayden Carruth's claim that a poem's "genuine passion does not come from the constricted ego, which can only tie itself in knots and has no innate recourse but suicide. It comes from the transcended ego in an ecstasy of concern" (Miller, 19).

In focusing on the pain of a ruptured romantic relationship and a problematic mother-daughter relationship, *The Glass Essay* is quite intimate and personal, yet it is wary of making claims about the nature of the self that experiences that pain. Although the poem's short first section is entitled "I," it subtly—with a single word—hints at the difficulty the poem will have defining just what that "I" is.

> I
>
> I can hear little clicks inside my dream.
> Night drips its silver tap
> down the back.
> At 4 A.M. I wake. Thinking
>
> of the man who
> left in September.
> His name was Law.
>
> My face in the bathroom mirror
> has white streaks down it.
> I rinse the face and return to bed.
> Tomorrow I am going to visit my mother. (1)

In the penultimate line, one would expect Carson to write, "I rinse *my* face." Her use of the impersonal article "the" suggests the distance between the speaker and a clear conception of herself—the self that fell in love with a man and then was damaged by his departure. This lack of certainty is suggested throughout the poem, so *The Glass Essay* can be read as a search for knowledge about the nature of the self and about the significance of the impact of experiences on that self. However, by poem's end, the speaker has discovered no easy answers. Here are the last lines of the poem.

> Something had gone through me and out and I could not own it.
> "No need now to tremble for the hard frost and the keen wind.
> Emily does not feel them,"
> wrote Charlotte the day after burying her sister.
> Emily had shaken free.
> A soul can do that.
> Whether it goes to join Thou and sit on the porch for all eternity
> enjoying jokes and kisses and beautiful cold spring evenings,
> you and I will never know. But I can tell you what I saw.
> Nude #13 arrived when I was not watching for it.
> It came at night.
> Very much like Nude #1.
> And yet utterly different.
> I saw a high hill and on it a form shaped against hard air.

It could have been just a pole with some old cloth attached,
but as I came closer
I saw it was a human body
trying to stand against winds so terrible that the flesh was blowing off
the bones.
And there was no pain.
The wind
was cleansing the bones.
They stood forth silver and necessary.
It was not my body, not a woman's body, it was the body of us all.
It walked out of the light. (38)

"Something had gone through me and out," she says, "and I could not own it." The experience that this thirty-eight-page poem has recounted and examined is finally summarized as being, vaguely, merely "[s]omething," and the fact of the speaker being unable to "own it" implies not simply that its existence within her was impermanent but that her knowledge of it must remain incomplete. Throughout the poem, the speaker describes various "naked glimpses of [her] soul" that she calls "Nudes." In the end, the final Nude is a figure whose bones "stood forth silver and necessary. / It was not my body, not a woman's body, it was the body of us all." The poem's investigation of the nature of the speaker's self as she has confronted intimate experiences peculiar to her has, paradoxically, culminated in this: a romantic vision of that self as being genderless, egoless, united with all of humanity. Such a notion echoes Emerson's belief in the capacity of the self to become a "transparent eyeball," to transcend "all mean egotism," and to feel its essential connection with all things (6). The idea of a shared humanity—and its attendant implication that there are essential human experiences that art can speak of—isn't very fashionable these days, but it is an idea with which some of our best poets sympathize. A poet does not have to share with Emerson a belief in a transcendent spiritual reality to believe in a universal *human* reality that can be suggested poetically. Galway Kinnell puts it this way, with a nod to Emerson's language.

Often a poem at least starts out being about oneself, about one's experience, a fragment of autobiography. But then, if it's really a poem, it goes deeper than personality. It takes on that strange voice, intensely personal yet common to everyone, in which all rituals are spoken. A poem expresses one's most private feelings; and these turn out to be the feelings of everyone else as well. The separate egos vanish. The poem becomes simply the voice of a creature on earth speaking. (6)

Carson's *The Glass Essay* transcends its private subject matter and becomes communal in part because of the "strange voice" in it that is nonetheless recognizably human. It is a voice whose signature is a clipped syntax that suggests at once an objective mind examining reality closely and volcanic emotions trying desperately to restrain themselves. This conflict is emphasized, too, by the poem's odd juxtaposition of modes of discourse and tone. In the following passage, one line barely articulates a feeling through monosyllabic words and a sentiment that might be drawn from a preteen's diary entry, but it is followed by a line whose understated, almost dismissive tone suggests the sound of the self turning away from—or apologizing for—its deepest concerns.

> When Law left I felt so bad I thought I would die.
> This is not uncommon. (8)

That guarded tone, that apparent veering away by the speaker from a confrontation with her inchoate and overwhelming emotions, is not an evasion; it is the sound of a self that is ambiguous and multiple in its concerns and conceptions. It is a tone that serves as a foil for the poem's more searing, emotionally bare passages, giving those sections the quality of hard-earned unveilings of difficult truths. It comes as something of a surprise, for instance, when, eleven pages into the poem, the speaker proclaims:

> Everything I know about love and its necessities
> I learned in that one moment
> when I found myself
> thrusting my little burning red backside like a baboon
> at a man who no longer cherished me. (11–12)

The Glass Essay does not deny that an important function of poetry is to examine and express the complicated nature of the interior life, and it does not imply that such a goal cannot be achieved through poetic expression. It does, however, persuade us that the self is perhaps essentially unknowable—or at least that to discover and define the self is no easy task and poetry can honor this truth.

With the famously strange and shape-shifting work of John Ashbery, one desires to get a toehold somewhere. One wants a firm place from which to begin reading. Here is a passage from his poem "Houseboat Days" that can be taken as a statement of purpose.

> But I don't take much stock in things
> Beyond the weather and the certainties of living and dying:

The rest is optional. To praise this, to blame that,
Leads one subtly away from the beginning, where
We must stay, in motion. (231)

If we "stay" yet are "in motion," we are going to be slippery prey indeed, difficult to pin down. The motion of Ashbery's poetry occurs in part through the seemingly random way he shifts pronouns—from singular to plural, from first to second to third person. By remaining in flux, Ashbery's poems refuse to settle into a particular angle of vision or into a particular conception of reality. However, this does not mean that Ashbery, as some of his critics would have it, glibly or coyly avoids meaning and engagement with real experience. When Ashbery's poetry is at its most persuasive and beguiling, it appears to be willing to bet its life on whatever notion is crossing its mind at the time, even if that notion will happen to be contradicted in the next line. The poems therefore feel intensely subjective, as if they record a very inner part of the self so separate from the social self that it is egoless, the place in which subjectivity expands to include not just the "I" but the "we" and the "you" and the "him," "her," and "they." Here is Ashbery's poem "Crazy Weather."

CRAZY WEATHER

It's this crazy weather we've been having:
Falling forward one minute, lying down the next
Among the loose grasses and soft, white, nameless flowers.
People have been making a garment out of it,
Stitching the white of lilacs together with lightning
At some anonymous crossroads. The sky calls
To the deaf earth. The proverbial disarray
Of morning corrects itself as you stand up.
You are wearing a text. The lines
Droop to your shoelaces and I shall never want or need
Any other literature than this poetry of mud
And ambitious reminiscences of times when it came easily
Through the then woods and ploughed fields and had
A simple unconscious dignity we can never hope to
Approximate now except in narrow ravines nobody
Will inspect where some late sample of the rare,
Uninteresting specimen might still be putting out shoots, for all
we know. (221)

Although he is unlike Whitman in many ways, Ashbery shares with him a sense of the self's multiplicity. Whitman says, "I am large, I contain multitudes" (246); Ashbery finds room in his poems for entire constellations of voices and perspectives. Also, as Whitman was fond of mixing formal and demotic speech, mixing high and low diction, so is Ashbery. We might say of his work that the "I" is not so much the source of the poems as it is the target; it is the magnet that, willy-nilly, pulls toward itself all sorts of images and phrases. The "I" does not proclaim its beliefs; it collects possibilities. That does not mean there is no "self" in an Ashbery poem. There is; he is not merely playing word games. But the poems are interested not so much in expressing the thoughts and feelings of an identifiable, coherent self as in suggesting what it is like to *experience* thoughts and feelings. The poems therefore move quickly and change course suddenly.

In "Crazy Weather," Ashbery begins with a familiar vernacular expression—"It's this crazy weather we've been having"—and already the pronouns are introducing an odd sense of mystery. Who are "we"? we might ask. Moreover, what about that floating, unmoored pronoun "It"? *What* is "this crazy weather we've been having"? From there, though, the poem mainly continues to evade our attempts to connect the pronouns to anything or anyone in particular. The "we" of the first line gives way to "People" in the fourth, then to "you" in the eighth and to "I" in the tenth before the poem circles back to "we" again in the last line. By then, however, one suspects the "we" aren't quite the same "we" the poem started with. The slipperiness of the pronouns mitigates against our inclination to read a literal narrative into the poem, to try to distinguish among characters and to place them in relation to each other. The poem is nonetheless about something more than mere language play; among other things, it is about the unlikeliness of ever detecting and conveying a stable truth, a subject that in Ashbery's work is given, by turns, a melancholy and a comic cast. "Crazy Weather" is about poetry, about perception, about longing—and there is an integrity to the way it circles *around* experience, the way it knows that, in a poem, the content of experience can only be gestured at. In remaining in motion, Ashbery's poem does not settle easily into a single stance, into an implication that the self can absorb experience, distill the truth from it, and then deliver that truth authoritatively in language. The self remains provisional, so the poem must, too, and the effect of this is a confrontation with what it feels like to be alive, not an evasion of it. As James Longenbach has written of Ashbery, "[H]is poems feel spoken even if they lack an easily identified speaker: their disjunctive manner does not preclude the fiction of the human subject, however intricately constructed the manner might suggest that fiction to be. This is why Ashbery's poems, no matter how obscure, no matter how aligned with what we think of as the dryer responsibilities of avant-garde poetry, are always ripe with pathos" (28).

When I, as a poet, say "I," that I is not me, exactly. I am not sure what it is until the poem starts giving me clues. Sometimes the "I" is someone I'd like to be or someone I hope I'm not or someone I fear I might become if I keep living in this way or someone I've fooled myself into thinking I was once. Sometimes it's a dog. If I presume to know too much about this "I" at the beginning, though, the poem is likely to fail; it will lack the energy and tension that come from mystery and discovery. For the poet, it is a good idea, while writing, to remain consciously ignorant for as long as possible—because, after all, we can trust that the place in us from which true poems come is never ignorant. Two centuries ago, Thomas Carlyle wrote, "Unconsciousness is the sign of creation. . . . So deep, in this existence of ours, is the significance of mystery" (qtd. in Abrams, 217). This is old news but worth repeating. The self, no matter our various notions about it, ultimately keeps its secrets. That is one of the best reasons to write and read poetry. In one of her many poems exploring the outer reaches of consciousness—examining, in other words, what it is like to be a thinking and feeling self—Emily Dickinson describes how "I, and Silence," are "some strange Race / Wrecked, solitary, here" (#280, 129). Perhaps the self exists most fully in silence. But if this "strange race"—this "I" and this silence—can speak, its language is surely poetry.

WORKS CITED

Abrams, M. H. *The Mirror and the Lamp: Romantic Theory and the Critical Tradition.* Oxford: Oxford University Press, 1953.

Ashbery, John. *Selected Poems.* New York: Viking, 1985.

Bell, Marvin. "Thirty-two Statements about Writing Poetry (Work in Progress)." *Writer's Chronicle,* special commemorative issue, 2002, 13.

Carson, Anne. *The Glass Essay.* In *Glass, Irony, and God.* New York: New Directions, 1995. 1—38.

Dickinson, Emily. #280 ("I felt a Funeral, in My Brain"). In *The Complete Poems of Emily Dickinson.* Edited by Thomas H. Johnson. Boston: Little, Brown, 1960. 128–29.

Dickinson, Emily. "To T. W. Higginson." In *Emily Dickinson: Selected Letters.* Edited by Thomas H. Johnson. Cambridge: Harvard University Press, 1986. 175–76. Letter 268, July 1862.

Emerson, Ralph Waldo. *Nature.* In *Ralph Waldo Emerson: Selected Prose and Poetry.* Edited by Reginald L. Cook. 2nd ed. San Francisco: Rinehart, 1969. 3–38.

Gannon, Mary. "Anne Carson: Beauty Prefers an Edge." *Poets and Writers,* March–April 2001, 26–33.

Hamilton, Ian. *Robert Lowell: A Life.* New York: Random House, 1982.

Kinnell, Galway. *Walking down the Stairs: Selections from Interviews.* Ann Arbor: University of Michigan Press, 1978.

Longenbach, James. "Disjunction in Poetry." *Raritan* 20, no. 4 (spring 2001): 20–36.

Miller, Matthew. "An Interview with Hayden Carruth." *Writer's Chronicle,* September 2001, 12–19.

Rimbaud, Arthur. Letter to Georges Izambard, May 13, 1871. In *Arthur Rimbaud: Collected Works.* Translated by Paul Schmidt. New York: Harper, 1976. 100–101.

Simic, Charles. "Cameo Appearance." In *Walking the Black Cat.* San Diego: Harcourt Brace, 1996. 6.

Simic, Charles. "The Initiate." In *The Book of Gods and Devils.* San Diego: Harcourt Brace, 1990. 59–61.

Simic, Charles. *Orphan Factory: Essays and Memoirs.* Ann Arbor: University of Michigan Press, 1997.

Simic, Charles. *The Uncertain Certainty.* Ann Arbor: University of Michigan Press, 1985.

Weigl, Bruce, ed. *Charles Simic: Essays on the Poetry.* Ann Arbor: University of Michigan Press, 1996.

Whitman, Walt. *Complete Poetry and Collected Prose.* New York: Library of America, 1982.

Williams, William Carlos. *The Collected Poems of William Carlos Williams.* Edited by A. Walton Litz and Christopher MacGowan. Vol. 1. New York: New Directions, 1986.

Wright, Charles. Letter to the author, 6 May 2002.

HEATHER MCHUGH

Poise and Suspense

From the Latin *pendere*—meaning "to weigh" something, hold it in hand or mind, apprising ourselves, by appraising it—from this *pendere* we get the word *pensive*. Wonder feels light, but a pensum is pondered. The Thinker is stooped.

But a poet's an odd sort of thinker—his sense informed by many senses—who wonders at the ponderable's shore. He gets down to business by rising to an occasion—meaning to have it two ways at the very least. He gets a line on the barely ponderable wonder, feels his way along the line, the way it weighs back to his hand and mind. Maybe he plays with how it hangs—from whatever heaven into whatever heaviness. This feeling around in form is a poet's way of thinking. At its best, the touched instrument is the touching one. If the artist is moved, he can move others.

Allen Ginsberg told us "Mind is shapely," and to that the wise men always added that feeling without thought was blind but thought without feeling merciless. The most delicious insights are conceived when a kilo of incarnation and a kick of cogitation come together.

DELIGHT IN DISORDER

A sweet disorder in the dresse
Kindles in cloathes a wantonnesse:
A Lawne about the shoulders thrown
Into a fine distraction:
An erring Lace, which here and there
Enthralls the Crimson Stomacher:
A Cuffe neglectfull, and thereby
Ribbands to flow confusedly:
A winning wave (deserving Note)
In the tempestuous petticote:
A carelesse shooe-string, in whose tye
I see a wilde civility:
Doe more bewitch me, then when Art
Is too precise in every part.

266

In Robert Herrick's "Delight in Disorder," the string is the emblem of the singing lover—it's the wild civility, itself—able to bind the beloved's foot or flow like those bloody ribbands there. The crimson stomacher your footnotes tell you is a sort of cummerbund might well arouse in you the thought of other reddenings—flows of fertility, or a redheaded bludgeon, the woman and man heartbeaten together. The line of shawl or scarf she casts about her shoulders for attraction causes some distraction, too—as order and laxity attract each other, and the overprecise, by comparison, is sterile.

In this poem, the beloved is erring, neglectful, confused, tempestuous, careless, and wild—but only by virtue of lace, cuff, ribbands, petticoat, and shoestrings. She's a very storm of strings. Hers are the ties that do *not* bind; rather they beg to be further undone—she's something of a scarlet woman—and her subjective genitive gives rise to her objective genitive. Thus do grammarians get excited.

Bound up in formal ways, a poem is unbound—by that I mean it's untoward, it's not tendentious, and it takes certain liberties with the language others use for constraint. It has a chance at the boundless, too, the moment it leaps into another heart or mind. (Forgive those quaint nouns: I don't know the word for that compound of sensibility where art at once resides and is moving.)

In that all-at-onceness of the oxymoron's lovely double bind ("a wild civility"), you sense that a bound's part noun, part verb. So, too, see Pound.

THE GARRET

Come, let us pity those who are better off than we are;
come, my friend, and remember
that the rich have butlers and no friends,
and we have friends and no butlers.
Come, let us pity the married and the unmarried.
Dawn enters with little feet
like a gilded Pavlova,
and I am near my desire.
Nor has life in it aught better
than this hour of clear coolness,
the hour of waking together.

THE GARDEN

Like a skein of loose silk blown against a wall
She walks by the railing of a path in Kensington Gardens,
And she is dying piece-meal
Of a sort of emotional anemia.

And round about there is a rabble
Of the filthy, sturdy, unkillable infants of the very poor.
They shall inherit the earth.

In her is the end of breeding
her boredom is exquisite and excessive.

She would like some one to speak to her,
And is almost afraid that I
Will commit that indiscretion.

The freshness of these poems arises from the almost palpable
"being of two minds" in them, a canny counterpoise of carnal seduction with mindful calm. In "The Garret," the mutual exclusiveness of
butlers and friends is weighed in one and then another way; and just
when we expect some commanding synopsis (such as "come let us pity
butlers and friends alike") we get the sudden non sequitur "Come, let
us pity the married and the unmarried"—a shift of object all the more
surprising for its imperative's perfect parallel construction with the
poem's first line. Now it's up to the reader to weigh the relations
between one social contract and another. There's no one obvious
choice, or even pair of choices, being peddled here.

We favor symmetry; our sense of evenhandedness requires two
hands: we construct our ethical and intellectual balance on a law of
opposites. But here Pound's arrangement of the terms requires us to
poise love and liberty, family and freedom, wealth and virtue in richer
ways than usual, ways that resist mutual exclusiveness. He'd like the girl
to be sturdier and more fertile—but admires her exquisiteness too. Let
me better illustrate my point.

Perhaps you think at first reading that "I am near my desire" means
I am near my beloved—certainly "waking together," the last two
words of the poem, seems to support such a reading. Having the riches
of a lover's company in one's garret, one might well think the merely
butlered CEO the less fortunate in his echoing mansion. But why add
"the married AND the unmarried" to the bargain? In view of that new
counterpoise, the second stanza could be said to weigh in on either
side: one might well love most the one to whom one is NOT married,
whether because one is single or because the lying together is extra-
matrimonial. Moreover "my desire" can weigh in on the solitary's side
of the argument: it's possible that to have ANY company is to have
one's attention impoverished, since without a lot of heavy breathing
and distraction one wakes at the hour of coolness (not heat) and clear-
ness (not carnal clouding). In that case, the hour of clear coolness
becomes not only a descriptor in an aubade but a desideratum in a

philosophical ambition, and the waking together means a broader waking than waking with a broad. That is, it could mean waking with the world, waking when all awake, rich and poor alike, on whom Dawn visits her coolest golds. Perhaps that love is richest of all since from the garret it has come to comprehend the globe.

In "In The Garden," Pound sensationally sets up the social counterpoise of two domains—that of "the sturdy unkillable children of the very poor" and that of the figure of the lassitudinous leisured lady in whom he sees "the end of breeding." He's the watcher between opposing worlds. In "the end of breeding," we understand he's playing two figures at once—that of a woman and that of a whole idea of womanhood—on the one hand an individually contracepted and contemporary girl and on the other the representative figure of an age of privilege. "The end of breeding" is in the first instance more specifically gynecological and in the second more generally sociological. The urchins who bubble up around this figure are not her children—he's sketching the demographics of poverty that will overwhelm this one effete figure in time. And Pound ends the poem by focusing on the woman's *own* underlying extinguishability—both yearning for company and afraid of her own yearning. This is no sturdy fertile figure. (The historical vulnerability of this figure of refined individual sensibility is weighed by any number of writers in times of social change and revolution—look at Lawrence, look at Celan, look at Mandelstam. And maybe every time is a time of revolution since even within individual human lives there are always developmental revolutions, ages of change, eras when we go gangbusting and grandstanding over more intricate understandings or inclinations—throwing away balance, broad-mindedness, discretion, in a rush of passion—or, on the other hand, times when solitude annihilates solicitude or ambivalence becomes indifference.)

Fear of what it desires is the doom of exquisite sensibility. Biology dictates some of this: to recoil from earthiness is to undermine your own animal vigor. But animals live on airs as well—and cell structures full of lovely aqueducts and struts. In every revolution, years of delicate work may be dispatched by the big brute forces of history. Think of Lavoisier, the pioneer in chemistry, guillotined by those who thought his sympathies too royal. Think of Archimedes, the Greek mathematician, engineer, and physicist, drawing certain figures in sand when a soldier rushes in and demands to know his name. According to the account of Valerius Maximus a few years after the death of Christ, Archimedes puts up his hands and famously says, "I beg you, don't disturb these circles." Alas, the next figure he cuts is as a corpse for the soldier strikes him dead. A simple slash dispatches the figurer's years. Passionate feeling overloves and rages; exquisite mind underloves and rues. Each is as much a danger to itself as to others. But in the best abiding human enterprises, certainly in the arts and sciences, it often seems that the near oxymorons best govern the health of our engagements— the oxymorons of exquisite feeling and passionate mind.

Such internal counterpoises compose our delight. For a poem must seem both necessary and surprising—and to be both of those things at once is no snap of the fingers (against an opposable thumb. The two words *poise* and *suspense,* to which this bouquet of readings is dedicated, both come, as *pensive* does, from the Latin *pendere,* "to weigh." And in the hands of a master of avoirdupois what constitutes a poetic pendulum—what its precise weights and reaches are—may itself surprise us, create a sense of unforeseen necessity. In the following poem by the contemporary American poet Louis Simpson, the biggest surprise, given its inferrably percussive backdrop, is its narrator's ultimate recourse to instrumental tedium. It's like a concerto carefully arranged for tympani and ennui. The bottom line—that nothing happens—is itself the surprise. There's no flatter last line in American poetry—and few as powerful.

ON THE LAWN AT THE VILLA

On the lawn at the villa—
That's the way to start, eh, reader?
We know where we stand—somewhere expensive—
You and I imperturbes, as Walt would say,
Before the diversions of wealth, you and I engage

On the lawn at the villa
Sat a manufacturer of explosives,
His wife from Paris,
And a young man named Bruno,

And myself, being American,
Willing to talk to these malefactors,
The manufacturer of explosives, and so on,
But somehow superior. By that I mean democratic.
It's complicated, being an American,
Having the money and the bad conscience, both at the same time.
Perhaps, after all, this is not the right subject for a poem.

We were all sitting there paralyzed
In the hot Tuscan afternoon
And the bodies of the machine-gun crew were draped over the balcony.
So we sat there all afternoon.

The poem is both funny and frightening—its narrator both titillating and dull. There's a buildup of momentum in the reader from the cumulative weight of important details (casually and even indifferently revealed by the narrator). This accumulation ultimately makes us impatient to arrive at fully expressed gesture or action. But the poem withholds from us the release we crave—and the counterweight of this withholding itself feels explosive.

Among narrators (always to be distinguished from the poets!), this one is the sort to toy around with art—as the "manufacturer of explosives" plays around with the Fourth of July. Self-consciously imitating and trying on for size first one style and then another—"and a young man named Bruno"!—he nevertheless turns away fast when, as happens in the course of a writer's engagement with his medium, he comes face to face with the most urgent premises or understory. The pattern of his reversions reveals something about himself rather than his characters, although in the course of a lurching, conspiratorial chatter he would rather repress it. Preoccupied with the surfaces of a staging, this is a character who flits from here to there, adjusting the lighting, never quite seeing the light. Chattering about how a story should be told, he pretends to jaunty narrative strategies (was it Chesterton who said that the artistic temperament is an affliction of amateurs?). And this guy is scurrilously chummy—"on the lawn at the villa—that's the way to start, eh reader? We know where we stand . . ." He treats Whitman as a snob and the scenery of war as interior decor, poetic occasion as camouflage.

But of course "knowing where we stand" means more than your realty guru or self-help book or GPS device can buy. This is a crucial point for art. It's not sufficient to affect a style, join an aesthetic, sign on to a manifesto, buy a formula, trot out your modish modus operandi. The enterprise cannot neglect the true weight and gravity of its undertaking, as revealed in the course of the writer's own discovery of his subject, inside his writing.

By contrast, this character is covering more than he's discovering; he's arranging the drapery around an atrocity, missing the heart of the matter that we, the readers, cannot miss. When the soldiers' bodies are treated only as so much drapery, the metaphor itself must damn him. It suggests a merely decorative interest in them as artsy figures, not human ones, and we can't help recognizing that some larger thing has been ignored—can't help craving its acknowledgment. For of course we care, as he seems not to, about whether these soldiers are living or dead. Their bodies are not just drapery to us.

That's the most compelling claim on our attention, the most compelling call here, the call to human response, and it is conspicuously ignored, sometimes even willfully suppressed, as every time self-knowledge rears its ugly head the narrator beats a retreat—"perhaps this is not the best subject for a poem." And it's worth noting, in any era in which self-consciousness becomes more of a fashion than a failing, how self-construction can become a self-deception and a metapoetic occasion an evasion. As the poem ends, most readers feel a wallop of frustration. To have to be stuck with, have to end on, such banality and such paralysis!—just at the moment of greatest calling. It's to Simpson's credit that we feel this something so fiercely in the face of such a nothing. This narrator's wish for an escapist mechanism has turned all telling moments into telling-moments: pattern into mere patter. Simpson's strategy of permitting his narrator to fail even as a storyteller, failing to deliver on all suspense and merely plopping down into the paralytic chaise longue, amounts to its own scathing remark on the means and milieu of Nothing Doing. Notice how much hangs on the word *so*—and by what a thin thread. The suspense is palpable—and fuels our fury at the narrator's refusal.

Artistic invention is deployed in the service of a serious realization—it's important to admit how invention and realization cooperate in art. The artistic calling can be blunted by any of a number of other drives—toward escapism, for example, or toward partisan preempting. You can see Louis Simpson again addressing that dilemma in the poem that follows.

A STORY ABOUT CHICKEN SOUP

In my grandmother's house there was always chicken soup
And talk of the old country—mud and boards,
Poverty,
The snow falling down the necks of lovers.

Now and then, out of her savings
She sent them a dowry. Imagine
The rice-powdered faces!
And the smell of the bride, like chicken soup.

But the Germans killed them.
I know it's in bad taste to say it,
But it's true. The Germans killed them all.

★

In the ruins of Berchtesgaden
A child with yellow hair
Ran out of a doorway.

A German girl-child—
Cuckoo, all skin and bones—
Not even enough to make chicken soup.
She sat by the stream and smiled.

Then as we splashed in the sun
She laughed at us.
We had killed her mechanical brothers,
So we forgave her.

★

The sun is shining.
The shadows of the lovers have disappeared.
They are all eyes; they have some demand on me—
They want me to be more serious than I want to be.
They want me to stick in their mudhole
Where no one is elegant.
They want me to wear old clothes,
They want me to be poor, to sleep in a room with many others—

Not to walk in the painted sunshine
To a summer house,
But to live in the tragic world forever.

Here's another crucial CAUSAL "so": "We had killed her
mechanical brothers / So we forgave her." Boil that down—"we had
killed so we forgave"—and you feel the weight in that little conjunction. The poem as a whole is preoccupied with the counterclaims of
two worlds—on the one hand that of the elders who remember the old
country's darker times and places and on the other that of the young
who have had the good fortune to grow up in brighter ones. (In a
sense, it's the universal counterclaiming of experience and innocence.)
To heft, to lift, two such worlds at once, in an effort to weigh them,
would put a lot of pressure on any sensitive soul. Many will be tempted
to dump one side in favor of the other—become self-righteous or
espousing. But the weight of the crux of the matter itself will be diminished. (The reason Christ's an important figure is precisely that he carries the cross: the coincidence in one conception of two contraries—
whether you call them soul and body, or heaven and earth, or god and
man, the two sides of a counterpoise weigh heavily on that figure.)
Simpson's characters, of course, are reeling from the wars of twentieth-
century Europe; every era and society brings to bear the demands of
history itself, and these forces press in around the individual. Berchtesgaden, once just a beautiful resort, became the retreat of the senior
Nazis and therefore was seized by the Americans so that what was orig-

inally notable for its peace and beauty came to be redefined by wartime. Between the claims of age and youth, old and new worlds, wartime and peacetime, the poem tilts back and forth. Ultimately the contraries cross-fertilize: the experience of the aged ones enters the world of the young and vice versa; the new world's citizens bring the old world with them; and so on. Dark with history, remarked by memory, the old ask to be remembered. Missing history but glittering with futures, the young ask to stay carefree. The narrator can have no rest: he knows how thin the veneer is, and how art can conspire, in the dream of the summerhouse.

Must art, then, look back or look forward? Is it art's responsibility to follow the dreamer and shoot for ever-refining happiness or to speak for the drowner in ever-repeating sorrows? A hermeneutics of single-mindedness, answering the question only one way or the other, can only diminish the premises—for they are the premises of life itself, a compound of grief and hope. In Simpson, as elsewhere in Pound, you'll find a third figure added to the balance. That's the figure of the very young child, a figure of unmediated compounding, perfect paradox: the child is the incarnation of joyful vulnerability, sensual innocence—states to which the adults may advert but can never themselves return. The child splashes around as if in Eden already or forever. The others, the opposed adults, seem adulterated by comparison—the flow of time protects her from them, though she does not live in time at all (only in the moment). Neither of the two schools of adulthood can forget time or causality, the genetic mechanics of her being, the tendentiousness and jockeying of oppositions—but she's unschooled, she's the true alternative to tendentiousness of either stripe—the *tertium quid*. For her, it's no agony of choice, no Manichaean black or white: given a mud hole, she simply *sees* a sun splash.

When Helen Keller could suddenly see with her fingertips, she said something extraordinary: she said she "felt . . . a thrill of returning thought"—a thrill of thought!—in which "the mystery of language was revealed." She said that when she understood the word *water*, recognized it in its name, "nothingness was blotted out." What a beautiful double negative that is!—and it's not just physical blindness she's referring to. Remember Borges too—why is it so many visionaries are blind? Asked how it felt to be sightless, he said it was a confinement at times, yes, but also "a liberation, a solitude propitious to invention, a key and an algebra." Even in conversation, Borges is astonishingly Borgesian! *We've* forgotten the world we knew firsthand, before the one hand and the other tore the world apart; forgotten how we felt our way around its sphere, a world Keller says her fingers saw as "alive, ruddy, satisfying." Ruddy! Now there's a palpable regard! But what do ordinary sighted grown-ups see? Here is Shirley Kaufman's "The Blue Shirt."

THE BLUE SHIRT

See that man with the basket
of fruit and vegetables.

You mean by the Roman arch?

The one with the blue shirt
and sandals.

By the Sixth Station of the Cross?

With the child eating a banana.

Where Veronica wiped the sweat
from His face with her handkerchief?

No. No. The blue shirt,
the basket of vegetables.

Each of these two adults sees only the meanings he's already made of the world. The two of them can't get their coordinates to jibe, however much each tries to bring the other to submit to his vocabulary: standing on the very same plot of land, they fail to find a common ground. Each persists in seeing "where he stands" in vehemently exclusive terms—their narratives have premises they can't get past, to make a present, much less a future. (It's no accident this poet lives in Israel or that Cain and Abel occupied the Mesopotamian region we now call Iraq. There's always an other—our brother—ever since Eve.) One of the characters in Kaufman's little story sees the world as animated by history and faith; the other brings eyes only for the immediate sensory evidence. Beginning students almost always want to champion this materialist way of seeing. They're impatient with the character who speaks second in the poem. But the first speaker is the one who begins without question—begins with an imperative not an inquiry—and when the other tries to follow, in his own language, the first speaker gets more and more abrupt. The imperative and the interrogative modes don't see the world the same way—and by the end of the poem, before the conversation has even had a chance to begin, the one who opened the conversation seems almost ready to break out in battle. Notice how Kaufman entitles the poem—The Blue Shirt—the way warring sides are sometimes entitled. The one who started by mildly indicating a whole man ends by wiping out the human figure from his indication; whereas the one who began with a ruin ends with a gesture of human sympathy; their paths have crossed, and yet they've failed to meet. Do we know where we stand? Somewhere expensive.

And then there's Su Tung-P'o—who during the Sung dynasty designed lakeside parks in China and wrote pastoral verses. He also wrote satires, and it was the satires that got him into trouble—rulers demand to be laughed with not laughed at. He was imprisoned, and then exiled, more than once. Each time he lost his home, scholars observe, he seemed to refocus on a simpler set of pleasures, find grounds for more illuminated thought—the deeper the brighter, in that sense of senses, where the thought and the felt can happen in one flash.

(After Su Tung-P'o)

One midnight in the spring! An hour
is worth a thousand golden coins . . .
The moon is shadowed, senses
Clearly flowering. Upstairs,
unwound from flutes and
throats—some silken
threads of sound.
And where the
garden holds
most still:
a swing.

Using the available translations, I myself fashioned this version of the poem, staying as faithful as possible to its spirit, as I understood it across time, and to that of the American English of our day. Su Tung-P'o was born in 1036. In another thirty years, he'll be a thousand. The way we use the word *poise* today—meaning "steadiness" or "composure"—was first recorded in English about six hundred years after Su Tung-P'o, though he remains one of that sense's best illustrations. Our usage came from the notion of something equally weighted on either side. In that sense of the word, any poise would be an equipoise. In Su Tung-P'o you feel that steady lateral balance is crossed by a moving vertical—full of the gravity with which celestial bodies work on terrestrial ones. So line and sphere both shape the enterprise—the line we make, to keep our balance, arms outstretched, and the spheres that spirit us up and ground us down. All poise, all equipoise, all gravity, all suspense, all life and art will draw opposing forces into an encounter. If you think you know what's happening, you won't feel two ways about it—can't feel two ways about it. You'll narrow it down to the known.

Despite everything I knew and felt, two of my dearest friends died gasping for air. Another couldn't stop her pain with morphine, so she disconnected her feeding tube. Still another has the same kind of cancer, and after a heartening remission it's back with a vengeance. Two other friends are sitting with their niece and nephew, who have just had to pull the plug on their mother's life support. All of them are sitting there at the mother's bedside as I write, enduring the umpteenth day of death. It's not a snap. My mother-in-law, while visiting us at our summer home last September, fell down the stairs at 2:00 am, alone, and died—she lay where we found her, five hours later, at the bottom of the stairs, in her moon-and-stars pajamas. The idea of death is always a simile—old as the hills. It can't hurt me. But the images have to be borne, and they are unbearable. In them, knowing and feeling fight for my soul, as if one or the other could win it. The evidences are as recalcitrant as they are unignorable. I suffer them as I will never suffer my own dying. In them, I feel the legacy of what befalls us—the Latin *cadere*, "to fall," gives us all that "is the case"—casualty and cadaver too—and even grammatical case, as I was recently amazed to discover, comes not from the word meaning box but from the past participle of *cadere*, making nouns more fundamentally moving than we like to imagine.

George Herbert lived in the golden age of polyphony and counterpoint and could have heard Dowland's lute and lilt in his lifetime. There's a good fortune. But he didn't live to see his forties. And, when that became clear, how did he say what he felt? Were thought and feeling hammered down, by conviction or rage, to one blind point? No way. When feeling no longer evades, and thinking no longer avails, the two become woven together. You feel knowing can't save you; you know feeling can't save you. Their famous battles fall away, and in a flash or stretch, depending how things go with you, you do a lot at once: holding back while you hold forth, bearing down while you bear up.

The greatest works in literature pull against a powerful sense of casualty. You must carry your weight in your life, in your work. That's gravity pulling you down: it gives you your heft. That's high spirits or levity pulling you up: it gives you your lift. Feeling along the vertical you get suspense, but feeling along the horizontal you get poise: having the weight of experience on the one hand and the wishes of innocence on the other. Reader and writer both are bound along these lines. We're bound together, bound away. We fell from a state of weightlessness—and were raised from birth. Suspense is a tie to the sky, as surely as to earth, which is where George Herbert squarely places us.

BITTER SWEET

Ah, my dear angry Lord,
Since thou dost love, yet strike;
Cast down, yet help afford;
Sure I will do the like.

I will complain, yet praise;
I will bewail, approve;
And all my sour-sweet days
I will lament and love.

JAMES LONGENBACH

Purity, Restraint, Stillness

Celebrating the painter Elstir, the narrator of *In Search of Lost Time* suggests that for the great artist the work of painting and the act of being alive are indistinguishable. For each of us, says Proust, there may be "certain bodies, certain callings, certain rhythms that are specially privileged, realizing so naturally our ideal that even without genius, merely by copying the movement of a shoulder, the tension of a neck, we can achieve a masterpiece." The implication here is that art is not the product of the will. More than lack of ambition, it is the inability to surrender to our characteristic callings and rhythms that keeps us from fulfilling our promise.

The word *surrender* makes this achievement sound easy, as if the victory of each day were to wake up looking exactly like yourself. But even if we all possess certain rhythms, certain callings, not everyone is able to exist in the simple act of recognizing them. The surrender of the will is itself impossible merely to will, and we may struggle with the act of surrender more deeply than we struggle with the act of rebellion. W. B. Yeats called the moment of recognizing oneself a "withering into the truth," and the word *wither* seems just right, for the discovery does not feel like a blossoming. Nor does it happen only once, like an inoculation. Proust's Elstir does not inhabit himself truly until he has achieved great age.

Writers have withered into variety, excess, and vulgarity; writers have withered into purity, restraint, and stillness. Why do the latter values so often get bad press, even from artists who embrace those values themselves? In my own experience, stillness can be difficult to separate from dullness, restraint from lack of vision or adequate technique; a young writer may embrace the glamour of risk in order to avoid parsing these discriminations. What's more, the association of artistic achievement with heroic willfulness is endemic, and it is clung to in the United States with a fierceness that belies its fragility. Lacking a thousand years of artistic craftsmanship to fall back on, the American artist is called great when he is at the frontier, taking the risk, disdaining the status quo but also landing the movie deal. What happens to the American poet who is destined to wither into stillness and restraint, the poet whose deepest inclination is to associate risk with submission?

In his long poem *Hugh Selwyn Mauberley,* Ezra Pound offers two artist figures, both of whom were masks for competing aspects of Pound's artistic identity: the effete Mauberley, who is devoted to aesthetic perfection; and the aggressive E. P., who transgresses the small parameters of perfection. Here, in some of the most rhythmically subtle lines Pound ever wrote, is Mauberley's fate.

> Thick foliage
> Placid beneath warm suns,
> Tawn fore-shores
> Washed in the cobalt of oblivions;
>
> Or through dawn-mist
> The grey and rose
> Of the juridical
> Flamingoes;
>
> A consciousness disjunct,
> Being but this overblotted
> Series
> Of intermittences;
>
> Coracle of Pacific voyages,
> The unforecasted beach;
> Then on an oar
> Read this:
>
> "I was
> And I no more exist;
> Here drifted
> An hedonist."

These quatrains are generally rhymed XAXA, but they are metered variously, so that we are sometimes asked to hear more stresses in the lines than are actually there. Listening to the final quatrain, for instance, we crave three firm stresses in the final line so that it matches the second line, with which it rhymes so crisply; as a result, we put an unnaturally heavy stress on the first syllable of the final line ("an") and feel a gaping caesura between this syllable and the next, which also needs to be stressed. The line floats away, drawn out in a languorous hesitancy much like the sensibility the poem describes.

But, while this section of the poem is meant to characterize Mauberley's failure (he is the shipwrecked aesthete, going nowhere, in contrast to the Odyssean E. P.), the poem also asks us to admire the exquisite restraint of this writing, a restraint of which Pound continued to be capable but in which he indulged with increasing reluctance. The rougher, more worldly sections of *Hugh Selwyn Mauberley* ("usury age-old and age-thick / and liars in public places") forecast both the sound and the values the *Cantos,* the long poem to which Pound devoted the last fifty years of his life. Ultimately, as much as he valued the stillness he first embodied in his early imagist poems and then associated with his alter ego Mauberley, Pound wanted to be a legislator not a crafts-man. He turned away from his characteristic callings and rhythms, will-ing a poetry of immense energy rather than succumbing to the stillness that truly distinguishes him.

Hugh Selwyn Mauberley is probably the best poem ever written about midlife crisis, but Pound was divided against himself from the start. As a young man, he told his mother that his ambition was to write the epic of the West, but at the same time he was entranced by the purest diction and syntax that the final decade of the nineteenth cen-tury had to offer. Listen to an early poem by W. B. Yeats, originally called "Breasal the Fisherman," to which the young Pound was devoted.

> Although you hide in the ebb and flow
> Of the pale tide when the moon is set,
> The people of coming days will know
> About the casting out of my net,
> And how you have leaped times out of mind
> Over the little silver cords,
> And think that you were hard and unkind,
> And blame you with many bitter words.

That's one sentence stretched over eight tetrameter lines: the metrical pattern and rhyme scheme never ruffle the syntax, which remains limpidly clear. At the same time, the metrical pattern is everywhere ruffled: though the overall feeling of the poem is iambic, not one of the lines is perfectly iambic. In the first line, the third foot is anapestic. In the second line, the first and third feet are anapests. In the third line, the second foot is anapestic, and in the fourth line the fourth foot is anapestic. That second line ("Of the pale tide when the moon is set") is made even wilder by the lack of an unstressed syllable between "pale" and "tide."

Those words are very plain, strategically so. One of the great advantages of the English language, as a palate for poetry, is its multiplicity of roots: we are used to hearing our original Anglo-Saxon words nestled against imported French or Latinate words in our poetry ("seas incarnadine"), and if Shakespeare seems like the master of this effect it is because the power of most English poetry depends on it. If we find the effect in English translations of Baudelaire or Dante, we are hearing something that poems written in French or Italian could never do since those languages are derived almost exclusively from Latin alone. But, while it's difficult to write English poetry without taking advantage of contrasting roots, this is exactly what Yeats does in "Breasal and the Fisherman," in which there are almost no words that are not derived from the language's Anglo-Saxon base: "ebb," "flow," "tide," "moon," "set." This limitation drives the poem's rhythmic sophistication: without the subtle variation of the metrical pattern through which the syntax moves, the poem's almost unrelievedly monosyllabic diction would fall flat.

It's a commonplace to think of Pound's early imagist poems as standing in opposition to the rhymed and metered poetry that preceded them, but Pound carved his imagist poetry out of little poems such as "Breasal the Fisherman." Listen to Pound's well-known "In a Station of the Metro," in which a small army of Anglo-Saxon monosyllables faces off against the Latinate "apparition" and "petals."

> The apparition of these faces in the crowd;
> Petals on a wet, black bough.

There is no real syntax here; the poem is all stillness, a high lyric moment. Yet the two lines are marked by the same delicacy of rhythmic movement that distinguishes Yeats's poem. The second line could be scanned in a number of ways, but what matters is that we hear the initial stress on the first syllable of "petals," then three unstressed syllables, then three strongly stressed syllables in a row ("wet, black bough"). The first syllable in this punchy triplet pulls us backward by rhyming with the initial syllable in the line, while the second and third syllables are bound together by heavy alliteration. Together all three syllables progress in orderly fashion through vowels of increasing duration, moving from a vowel sound made in the back of the mouth ("wet") to the middle of the mouth ("black") to the front of the mouth ("bough"). The same thing happens in the first three stressed syllables in the second line of Yeats's poem ("pale," "tide," "moon"), the vowel sounds moving from the back to the middle to the front of the mouth. This physical progression of sound in the mouth is the sensation of great poetry: "Season of mists and mellow fruitfulness," begins Keats's

ode "To Autumn," the sequence of vowel sounds once again gratifying our mouths with the seduction of orderly movement.

I don't often hear these sounds in later Pound, but I do hear them
in middle-period Yeats.

> The trees are in their autumn beauty,
> The woodland paths are dry,
> Under the October twilight the water
> Mirrors a still sky;
> Upon the brimming water among the stones
> Are nine-and-fifty swans.

And I hear them in later Yeats as well.

> Under my window-ledge the waters race,
> Otters below and moor-hens on the top,
> Run for a mile undimmed in Heaven's face
> Then darkening through "dark" Raftery's "cellar" drop,
> Run underground, rise in a rocky place
> In Coole demesne, and there to finish up
> Spread to a lake and drop into a hole.
> What's water but the generated soul?

Yeats is notoriously a poet who changed, but from the beginning until
the end of his career he delighted in stanzas (or complete poems) compromising one syntactical swoop. While the stanza from "Coole and
Ballylee, 1931" is obviously two sentences, the final one-liner alerts us
to the length of the sentence preceding it, highlighting its elegant
attenuation. And, while the stanza is cast in octava rima, the stanza
Byron used for *Don Juan*, Yeats's syntax retains the clarity of discursive
prose: it travels through the intricate stanza as effortlessly as the underground river it describes.

In the stanza from "The Wild Swans at Coole," Yeats cheats a little since the punctuation joins what could be independent clauses—
clauses in which the syntax is shockingly mundane: the trees are, the
paths are, the swans are. This poem is standing still. What's more, Yeats
is working not with a highly literary stanza such as octava rima but with
our most predictable stanza: the first four lines are cast in common
measure, the stanza we associate with ballads and hymns—iambic
tetrameter lines ending in unstressed syllables alternating with iambic
trimeter lines ending in stressed syllables. No great poem in the language begins by so dramatically relinquishing the means of verbal
power.

> The woods are in their autumn beauty;
> The woodland paths are dry.

After hearing these lines, you expect something like "This poet will write poetry / Until the day he dies." But the third line disrupts our expectations. Yeats flips its initial iamb into a trochee ("under"), then follows this inverted foot with an anapest, giving us three unstressed syllables in a row ("Under the October"). The line's final foot is also larded with unstressed syllables, making the whole line feel weirdly flat in a different way—not rhythmically predictable but lacking in tension: "Under an October twilight the water." The next line begins again with a trochee ("mirrors"), but ends with a spondee ("still sky"). Lacking its share of unstressed syllables while flaunting its stresses, this line feels punchy, especially after the flaccid line preceding it: "Mirrors a still sky." But then the penultimate line settles into the mostly iambic regularity with which the stanza began, heralding the return of the verb to be: "Are nine-and-fifty swans." If he'd wanted to, Yeats could have written "Are fifty-nine swans," making a trimeter line with more rhythmic energy. Why didn't he? Why did Yeats go to such lengths to keep the language of this poem from taking flight?

This poem's diction is not as resolutely Anglo-Saxon as that of "Breasal the Fisherman," but combined with the bland syntax, the bald repetitions, and the lost opportunities for rhythmic variation its purity sets a stage in which even the most restrained disruption of the poem's decorum is going to feel like a thunderclap. The storm breaks loose in the second line of the poem's final stanza.

> But now they drift on the still water,
> Mysterious, beautiful.

These Latinate words—"mysterious, beautiful"—are not in themselves terribly unusual or challenging, but the poem makes them feel that way. The sound of these two words, wedged together to make one elegant trimeter line, feels incantatory, revelatory, a release from the poem's almost relentlessly stolid verbal landscape.

Yeats is by no means the only poet to explore this effect. Andrew Marvell employs it for satirical ends in "Last Instructions to the Painter" when he says that a diplomatic letter "instructs our (verse the name abhors) / Plenipotentiary ambassadors." The strategically delayed use of Latinate diction often sounds funny, but Yeats manages to keep the effect in service of mystery and incantation. In the second movement of "The Tower," these lines of predominately monosyllabic, Anglo-Saxon diction once again provide a runway for the sonic boom of revelation.

> Death and life were not
> Till man made up the whole,
> Made lock, stock and barrel
> Out of his bitter soul,
> Aye, sun and moon and star, all,
> And further add to that
> That, being dead, we rise,
> Dream and so create
> Translunar Paradise.

When I was a student, I was taught to think of the plain style in English poetry as something epitomized in the Renaissance by Ben Jonson and championed more recently by poets such as Yvor Winters and Thom Gunn. I was taught to think of Yeats as a poet of large-scale rhetorical effects, and at times he is. But no matter how arcane his cosmology, no matter how obscure his thought, Yeats's sentences exhibit a restraint related to but different from the plain style, a restraint we don't inevitably associate with a poetry of cognitive wildness. So do William Blake's.

> O Rose, thou art sick;
> The invisible worm
> That flies in the night
> In the howling storm,
>
> Has found out thy bed
> Of crimson joy,
> And his dark secret love
> Does thy life destroy.

So do Andrew Marvell's.

> What wondrous life in this I lead!
> Ripe apples drop about my head;
> The luscious clusters of the vine
> Upon my mouth do crush their wine;
> The nectarine, and curious peach,
> Into my hands themselves do reach;
> Stumbling on melons, as I pass,
> Ensnared with flowers, I fall on grass.

What exactly do these poems have in common?

The poets I've examined were influenced by the plain style, but each of them sits uncomfortably to the side of that tradition. Rather than fostering a poetry of direct statement, they employ extremely restrained diction in order to suggest something other, something spooky or mythic, than what the language of the poem also denotes. Reading "The Sick Rose," we know immediately that this rose is an emblem for certain notions about human sexuality, though we also know it is a rose. Reading "The Wild Swans at Coole," we feel that the woods, the path, and the swans are luring us into a landscape at once physical and spiritual. The poems don't require any allegorical machinery to establish this effect: the restraint of the language itself— the immediate sense that we are being told far less than we could be told—establishes a decorum in which the clear sense of what is being said raises the mysterious specter of why it is being said.

Though it is the briefest of the poems I've examined, Pound's "In a Station of the Metro" is the most explicit about this procedure since it tells us that the petals on the bough are an apparition of something other than themselves. Yeats's "Coole and Ballylee, 1931" is the most self-conscious about this procedure: the one-line sentence that con-cludes the opening stanza is almost sly ("What's water but the gener-ated soul?") since by the time we've reached this line we've realized that, however brilliantly the poem is describing the intricate pathway of water, it's also conjuring a world elsewhere. The rhyme of "hole" with "soul" says it all: the language of the poem rises to heaven because it cleaves to the earth.

Marvell is for me the greatest master of this effect in the English language. The very title of "The Garden," a poem whose complexities I can only gesture toward, feels at once satisfyingly concrete and at the same time immensely suggestive. In the stanza I've quoted from the middle of the poem, we are treated to a cornucopia of sensuous detail—ripe apples, vines, nectarines, the curious peach—all of it deliv-ered to us wrapped in lapidary couplets of seemingly effortless simplic-ity. But while we feel seduced by the sensuous world, just as the speaker of the poem is treated to its solicitude, we feel simultaneously that we are entering translunar paradise—a world in which the physi-cal act of falling on the grass, sinking into its lusciousness, feels inex-plicably evocative of a spiritual threshold.

The next stanza confirms this feeling, for it is itself about the mind discovering its separation from the body.

Meanwhile the mind, from pleasures less,

Withdraws into its happiness:
The mind, that ocean where each kind
Does straight its own resemblance find;
Yet it creates, transcending these,
Far other worlds, and other seas,
Annihilating all that's made
To a green thought in a green shade.

The syntax of this poem could not be more perspicuous; the diction could not be more precise. But, as in the lines by Yeats and Blake, the language feels inexplicably complex by virtue of its restraint, by virtue of implications it raises but does not acknowledge having raised. The poem does not feel like a puzzle to be solved for its aura of other-worldliness is dispelled neither by multiple readings nor by the armada of literary critics who have attended to its language so lovingly. The final four lines of this stanza are paradigmatic: the first and third lines are dominated by complex Latinate words ("transcending," "annihilat-ing") while the second and fourth lines are made exclusively of simple Anglo-Saxon words, the most important word in each line used twice ("other," "green"). The monosyllabic diction of the final line could not be plainer, but its meaning feels at least as complex as the more obviously rich line preceding it. To be asked to consider the relation-ship of a "green thought" and a "green shade" is to feel the simple word *green* grow thick with connotation; the meaning of the line feels at once utterly plain and endlessly elusive. Like the soul, to which the poem turns in the next stanza, this line luxuriates in "the various light."

For years I knew "The Garden" better than I knew myself. For when I happened recently to return to Marvell I was thrilled to dis-cover that everything I love about poetry is epitomized by this poem. It was as if the poem were a house I'd lived in all my life without knowing it. It was as if the poem (along with the poems I've associated with it) so determined the satisfaction I derive from poetry that the deepest act of artistic originality was inevitably an act of recapitulation. If we all possess, as Proust suggests of Elstir, our particular callings, our particular rhythms, they are not original to us. The world makes us, but until we're able to wither into the limitations of ourselves, we cannot see the world.

Some of the poems that shaped me are metered and rhymed, while others are written in free verse of varying kinds. In each case, what cap-tured me was a quality of diction and syntax, and that quality could be found as much in the free verse of "In a Station of the Metro" as in the quatrains of *Hugh Selwyn Mauberley*. In the wake of the various mod-

ernist disruptions of poetic decorum, however, stillness and restraint
became associated with the kind of poems we call traditional while
energy and excess were claimed by the poems we call experimental.
Hugh Selwyn Mauberley embodied this predicament for us almost a hundred years ago, and it shows few signs of abating. Today the ambitious
young poet writes snap-crackle prose poems while twenty years ago
she wrote mordant quatrains. It's only a matter of moments before the
pendulum swings back.

How crucial, then, the unproscribable exception. How crucial the
poems that employ the language of the garden while embracing formal
innovation. Poems that serve literature rather than playing to taste. Listen to George Oppen's "Inlet," the last poem I will discuss.

> Mary in the noisy seascape
> Of the whitecaps
>
> Of another people's summer
> Talked of the theologians   so brave
> In the wilderness she said   and off the town pier
>
> Rounding that heavy coast of mountains
> The night drifts
> Over the rope's end
>
> Glass world
>
> Glass heaven
>
> Brilliant beneath the boat's round bilges
> In the surface of the water
> *Shepherds are good people let them sing*
>
> the little skirts life's breasts for what we can have
> Is each other
>
> Breath of the barnacles
> Over England
>
> over ocean
>
> breakwaters   hencoops

Oppen's diction is severely winnowed: only a handful of words derived
from French or Greek ("brilliant," "barnacle," "theology") disrupt this
English seascape, which is dominated by nouns that sound like Anglo-
Saxon kennings ("whitecap," "breakwaters," "hencoops"). The syntax
is similarly plain, its difficulties not a matter of subordination but of
compression and juxtaposition. Prepositions direct us up or down.

Mary is in a boat talking about theologians in the wilderness. Over the boat drifts night. Beneath the boat lies heaven. Over the land floats the breath of barnacles. Over the sea float hencoops—or at least we're tempted to see them floating there by the accumulation of unpunctuated prepositional phrases. Like "The Seafarer," the Anglo-Saxon poem that Oppen inevitably invokes, "Inlet" is about finding the earth in the sky, the spiritual in the physical, and the poem's language embodies the discovery the poem describes. Working in the opposite direction from Yeats, Oppen makes the most ordinary Anglo-Saxon words sound like revelation: "breakwaters," "hencoops." The poet who rounds the "heavy coast of mountains" to see "heaven / Brilliant beneath the boat's round bilges" knows that the words *heavy* and *heaven* are derived from the same word, that *heaven* is an archaic past participle of *heave*. With its multiplicity of roots, English is one of the few Indo-European languages with different words for heaven and sky: in English, whatever is in heaven has been heaved there from the world below.

Each poem I've discussed has enacted this heavy lifting. Precision, they suggest, is not opposed to mystery. In fact, mystery depends on our attention to the particular nature of particular English words—on the way in which our language permits us to hear one kind of word (big, small) as strategically plainer and possibly even less interesting than another kind of word that means about the same thing (immense, minute). These kinds of choices are made in all English poems, not to mention everyday speech; but not all poems take strategic advantage of those choices, making what might otherwise seem like a retreat to purity, stillness, and restraint feel laden with connotation. "Shepherds are honest people, let them sing," said the seventeenth-century poet George Herbert, Marvell's contemporary. Slightly misquoting this line in "Inlet," Oppen knew as well as Herbert did that rustic shepherds are notorious for saying elaborate things whenever they show up in poems. Plainness, these poets suggest, is never simple.

Neither is the road on which a poet travels to this realization, obvious as it might seem. Although he ended his life with the dignity of Proust's Elstir, Oppen waited half a lifetime to wither into the truth of himself. As a young man, he published the preternaturally sophisticated *Discrete Series* in 1934. Then commenced a silence that didn't end until almost three decades later with the appearance of Oppen's second book, *The Materials,* in 1962. Exactly what made poems return to him seems obscure; even the explanations Oppen himself provided strike me as insufficient, and I suspect that his late withering seemed as mysterious to him as it does to anyone else. Less obscure to me is the sense that Oppen's career magnifies what is at stake when any writer faces the empty page then finds it full. More threatening is my suspicion that Oppen's complete surrender of the will to write was itself the fuel for his astonishing achievement.

Not everyone is by nature so stoic, nor does anyone need to be— unless such stoicism distinguishes him truly. My point today is not that anyone ought necessarily to strive to write like Oppen or Marvell or any other writer. Nor is it my intention to hold up the values of purity, stillness, and restraint as inevitably superior to any other values—except inasmuch as these values seem more compatible with the acts of submission on which great art depends. "Idolatry of the forms which had inspired it," says Proust, "a tendency to take the line of least resistance, must gradually undermine an Elstir's progress." Stillness and restraint will move you if such values distinguish the poems you must write— against your own will. Oppen or Marvell will matter if you learn to hear yourself by listening to them. The greatest poems we will write already exist, and the work of a lifetime is to become meek enough to recognize them as our own.

NOTES

First appeared in *Virginia Quarterly Review* 82, no. 3 (summer 2006).

Contributors

Agha Shahid Ali, a Kashmiri American, was born in New Delhi in 1949 and grew up in Kashmir. He taught at the University of Utah and in the MFA program at Warren Wilson College, as well as at Hamilton College and the University of Massachusetts-Amherst His poetry collections included *The Half-Inch Himalayas, A Nostalgist's Map of America, The Country Without a Post Office,* and *Rooms Are Never Finished,* which was a finalist for the National Book Award in 2001, the year of his death. He also translated the poetry of Faiz Ahmed Faiz, collected in *The Rebel's Silhouette: Selected Poems,* and edited *Ravishing DisUnities: Real Ghazals in English.* He received Guggenheim and Ingram-Merrill fellowships among other honors during his lifetime. A posthumous collection, entitled *Call Me Ishmael Tonight,* appeared in 2003.

Marianne Boruch's five poetry collections include *Poems: New and Selected* (Oberlin, 2004). She has also published two books of essays on poetry, *Poetry's Old Air* (Poets on Poetry Series, Michigan, 1995), and *In the Blue Pharmacy* (Trinity, 2005). Awarded a Guggenheim fellowship in 2005, she has also received fellowships from the National Endowment for the Arts and two Pushcart Prizes. She teaches in the MFA programs at Purdue University and Warren Wilson College.

Carl Dennis is the author of nine books of poetry, including, most recently, *New and Selected Poems, 1974–2004* (Penguin, 2004). His previous book, *Practical Gods* (Penguin, 2001), was awarded the Pulitzer Prize in poetry in 2002. A recipient of fellowships from the Guggenheim Foundation and the National Endowment for the Arts, in 2000 he received the Ruth Lilly Prize from *Poetry* magazine and the Modern Poetry Association for his contributions to American poetry. He is Artist in Residence at the State University of New York at Buffalo and has often taught in the faculty of the MFA program at Warren Wilson College.

Stephen Dobyns is the author of twelve books of poems, twenty novels, one book of short stories, and a book of essays on poetry: *Best Words, Best Order.* He lives in Rhode Island.

Chris Forhan is the author of two books of poems, *The Actual Moon, the Actual Stars* (Northeastern, 2003), which won the Samuel French Morse Poetry Prize, and *Forgive Us Our Happiness* (New England, 1999), which won the Katherine Bakeless Nason Prize. He is also the author of two chapbooks, *x* and *Crumbs of Bread,* and has won a Pushcart Prize and a Washington State Book Award. He teaches at Auburn University.

Tony Hoagland's most recent collection of poems, *What Narcissism Means to Me* (2003, Graywolf), was a finalist for the National Book Critics Circle Award. He teaches in the graduate writing program of the University of Houston and the MFA program at Warren Wilson College. A book of prose about poetry, *Real Sofistikashun,* was published by Graywolf in 2006.

A. Van Jordan is the author of *Rise* by Tia Chucha, 2001, which won the PEN/Oakland Josephine Miles Award, and M-A-C-N-O-L-I-A (Norton, 2004), which won an Anisfield-Wolf Book Award. He is also a recipient of a Whiting Writers Award and a Pushcart Prize. He teaches at the University of Texas at Austin and in the MFA program at Warren Wilson College.

Laura Kasciske's most recent collection of poems, *Gardening in the Dark,* was published in 2004 by Ausable Press. She has published five previous collections and four novels and has been the recipient of two fellowships from the National Endowment for the Arts, three Pushcart Prizes, the Alice Faye DiCastagnola Prize from the Poetry Society of American, and the Bobst Award for Emerging Writers from New York University. She teaches in the MFA program at Warren Wilson College, and in the Residential College and MFA program at the University of Michigan. She lives in Chelsea, Michigan.

Larry Levis published five collections of poems during his lifetime. *Elegy* was published posthumously after his death in 1996. He was Professor of English at Virginia Commonwealth University, and he taught at the University of Missouri, the University of Utah, the University of Iowa, and in the MFA program at Warren Wilson College. His awards include the U.S. Award of the International Poetry Forum, a Lamont Prize, and selection for the National Poetry Series. He received fellowships from the National Endowment for the Arts and the Guggenheim Foundation.

James Longenbach is the author of three books of poems, most recently *Draft of a Letter* (Chicago, 2007), and five books of literary criticism, most recently *The Resistance to Poetry* (Chicago, 2004). *The Art of the Poetic Line* is forthcoming from Graywolf. He has been a Visiting Fellow at Worcester College and Oxford University and the Bain-Swiggett Professor of Poetry at Princeton University. He is currently the Joseph H. Gilmore Professor of English at the University of Rochester.

Heather McHugh is the Milliman Distinguished Writer-in-Residence at the University of Washington in Seattle and a frequent summer visitor at the MFA for writers at Warren Wilson College near Asheville, NC. Her latest collection of poems is *Eyeshot* (which was a finalist for the Pulitzer Prize). With her husband, Nikolai Popov, she translated poems of Paul Celan (in a volume entitled *Glottal Stop*, which won the Griffin International Poetry Prize in 2001). She is a fellow of the American Academy of Arts and Sciences.

Daniel Tobin is the author of four books of poems, *Where the World Is Made*, cowinner of the 1998 Katherine Bakeless Nason Prize; *Double Life* (Louisiana State, 2004); *The Narrows* (Four Way, 2005); and *Second Things* (forthcoming), as well as *Passage to the Center: Imagination and the Sacred in the Poetry of Seamus Heaney* (Kentucky, 1999). He edited *The Book of Irish American Poetry from the Eighteenth Century to the Present* (Notre Dame, 2007) and *Light in Hand: The Selected Poems of Lola Ridge* (Quale, 2007). Among his awards are the "The Discovery/*Nation* Award," the Robert Penn Warren Award, a creative writing fellowship from the National Endowment for the Arts, and the Robert Frost Fellowship. He is Chair of the Department of Writing, Literature, and Publishing at Emerson College.

Pimone Triplett is the author of *The Price of Light* (Four Way, 2005), winner of the Larry Levis Poetry Prize. She is also the author of *Ruining the Picture* (Triquarterly/Northwestern, 1998). Her poems have appeared in *Yale Review, Paris Review, Agni, Poetry,* and many other journals. She attended Sarah Lawrence College and received an MFA from the University of Iowa. Currently, she is Assistant Professor of Creative Writing at the University of Washington and teaches in the MFA program at Warren Wilson College.

Ellen Bryant Voigt has published six volumes of poetry: *Claiming Kin* (1976); *The Forces of Plenty* (1983); *The Lotus Flowers* (1987); *Two Trees*

(1992); *Kyrie* (1995), a finalist for the National Book Critics' Circle Award; *Shadow of Heaven* (Norton, 2002), a finalist for the National Book Award, and *Messenger: New and Selected Poems* (Norton, 2007). She also coedited an anthology of essays, *Poets Teaching Poets: Self and the World,* and collected her own essays on craft in *The Flexible Lyric* (Georgia, 1999). For her poems, which have been published in the *New Yorker, Atlantic, New England Review, Southern Review,* and *Slate,* she has received the Emily Clark Balch Award, the Hanes Poetry Award, the Teasdale Award, three Pushcart Prizes, inclusion in Scribner's *Best American Poetry,* an Award in Literature from the American Academy of Arts and Letters, and grants from the National Endowment of the Arts, the Guggenheim Foundation, and the Lila Wallace–Reader's Digest Fund. Voigt designed and directed the nation's first low-residency MFA writing program, at Goddard College, and she now teaches in its reincarnation at Warren Wilson College. She has also taught at Iowa Wesleyan College, the Massachusetts Institute of Technology, the University of Cincinnati, the Breadloaf Writers Conference, and in brief residencies at numerous colleges and universities. A former Vermont State Poet, she has been inducted into the Fellowship of Southern Writers and named a Chancellor of the Academy of American Poets.

Alan Williamson teaches at the University of California at Davis, as well as in the MFA program at Warren Wilson College. He is the author of five books of poetry, most recently *The Pattern More Complicated: New and Selected Poems* (Chicago, 2004), and of five books of criticism or essays, most recently *Westernness: A Meditation* (Virginia, 2006).

Eleanor Wilner's most recent books are *The Girl with Bees in Her Hair* (Copper Canyon, 2004) and *Reversing the Spell: New and Selected Poems* (Copper Canyon, 1998). Her awards include MacArthur and National Endowment for the Arts Fellowships, the Juniper Prize, and Pushcart Prizes; she has taught at many colleges and universities, most recently at the University of Chicago, Northwestern University, and Smith College. For close to twenty years, she has been on the poetry faculty of the MFA program at Warren Wilson College.

Dean Young has published seven books of poems, most recently *Elegy on Toy Piano* (Pittsburgh), which was a finalist for the 2006 Pulitzer Prize, and *embryoyo* (Believer, 2007). His poems have appeared in *American Poetry Review, Paris Review, Ploughshares, Paris Review,*

Threepenny Review, and many other journals. He has received fellow-ships from the Guggenheim Foundation and the National Endowment for the Arts and teaches at the Iowa Writers' Workshop and the MFA program at Warren Wilson College.

Index

Owen, Wilfred, 127
oxymoron, 5, 267, 270

Pagis, Dan, 153
pantoum, 179
parallelism, 221–22, 230, 232, 268
paraphrase, 20, 188, 204
parody, 66, 70–71, 73, 109
pastoral, 100, 239, 276
pattern, 24–25, 30, 52–53, 62, 66,
    85, 175, 187–88, 205, 208,
    217–20, 223, 225–26, 228,
    230–34, 271–72, 281–82
Perkins, David, 185
persona, 44, 52–53, 75, 166
Pessoa, Fernando, 145
Petrarch, Francesco, 199, 221
Philip, M. Nourbese, 68–72
Picasso, Pablo, 83, 153
Pinsky, Robert, 108, 118–19
pitch, 30, 202–3, 209–11, 213–14
Plath, Sylvia, 28, 52, 108, 139, 172,
    252
Plato, 176–78
political, 24, 68–69, 73, 84, 99–100,
    105, 120–21, 124–25, 130, 144,
    152–55, 158, 160, 172, 174
polysyllabic, 200, 219
postmodern, 2, 69, 76, 113–16, 118,
    172, 176, 182, 184, 188
Pound, Ezra, 2, 5, 34, 139, 155,
    174–75, 179, 181–82, 184–85,
    234, 267–69, 274, 280–83, 286
Pope, Alexander, 219
projective verse, 182–85, 187, 192
prose poetry, 72, 170, 288
prosody, 16, 203, 216, 234, 241
Proust, Marcel, 279, 287, 289–90
pyrrhic, 204–5, 207, 213
Pushkin, Aleksandr, 154

quatrain, 182, 189, 199, 210, 220–21,
    280, 287–88

Ray, Man, 130
Ray, Satyajit, 149–50
realism, 84–85, 91, 119, 129–30
Reddy, Shrikanth, 75–76
repetition, 12, 17, 25, 31, 34, 37,

110, 175, 180, 218, 221, 226–28,
    234, 284
representation, 67, 97–98, 105, 136,
    138, 150
rhyme, 17, 48, 66, 70, 174, 182, 197,
    199, 201–2, 208, 220–28, 230–34,
    280–82, 286–87
rhythm, 16, 30–32, 40, 62, 67, 75,
    85, 88–89, 92, 126, 176–78, 182,
    185, 187–88, 204, 213, 216–17,
    219–23, 226, 228, 233–34, 252,
    255, 279–82, 284, 287
Rich, Adrienne, 38, 97
Richter, Hans, 128
Rigaut, James, 128
right-branching, 221–23, 226–27,
    231–32
Rimbaud, Arthur, 125–26, 252
Romanticism, 15, 61–62, 66, 73,
    125–26, 158, 181, 236, 243–44,
    252
Roy, Arundhati, 147
Rumi, 151, 154
Rushdie, Salman, 63–65, 76, 145,
    147, 149–54

Sacks, Peter, 96–97, 99
Said, Edward, 147–48
satire, 41, 136, 276, 284
Schmidt, Michael, 58
Seghor, Leopold, 81, 83–84, 92–93
self, 14–15, 18, 40, 53, 61–63, 66,
    69–72, 74, 76, 97, 111, 117, 126,
    129–30, 138–39, 141–42, 163,
    165–69, 175, 240, 250–51, 255–64
sestina, 146, 179, 189
Sexton, Anne, 252
Shakespeare, William, 1, 113, 114,
    132, 144–45, 150, 152, 154, 156,
    158–59, 176, 182, 210, 219–24,
    234, 282
Shapiro, Alan, 23, 26
Shapiro, Karl, 4, 27
Simic, Charles, 5, 255–57
Simmons, James, 104
Simms, Laura, 53
Simon, Rachel M., 165
Simpson, Louis, 5, 270, 272–74
Snyder, Gary, 113

sonnet, 16–17, 31, 36, 77, 142, 146, 154, 158–59, 176, 179, 181–82, 185, 189, 199, 204, 210, 219, 223, 234, 240–41, 244

Soupault, Philippe, 133

Soyinka, Wole, 149, 154

speaker, 5, 13, 15–19, 21, 24, 26, 31, 41, 45, 52, 94, 109, 112, 114–18, 124, 166, 169, 171, 178, 180, 199, 202, 206, 210, 236–45, 248–49, 250–51, 253–56, 257–61, 263, 275, 286

speech-act theory, 237, 245

spondaic, 176, 223

spondee, 32, 39, 94, 204–5, 207, 213, 223, 229, 231–33, 284

stanza, 16, 25, 27, 39, 55, 125, 166, 176, 178, 181–82, 184, 186, 197, 201–2, 205–9, 211–14, 219–22, 224, 226, 228, 230–32, 239–40, 242–43, 268, 283–84, 286–87

Steele, Timothy, 174–77, 181

Stevens, Wallace, 65, 153, 159, 188, 197

stichic, 197

Stoutenberg, Adrian, 30

Strand, Mark, 106

stress, 30–33, 39, 94, 178, 182, 202–7, 210, 213–14, 216, 219–23, 225–27, 229–31, 234, 241, 280–84

structure, 5, 27, 31, 54, 60, 104, 163–64, 169–70, 172, 181–82, 185–88, 190, 218–19, 223, 227, 229, 236, 238, 240–41, 244, 249

style, 2, 4, 61, 69–70, 72, 99, 108, 118, 161, 163, 167–68, 173, 175, 179, 271, 285–86

sublime, 4, 60–77, 148, 188

surrealism, 4, 44, 84–85, 91, 93–94, 108, 111, 118–19, 120–21, 124–26, 132–36, 138, 141–43, 144, 168–69, 257

Swift, Jonathan, 132

syllable, 31–33, 70, 94, 182–84, 188, 197, 199–211, 213–15, 219–20, 222–31, 234, 255, 280–84

symbol, 35, 62, 71, 97, 156, 228, 242–43

symmetry, 188, 197, 226, 231, 268

sympathy, 248, 276

syntax, 5, 149, 176–80, 183, 187, 200, 216–24, 226, 230–34, 255, 261, 281–84, 287–88

Taggard, Genevieve, 170–71

Tagore, Rabindranath, 154

tankha, 158

Tennyson, Alfred, Lord, 132

tercet, 36

texture, 109, 177–78, 187–90, 192, 203, 211–12, 222, 226

Thomas, Dylan, 109

timbre, 124, 202–3, 210–13

tone, 16, 37–39, 45, 52, 56, 65, 71, 87–88, 94, 104, 111, 166, 171, 178–79, 190, 205–6, 213–14, 216, 219, 232, 239, 243, 261

tradition, 2, 4–5, 15–16, 32, 60–61, 63, 68, 73, 75–77, 117, 147, 149, 151–52, 156, 174–80, 182, 184–88, 197, 203, 214, 219, 240, 244, 286, 288

tragedy, 17, 38, 118, 141, 148, 151, 236

trochaic, 16, 32, 178, 204

trochee, 16, 30, 94, 207–8, 231, 284

Trotsky, Leon, 159

Tuckerman, Frederick Goddard, 5, 244–45

Tung-P'o, Su, 276

Tzara, Tristan, 128–30

Vaché, Jacques, 128

Valéry, Paul, 198

Vallejo, César, 159, 168

Vargas Llosa, Mario, 91

verse, 67, 145, 151, 177, 182–83, 185–86, 188–89, 191–92, 203, 214, 219, 228, 253
  accentual verse, 219
  blank verse, 180, 184
  free verse, 146, 151, 175–77, 179, 181, 184–85, 187, 189, 191–92, 203, 214, 217, 287
  open verse, 182, 189, 217
  projective verse, 182–85, 187, 192

villanella, 179, 189, 192

Virgil, 105

Viswanathan, Gauri, 155
voice, 3, 16, 23, 26, 38, 40–41, 52,
  65, 92, 104, 114–15, 141, 143,
  153, 166, 169, 176, 179, 182–84,
  212, 223, 241, 250, 253, 257,
  260–61, 263
Voigt, Ellen Bryant, 1, 4, 187

Wakoski, Diane, 174–76
Walcott, Derek, 65–66, 149
Waldrep, G. C., 166
Walker, Alice, 159
Walrond, Eric, 83
White, Edmund, 153–54
White, Patrick, 149
Whitman, Walt, 5, 28, 34–36, 68,
  73, 141, 148, 174, 176, 218, 244,
  262–63, 271
Wilbur, Richard, 174, 179

Williams, C. K., 119
Williams, William Carlos, 4–5, 37,
  174, 177, 182, 184–85, 252–55
Winters, Yvor, 285
Winterson, Jeannette, 11
Wordsworth, William, 61–64, 75,
  77, 125–26, 177, 181, 243
Wright, Charles, 77, 118, 217,
  252
Wright, James, 108, 197–98
Wright, Orville, 33, 35, 37–38
Wright, Wilbur, 28–29, 35, 37–38
Wyatt, Thomas, 4, 199, 206–8

Yeats, William Butler, 4–5, 52, 55,
  74, 96, 106, 175–81, 183–84, 187,
  191, 208, 211, 252, 279, 281–87,
  289
Yenser, Stephen, 252